PALGRAVE STUDIES IN THEATRE AND PERFORMANCE HISTORY is a series devoted to the best of theatre/performance scholarship currently available, accessible, and free of jargon. It strives to include a wide range of topics, from the more traditional to those performance forms that in recent years have helped broaden the understanding of what theatre as a category might include (from variety forms as diverse as the circus and burlesque to street buskers, stage magic, and musical theatre, among many others). Although historical, critical, or analytical studies are of special interest, more theoretical projects, if not the dominant thrust of a study, but utilized as an important underpinning or as a historiographical or analytical method of exploration, are also of interest. Textual studies of drama or other types of less traditional performance texts are also germane to the series if placed in their cultural, historical, social, or political and economic context. There is no geographical focus for this series, and works of excellence of a diverse and international nature, including comparative studies, are sought.

The editor of the series is Don B. Wilmeth (Emeritus, Brown University), PhD, University of Illinois, who brings to the series over a dozen years as editor of a book series on American theatre and drama, in addition to his own extensive experience as an editor of books and journals. He is the author of several award-winning books and has received numerous career achievement awards, including one for sustained excellence in editing from the Association for Theatre in Higher Education.

Also in the series:

Undressed for Success by Brenda Foley
Theatre, Performance, and the Historical Avant-garde by Günter Berghaus
Theatre, Politics, and Markets in Fin-de-Siècle Paris by Sally Charnow
Ghosts of Theatre and Cinema in the Brain by Mark Pizzato
Moscow Theatres for Young People: A Cultural History of Ideological Coercion and Artistic Innovation, 1917–2000 by Manon van de Water
Absence and Memory in Colonial American Theatre by Odai Johnson
Vaudeville Wars: How the Keith-Albee and Orpheum Circuits Controlled the Big-Time and Its Performers by Arthur Frank Wertheim
Performance and Femininity in Eighteenth-Century German Women's Writing by Wendy Arons
Operatic China: Staging Chinese Identity across the Pacific by Daphne P. Lei
Transatlantic Stage Stars in Vaudeville and Variety: Celebrity Turns by Leigh Woods
Interrogating America through Theatre and Performance edited by William W. Demastes and Iris Smith Fischer
Plays in American Periodicals, 1890–1918 by Susan Harris Smith
Representation and Identity from Versailles to the Present: The Performing Subject by Alan Sikes
Directors and the New Musical Drama: British and American Musical Theatre in the 1980s and 90s by Miranda Lundskaer-Nielsen
Beyond the Golden Door: Jewish-American Drama and Jewish-American Experience by Julius Novick
American Puppet Modernism: Essays on the Material World in Performance by John Bell
On the Uses of the Fantastic in Modern Theatre: Cocteau, Oedipus, and the Monster by Irene Eynat-Confino

Staging Stigma: A Critical Examination of the American Freak Show
by Michael M. Chemers, foreword by Jim Ferris
Performing Magic on the Western Stage: From the Eighteenth-Century to the Present edited by Francesca Coppa, Larry Hass, and James Peck, foreword by Eugene Burger
Memory in Play: From Aeschylus to Sam Shepard by Attilio Favorini
Danjūrō's Girls: Women on the Kabuki Stage by Loren Edelson
Mendel's Theatre: Heredity, Eugenics, and Early Twentieth-Century American Drama by Tamsen Wolff
Theatre and Religion on Krishna's Stage: Performing in Vrindavan by David V. Mason
Rogue Performances: Staging the Underclasses in Early American Theatre Culture by Peter P. Reed
Broadway and Corporate Capitalism: The Rise of the Professional-Managerial Class, 1900–1920 by Michael Schwartz
Lady Macbeth in America: From the Stage to the White House by Gay Smith
Performing Bodies in Pain: Medieval and Post-Modern Martyrs, Mystics, and Artists by Marla Carlson
Early-Twentieth-Century Frontier Dramas on Broadway: Situating the Western Experience in Performing Arts by Richard Wattenberg
Staging the People: Community and Identity in the Federal Theatre Project by Elizabeth A. Osborne
Russian Culture and Theatrical Performance in America, 1891–1933 by Valleri J. Hohman
Baggy Pants Comedy: Burlesque and the Oral Tradition by Andrew Davis
Transposing Broadway: Jews, Assimilation, and the American Musical by Stuart J. Hecht
The Drama of Marriage: Gay Playwrights/Straight Unions from Oscar Wilde to the Present by John M. Clum
Mei Lanfang and the Twentieth-Century International Stage: Chinese Theatre Placed and Displaced by Min Tian
Hijikata Tatsumi and Butoh: Dancing in a Pool of Gray Grits by Bruce Baird
Staging Holocaust Resistance by Gene A. Plunka
Acts of Manhood: The Performance of Masculinity on the American Stage, 1828–1865 by Karl M. Kippola
Loss and Cultural Remains in Performance: The Ghosts of the Franklin Expedition by Heather Davis-Fisch
Uncle Tom's Cabin *on the American Stage and Screen* by John W. Frick
Theatre, Youth, and Culture: A Critical and Historical Exploration by Manon van de Water
Stage Designers in Early Twentieth-Century America: Artists, Activists, Cultural Critics by Christin Essin
Audrey Wood and the Playwrights by Milly S. Barranger
Performing Hybridity in Colonial-Modern China by Siyuan Liu
A Sustainable Theatre: Jasper Deeter at Hedgerow by Barry B. Witham

A Sustainable Theatre

Jasper Deeter at Hedgerow

Barry B. Witham

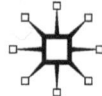

A SUSTAINABLE THEATRE
Copyright © Barry B. Witham, 2013.
All rights reserved.
First published in 2013 by
PALGRAVE MACMILLAN®
in the United States—a division of St. Martin's Press LLC,
175 Fifth Avenue, New York, NY 10010.

Where this book is distributed in the UK, Europe and the rest of the world, this is by Palgrave Macmillan, a division of Macmillan Publishers Limited, registered in England, company number 785998, of Houndmills, Basingstoke, Hampshire RG21 6XS.

Palgrave Macmillan is the global academic imprint of the above companies and has companies and representatives throughout the world.

Palgrave® and Macmillan® are registered trademarks in the United States, the United Kingdom, Europe and other countries.

ISBN: 978–0–230–34145–6

Library of Congress Cataloging-in-Publication Data

Witham, Barry, 1939–
   A sustainable theatre : Jasper Deeter at Hedgerow / Barry B. Witham.
      pages cm.—(Palgrave studies in theatre and performance history)
      ISBN 978–0–230–34145–6 (alk. paper)
    1. Hedgerow Theatre (Organization : Rose Valley, Pa.)—History.
2. Deeter, Jasper, –1972. 3. Theater—Pennsylvania—Rose Valley—History. I. Title.
PN2277.R672H439 2013
725'.8220974814—dc23   2012050305

A catalogue record of the book is available from the British Library.

Design by Newgen Imaging Systems (P) Ltd., Chennai, India.

First edition: June 2013
10 9 8 7 6 5 4 3 2 1

Transferred to Digital Printing in 2013

For Peggy

"Courage is reckoned the greatest of all virtues; because, without courage, there is no security for preserving any other." (*Boswell,* The Life of Johnson)

Contents

List of Illustrations	ix
Preface	xi
Acknowledgments	xv
Introduction	1
1. *Inheritors*: Growing a Theatre	13
2. *The Emperor Jones*: A Passion for Equality	27
3. *Winesburg, Ohio*: Democracy between the Hedgerows	43
4. *An American Tragedy*: Whose Social Conscience?	59
5. *The Cherokee Night*: Riggs and the Power of Place	73
6. *Too True to Be Good*: Consequences of Integrity	87
7. *Uncle Vanya*: A Way of Acting	101
8. *The Hedgerow Story*: Celebrity and Disappointment	115
9. Aftermath	129
Epilogue	141
Appendix A: Hedgerow Repertory 1923–1956	143
Appendix B: Repertory for Shaw Festival, *July 19– August 14, 1937*	149
Appendix C: Repertory Calendars	151
Notes	153
Bibliography	173
Index	179

Illustrations

1.1	*Inheritors* at Hedgerow, 1932	14
2.1	Arthur Rich and Jasper Deeter in *The Emperor Jones*	28
3.1	Sherwood Anderson and Jasper Deeter on the set of *Winesburg, Ohio*, 1934	44
4.1	Production photo *An American Tragedy*, 1935	60
5.1	Company photo, 1934	74
6.1	Jasper outside Hedgerow	88
7.1	Jasper Deeter and Rose Schulman taken in the early 1950s	102
8.1	Production photo, *Caucasian Chalk Circle*, 1948	124
9.1	Hedgerow exterior, 2002	130

Preface

In 1923, theatre visionary Jasper Deeter, joined by a group of idealistic actors, designers, and playwrights, founded Hedgerow Theatre. It was established as America's first resident repertory company, a seminal influence for the beginnings of the national regional theatre movement. Despite initial community resistance and the Great Depression, Deeter demonstrated clear resolve to make theatre an art and a way of life. For decades, Hedgerow has both thrived and struggled, training generations of theatre artists while keeping an unbroken performance calendar for 90 years. In fact, the National Theatre Communications Group Convention in Philadelphia recognized Hedgerow in 2002 as the "Mother of all Philadelphia Theatres" for spawning careers of generations of artists and a number of companies such as People's Light and Theatre Company and Freedom Theatre.

My grandmother, Nancy Moore, was a company member in the 1920s, a beautiful southern lady, whose life had been an endless ball of boys and glamour, and who was caught off-guard when Deeter challenged her every assumption and asked more of her than comfortable expression. With wounded pride, she packed to leave, but paused, decided to stay, and went on after Hedgerow to a career as novelist and writer for radio and television. She dedicated her work to detail, to characters coming to life, based on truth. Lessons she had learned at Hedgerow.

In 1962, my mother Janet Kelsey, her husband, and four little children moved to Rose Valley and became part of the community and an important part of the theatre. As a professional actress, she found in Hedgerow, a block away from home, the perfect place to grow both her talents and her little ones. Starting as Jasper's student, she progressed to leading lady, director, teacher, business manager, managing director, and partner—50 years of dedicated service. Even now running the alumni and community database, she is a constant adviser and reminder of how rooted one must be to grow Hedgerow.

I was 17 at the time and living with my grandmother (a teacher) and grandfather (a retired businessman), and we decided that I should stay to finish school. However, theatre was my lifeblood. As a fourth-generation actress on my father's side, I was acting in every local community theatre and earned my Equity card at the Robin Hood Theatre in Arden, Delaware. That fall, in my final year of school, my father, a New York actor, died. After the wake, on my way back by train to a technical rehearsal, I vowed to dedicate my life to acting in honor of my father, Jared Reed.

My world swirled around me, school by day, Gittel Mosca by night in *Two for the Seesaw*. The other character in the two-hander was named "Jerry" (my father's nickname). With the end of the show, I experienced a great void. What to do? I was torn between grieving and connecting with my father. My mother suggested that I come two nights a week and study with her teacher, Jasper Deeter.

What a universe opened for me then! The great man, skinny as a rail, with one leg draped over a knee, leaning forward to focus that giant mind on the scene at hand. I saw him pound on the table as he sent one woman in her twenties away in tears with, "Get out...I don't want to take your money. Leave. Get some experience!" Of course he meant life experience, of which I had relatively none. I worried that I would be the next one, but the truth he saw for me was different. "Focus" would become my battle cry, "channel" my watchword. One day, when I nearly knocked him over rushing into the door of the farmhouse/school, he looked at me with those penetrating eyes, and proclaimed, "You're like a discombobulated weather vane going four directions at the same time!" He'd nailed it. This is something I would have to work on all my life: eliminating distractions, clutter, too many meetings—time for focus. Even as I write this, appointments are colliding with reminiscence. But Jasper encouraged me to continue, put me into the advanced acting class where I had the great opportunity to act with him in several scenes: as Lavinia in *Inheritors*; Ellie in *Heartbreak House*; Anna Christie, with "Jap" as bartender and my mother as Marty Owen; I was so nervous about his critique that I walked out of the room. My mother later reported that he shrugged his shoulders and said, "What did I say?" to the merriment of all.

Jasper's words and direction have filled my life. Whether in person or retained through years of training at Carnegie Tech., on stage as actress, behind the scenes as director, or playwright, or running Hedgerow now. I had learned from "Jap" the three values that actors must have: humility, industry, and an aptitude for learning. With dedication to truth being the first and most important aspect of acting, I was able to travel the terrain of technique with ease. I knew that technique was always in service to truth. I learned from the renowned speech teacher, Edith Skinner, that "we learn to talk like kings and queens so we can talk like peasants," and "don't be too pedantic, only speech teachers talk that way." Because Jap had prepared me, I could take amazing teachers and apply their lessons to my basic understanding of his intellectual principles. "Focus on what, where, when and why," he'd say, "and let how take care of itself." While others were either too tame or sawing the air, I had learned that stimuli hit the central nervous system first or, as Jap called it, the "feeling" mind, then the body, eyes, face would respond and then talk would emerge as honest result of the human process. The text provides mere tips of the iceberg of the created human being. Again and again the lessons of Hedgerow have stayed with me through all my years of training, my decades as actress, director, teacher, and administrator.

Early on, of course, there were serious questions about whether the company would even survive. In 1923, there was a clear community schism in which Hedgerow was seen as an intruder by some, particularly the Rose Valley Chorus, which featured Jasper's sister as Katisha in *The Mikado*. The Arts and Crafts Community of Rose Valley, which Jasper would come to embrace, was suspicious of the outsiders, and a group of four community members connected with the chorus sought to deny him the right to the building. However, L. Stauffer Oliver, who owned the outstanding shares to the property, sided with Jasper, and the prospect of professional actors living and working with gifted local players ignited the imagination of the community.

Anna Kyte Price wrote in her diary that the name "Hedgerow" was inspired by Jasper Deeter's determined action. Jasper pounded his fist on the table and said, "If they won't let us play in the Guild hall, we'll play in the Hedgerows!" To be clear, a hedgerow is not a tidy hedge growing in a line, but a wild thing, reminiscent of the Irish hedge schools, which were sanctuaries for the young to learn their native, forbidden language, culture, and history. Naming the theatre "Hedgerow" was the first glimmer of its activist nature.

Jasper and his young troupe did get into the hall, housed in the old stone grist mill that became their signature theatre, and the power of Deeter and his company led to years of dedicated questioning, searching, and revealing truth. Whatever the stakes, an idea that could ignite minds toward a better way was the basis of the work at Hedgerow. Perseverance kept the company going. Peggy Oliver Shay recounts that her mother told her that in the 1930s Jasper was asked who was responsible for keeping the theatre alive.

Rather than mention her mother, he noted one of the four women who had actively fought against him. When her mother asked why, Jap said that he just couldn't wait for the leader of the pack to read this in the paper. He loved to play the imp! Humor was an important principle to the company. He loved to laugh, to entertain. Many alumni recall with great fondness the delight that he took in playing the piano in the great room at night.

At core I am an actress, who plays the roles she's given. My passion (or obsession) for this theatre keeps me playing in the hedgerows with the most wonderful, dedicated community and company. I feel that all the fund-raising, administration, scheduling, bookkeeping, restructuring a board, merging entities, and managing people—the jobs that have come my way—are so foreign to my basic nature. However, it has all been so worth it to watch this place grow, to remind people of Jasper Deeter and his incredible gritty peers, to see the alumni return, and to watch generations of theatre artists populate the field. I feel in many ways that I am simply a midwife to the legacy of Hedgerow. And Barry Witham's wonderful book makes that legacy vivid and provocative.

Jared Reed, my son and my father's namesake, is an emerging leader. We share a vision of Hedgerow; that the strengths of its past have been the strengths of its company—both resident and extended—to reach into the greater theatre world, to train the next generation of theatre professionals, and to bring joy to the region and the communities it serves. Hedgerow is still a rare place where the gifted and self-motivated can join and immediately be part of running a theatre—nothing is excluded from those who wish to learn. For one with "humility, industry and an aptitude for learning," Hedgerow is practical with enough opportunities to solve one's own puzzle.

As our alumni return to help Hedgerow grow toward one hundred, I feel blessed that Barry's book is allowing new generations to experience Jasper Deeter's ideas. Jap, we're trying to keep it going and growing. The mill theatre is still doing repertory, still operating year-round, and still producing the artists, craftspersons, audiences, and teachers of tomorrow. The old Hollingsworth homestead is still a working farm, producing crops of theatre artists of all ages. I hope readers will appreciate your passion for living and for igniting the mind toward greater personal truth. Time and again, I hear from alumni how Hedgerow affected their lives, helped them see their true calling, and gave them the grit to face life bravely. Henry Miller was right on target when he recalled that the premiere meeting ground for talent and minds was "the intrepid little Hedgerow Theatre."

PENELOPE REED

Acknowledgments

Gail Cohen is the most important historian of the Hedgerow Theatre and I am deeply indebted to her for establishing the Hedgerow archive at Boston University's Gotlieb Research Center. My thanks to all the staff at the Gotlieb for their courtesy and professionalism, especially Katelynn Vance, Adam Dixon, and Sean Noel who were unflappable and enormously helpful. At the Hedgerow Theatre in Moylan, Pennsylvania, I examined several boxes and files still uncatalogued, and I am grateful for the cooperation and support of Penelope Reed, Janet Kelsey, Susan Wefel, Rebecca Cureton, and Juliet Grey Kelsey. Penny Reed, the current artistic director of Hedgerow, was especially generous in sharing her thoughts about Jasper Deeter and in writing a preface to this volume.

Ruth Esherick Bascom and her husband, Mansfield, welcomed me into their beautiful home and answered many of my questions about the theatre and the Moylan-Media communities. I am particularly indebted to Ruth for her firsthand recollections about being a part of the Hedgerow company and for her vivid memories of Jasper Deeter and her distinguished father, Wharton Esherick.

Peter Carnahan sent me nearly 18 hours of interviews with Jasper Deeter teaching and reminiscing about the theatre, recorded over several weeks at Deeter's summer home in Summerdale, Pennsylvania, in 1966 and 1967. These magnetic tapes have now been transferred to CD format and will be donated to the Hedgerow archive at Boston University. Carnahan's own storied career in the American theatre can be accessed in his splendid autobiography, *Opposable Lives*.

Many people shared their memories of Hedgerow with me and were generous with photos, correspondence, and papers. Particular thanks to Mark Sfirri, Richard Wright, Joyce Mycka-Stettler, John Harvey, Tom McCarthy, Ann-Marie Spata, and Jack Wade.

Louis Lippa and David Ralphe were instrumental in steering me through more than 90 years of Hedgerow history. Each brought a valuable and sometimes conflicting point of view to the complex community that is Hedgerow, but both were in agreement—and in awe—of what Jasper Deeter accomplished.

Thanks to my colleagues at the University of Washington: Herb Blau, Jon Jory, Mark Jenkins, Odai Johnson, Stefka Mihaylova, Patrick Scheible, Andrew Tsao, Mark Weitzencamp, and Jack Wolcott for listening and making valuable suggestions; to Kathy Burch and Carol Dempsey for photographic advice, and to Ansley Sawyer and Nathan Witham for research assistance. And a special thanks to Joshua Polster, Lisa Jackson-Schebetta, and Michelle Granshaw, my final PhD advisees, who were patient with their advisor while negotiating their own careers.

I owe much to Don Wilmeth for his editing prowess, to Bob Schanke and Felicia Londre for encouraging me to pursue this project, and to my editors Robyn Curtis and Kristy Lilas for their critical acumen. Thanks also to Ian Smith at Seattle's Victory Studios, to Paul Eisenhauer at the Esherick Museum, to Andrea Gottschalk at the University of Pennsylvania Library and to Jonathan Shandell at Arcadia University who aided me in countless ways while pursuing his own interest in the phenomena of Hedgerow.

This book could not have been written without the enormous help of Kevin Hughes. His knowledge opened many doors, and his generosity in sharing files, manuscripts, and details of Hedgerow history continually challenged and encouraged me.

Finally, I am most grateful to Sue Bruns, whose day job is to supervise, accommodate, and educate the graduate student population at the University of Washington School of Drama, but who always finds time to read and burnish my prose as well as to patiently guide me through the on- and off-ramps of the Internet.

Sections of chapter 4 were first published in Barry Witham, "Theater, Environment, and the Thirties," in Wendy Arons and Theresa J. May, eds., *Readings in Performance and Ecology*, New York: Palgrave Macmillan, 2012, reproduced with permission of Palgrave Macmillan.

Introduction ❧

Rose Schulman was one of the true believers. She believed in Jasper Deeter's vision of a theatre that was about living a meaningful life, for its company and its audiences. For Deeter, the professional theatre in New York had become the embodiment of the industrial impulses that had remade labor in the nineteenth century, and the actor like the factory worker was only a cog in the machine. Broadway theatres in Deeter's mind were factories where casting was determined by type—which required little acting—and the productions were commercial *products* designed exclusively to make money. In response he had founded Hedgerow in 1923, a theatre that returned to the repertory system, which had once nourished American production, and to the landscape and environment of the rural United States. Hedgerow was a cooperative in almost every sense of that word. The company received room and board but no salary. They were not only cast in a variety of roles but also expected to cook and wash and paint and usher and park cars. For 30 years they made some extraordinary theatre in a tiny Rose Valley community outside of Philadelphia.

But the work was hard and sometimes even the true believers faltered. By the early 1950s—in spite of the parade of their accomplishments and her own emergence as a perceptive teacher and imaginative director—Rose Schulman was struggling with the demands of the life and the art to which she had dedicated her ambition.

> It is becoming increasingly difficult for me to work directly with people and live with them...For twenty years I have studied thoroughly the enduring reaction in myself and in others. Now I find that I do not wish to endure as much as I used to; therefore, my recourse is to give vent to them...I want a "place of my own." I would like a kitchen; a bathroom with a tub; a bedroom; and a place to work...Would and could the theater convert the third floor into an apartment for me? Or some other place on the premises?[1]

They lived communally in a converted farmhouse, a few hundred yards from the old stone mill that they had remodeled into a proscenium arch theatre with a concrete cyclorama and 16 rows of hard seats. The farmhouse had a spacious family room and kitchen as well as offices, storage spaces, and sleeping rooms. Their work calls began at 10:30 each morning and continued well into the night depending on their rehearsal and/or performance schedule. They grew vegetables and filled pantries with rice, peanut butter, jam, and cocoa. Their income was principally from their often meager box office, but their sustenance came from their commitment to each other and to the preservation of their theatre, a theatre that was dedicated in their imaginations to the best that made them human.

Rose Schulman did not get "her own place." The executive committee was sympathetic to her cri de coeur, but they felt that the financial situation of the theatre was just too precarious to invest in any immediate remodeling. She was disappointed, but like other believers she agreed to soldier on for the best interest of the theatre. Her dilemma was one that most of her colleagues would confront over the three decades that Hedgerow was producing a repertory calendar unmatched in the American theatre. As the reputation of the company soared in the 1930s, dozens of youngsters came to learn from Deeter, but most were unable to sustain his idea of theatre and moved on searching for success, celebrity, and material satisfaction. Those who stayed were rewarded but always struggled with thoughts of what they had given up. Miriam Philips, one of the most talented, articulated the struggle in a letter to the Hedgerow Board in January 1943.

> I am not always steadfast. Sometimes I wonder how long I shall have the strength to continue. I have often wanted the beautiful things that our life here could not provide; the freedom to spend myself foolishly, and to wander, just for fun. I have been tempted to give up the battle for the ultimate good and accept comfort and care, safety and security. But these desires are only temporary, and I have again and again knowingly and deliberately made the choice of this life, which is sometimes almost too hard to bear, because therein lies the greatest freedom; because when I think about what WE want, I am happier when I make the choice of what WE want together.[2]

But what was this "ultimate good" for which they strove? For Deeter, who was the driving force, it was simple. Theatre was a profession that could be fulfilling as a way of life and not as a tool to accumulate wealth and material possessions. Theatre, especially acting, was always about finding the "truth." But in order to do that acting had to be freed from the typecasting and easy clichés that had imprisoned it, and actors had to relearn their art and their craft. The actor is created by his roles, Deeter was fond of preaching, and thus the repertory system is the only model of theatre that will allow the actor to grow and discover. Therefore, it is only possible to achieve that growth if a company is committed to that purpose. "The intellectual purpose of our entire repertory, he wrote, is creating a situation in which living a better life may be possible."[3]

Rehearsals at Hedgerow were about discovery and finding the truth for the actor in each moment as well as the larger truth of the play. "You have to teach a person to see," he often remarked, "to tell them what to see is only a matter of taste."[4] Casting was often erratic in some people's minds because Deeter wanted to force actors outside the easy range that had conditioned them. Ann Harding, one of his protégées and subsequently a film star, remembered how she had questioned her casting in *Inheritors* because she was from a military family and her character had to defend conscientious objectors. "This isn't about you," he told her, "this is about finding the truth of the character you are playing."[5] Writers adored Deeter because he sought to discover the "truth" in their plays and devoted long, testing rehearsals to realizing it. Sherwood Anderson, remembering the "midnight rehearsals" for the world premiere of *Winesburg, Ohio* in 1934, wrote to Deeter praising his directing and recalling, "Once I heard you say that the parts make the actor and we must find out what the playwright is trying to say."[6] And Lynn Riggs, whose work Deeter admired and whose plays were frequently offered in the Hedgerow repertory, wrote him from Hollywood in 1932, "It's too bad you're such a fine director. After you the others seem piddling and empty."[7]

Hedgerow produced a variety of new plays as part of their storied repertory including the American premieres of Shaw's complete *Man and Superman*, Brecht's *Caucasian Chalk Circle*, Sherwood Anderson's *Winesburg, Ohio*, and the Dreiser-Piscator's *An American Tragedy*. Deeter was particularly interested in Shaw because he admired his dramaturgy, his willingness to wrestle with unpopular causes, and his iconoclastic treatment of conventional social attitudes. *Candida* was one of their first productions and remained in the active repertory for a number of years. *Heartbreak House* and *Too True to Be Good* were also among Deeter's favorites and became centerpieces of the summer Shaw festivals that Hedgerow popularized in the 1930s. Shaw was also a terrific vehicle for teaching actors about making honest choices, Deeter believed, and his plays spoke to the "truths" that could be revealed in the theatre. In keeping with his critique of Broadway, Deeter wrote to Shaw in 1941 that "Cornell makes a stained-glass pageant out of *St. Joan* which has nothing to do with the play. *Joan* is about when to laugh and when to pray" and further that "the Lunts did a smart *Arms and the Man* alerting the audience then delivering the expected epigram 'superbly' as the critics say but had nothing to do with the characters."[8]

Hedgerow was a remarkable theatre but much of its history has been overlooked because of Deeter's insistence on preserving its rural and repertory character. Eva LeGalliene worked there before establishing her own Civic Repertory in New York. Virginia Farmer, Herbert Biberman, and Morris Carnovsky all worked for Deeter before becoming part of the emerging Group Theatre. And the powerful Theatre Guild periodically squabbled with Deeter over production rights to Shaw and other prominent playwrights. Hedgerow had a school that trained actors and eventually had a roster of prominent alumni in film, theatre, and television. And perhaps most remarkably, Deeter pioneered a Negro Theatre Unit in 1929, which subsequently attracted a company of black actors who performed plays by Paul Green, Eugene O'Neill, and Countee Cullen in the bucolic Rose Valley community.

The erasure of Hedgerow, and to a degree Jasper Deeter, from many narratives about American theatre has to do with a tendency to view Hedgerow as one of many "little theatres" that came to prominence from 1911 to 1930. Inspired by the excesses of the Theatrical Syndicate, and their war with the Shubert Brothers, and motivated by the Independent and Art theatre movements in Europe, little theatres in America soon expanded outside New York experiments such as the Washington Square Players and the Provincetown Players and flourished in a variety of communities including Chicago, Cleveland, and Detroit. They in turn stimulated activity in colleges and universities where the study of theatre moved away from an extracurricular activity to an arena for legitimate academic pursuit. This combination of amateur art theatres, civic community ventures, and academic programs created a vast network of theatres across the United States, which was often defined in relation to—or in opposition to—the professional theatre of Broadway.

Many "little theatres" wanted to encourage and produce new plays in a way that would not just ape the star-vehicle traditions in New York, but which would uncover and nourish local artists and actors who would not just be driven by the monetary demands of a professionalized industry; and they wanted to serve as a conduit for introducing local audiences to the modernist, and often controversial, dramatists who were revolutionizing the European theatre: Ibsen, Chekhov, Strindberg, and Shaw. Each theatre was unique and distinct, of course, and many discovered that their ambitions were not matched by their accomplishments. Plays that had had a successful New York run often attracted bigger audiences and income, and many saw their talented amateurs depart for New York once their prominence was assured in the local community. But most of the little theatres shared a vision that the intense commercialization of the stage, symbolized by the monopoly of the Theatrical Syndicate, had forged an American theatre that had lost its critical center—the ability to function as *art*.

Hedgerow shared many of the qualities of dozens of other little theatres across the United States, and thus its accomplishments often got subsumed in the accomplishments of the movement. But in two critical ways Hedgerow was unique, and it is that uniqueness that inspired many of its accomplishments, successes, and failures. First, Hedgerow was founded as a genuine repertory company and maintained that calendar in the face of economic crises and temptations to long runs and starring systems for 30 years. Second, the theatre was imagined and shaped in a community that had a deep and rich commitment to the Arts and Crafts movement in American life. The Rose Valley was a planned experiment to return the creation of art/craft objects to individual artistic expression and to encourage in the artist a sense of integrity and self-worth. Its principal product was architecture and furniture in the heydays of the first decade of the twentieth century, but those impulses would find vivid and dramatic expression in a variety of activities, including the theatre.

The Rose Valley Association was officially incorporated in 1901 by William Price, a Philadelphia architect, and several of his colleagues who wished to establish a crafts-oriented community along the lines advocated by William Morris and John Ruskin in England. Morris and Ruskin were the principal inspiration for the whole Arts and Crafts movement that swept through the United States in the last decades of the nineteenth century. They believed that the industrial revolution had not only led to the mass production of arts and crafts objects but also to the dehumanization of those who created them. In addition, they believed that this process had been accelerated by the explosion of urban landscapes where the factory mentality had robbed human beings of their connections to nature and the land.

One of the ways to combat this industrialization was to return to rural environments and create communities dedicated to simplicity, hard work, an appreciation for the wealth of the land, and the creation of objects—pottery, furniture, or book bindings—by individual labor. Price purchased land and buildings in Delaware County outside Philadelphia to establish a community where the philosophy and the principals of the movement could be realized. The Rose Valley community soon became the centerpiece for one of the most active craft colonies in America.

As a formal association it lasted only a single decade, but its influence on the community was enormous and persists to the present day. Craftsmen moved to the Rose Valley seeking a better way of life, and the community grew and prospered with a kind of blueprint about what it meant to live a more humane existence. That blueprint invoked a shared understanding of principals that were informally passed along by word of mouth and articulated in *The Artsman,* the official magazine of the association.

Furniture, for example, was made by hand, of good oak, and fitted together with joints and mortises that relied on gravity and weight bearing. Wooden pegs and some glue were allowed, but the emphasis was on the craft of piecing things together that were simple and strong. This process reflected a philosophical notion that design was a process based on reason and the creativity of the craftsman, and that the end result was not only an object but also a realization that work is an intrinsic good. For Price and his colleagues, all work "must bear the most severe scrutiny as to the honesty and thoroughness of construction" because "realization of the human potential of the craftsman is an end in itself, the highest goal attainable."[9]

Of course, the issue of cost for such carefully crafted work and the problem of marketability were enormous problems for many Arts and Crafts practitioners. The famous Rose Valley Morris chairs ranged in price from $50 to $100, while the Sears and Roebuck reproductions could be had for a price ranging from $4.25 to $6.45.[10] Price believed that the quality of the product was its own strength but he was uncompromising about his notion that market demand was not a measure of worth. "If a product sells in the marketplace, very good; if it does not, however, this does not make the product bad. Work, in the last analysis, is to be judged not by the product but by the process by which it is produced."[11] Jasper Deeter would later both struggle with and embrace this notion as he crafted a permanent repertory of plays. When the plays did not attract large audiences, he would keep them in the repertory if he believed in them and in the rehearsal process that created them. He frequently referred to the theatre's mission to do important works even if the audience at first rejected them. He wrote to Shaw that sometimes when the plays were right and true, he had to "shove them down the throats of his audience."[12]

The Rose Valley Association formally disbanded in 1910, but its remnants and participants remained the guiding spirit in the community for decades. When Hedgerow made its first tentative steps into the community in 1923, performing in the old stone mill that had once been the community center, some were suspicious of their "professionalism." Price had encouraged an active theatre program but it was staffed by members of the community, and they viewed their amateur status as a positive expression of their lifestyle. But Deeter persisted, and by the mid-1920s, the Hedgerow Theatre had become a vital part of Rose Valley culture. Price died in 1910, but his family became active in Deeter's theatre and his son William was an important member of the company. The reclusive but brilliant sculptor Wharton Esherick, who was one of the most prominent advocates of the Crafts movement, designed furniture for the Green Room, scenery for the productions, and a pair of sculpted wooden horses that stood at the entrance of the theatre. His wife, Letty, was a member of the company for many years and taught dance, weaving, and progressive education at the Hedgerow School. And both their daughters—Ruth and Mary—performed in numerous productions. Deeter had a small corps of actors who had followed him to the Rose Valley from his days at the Provincetown Playhouse in New York, but he encouraged community participation in the theatre, and soon many locals embraced the idea of Hedgerow in the same way that Deeter embraced the philosophy of Price, the Rose Valley, and the *idea* of a life sustained by hard and honest work.

Today, "sustainability" is a concept that is discussed and contested over multiple cultural sites. But many of its roots are in the Arts and Crafts awakening. The bibliography of works that invoke sustainable practices has mushroomed in the wake of the environmental consciousness of the late twentieth century and the global warming debates of the twenty first. It has multiplied into carbon mathematics and notions of economic growth that factor the depletion of natural resources. At its base, however, sustainability is about the capacity to endure in a duel between human extractive needs and the preservation of the natural environment. Jasper Deeter never conceived of the multiple meanings that sustainability denoted for subsequent generations, but his work at Hedgerow was infused with a sensibility that speaks to contemporary notions. Not only did he insist that they survive on what they could earn in the community, but his work in the theatre was also guided by a respect for the power of the environment in human lives, and long before "placiality" became a dramatic concept, Deeter was stressing the importance of locale in understanding human behavior. He taught acting by focusing on the relationship between the "guts" of the actor and the locale and demanded that this be visible in the body. Guided by Wharton Esherick and others, Deeter came to understand the power of living in a kind of harmony with a natural world unblighted by urban progress.[13]

Deeter frequently referred to Hedgerow as the only "rooted growth" theatre in America. That meant, on the one hand, an organization that was sensitive to, and appreciative of, the rhythms of seasons and change. Spring invigorated him, and he always saw renewed opportunities in its arrival: "First the blade, then the ear, then the full grain in the ear. Spring is hope for the heart and rest for the mind... being close and friendly with the world around us."[14] They lived simply, growing their own vegetables and sharing the daily chores of cooking, cleaning, and maintaining their environment. They raised sheep for food and wool, made their own costumes, and pieced together stage settings from scrap lumber and canvas. This work was not only necessary but also *honest*, and in Deeter's mind gave meaning and dignity to what they did. And "rooted growth" was also about the way that they worked. Like good furniture they started with strong scripts and then in long, testing rehearsals built them into productions where acting became the key to revealing truths about human existence. Deeter's acting and directing notes (many of which are preserved in the Gotlieb archives at Boston University) are about seeking out honest behavioral choices in the given circumstances. He encouraged his actors to experiment with different choices. His mantra of "failure is a privilege" was well-known at Hedgerow, and he was insistent that the rehearsal process was one where trying and failing was fundamental to the process of growth. Productions were not discarded once they were opened to the public, but like the furniture and crafts that inspired them, were preserved in the repertory.[15] They were not about elaborate scenery or spectacular technical effects. Often they were platforms, simple set pieces, and detailed lighting effects on the Provincetown-inspired cyclorama. This not only reflected a physical stage that measured 12 by 17, and loaded through trap doors from the basement, but it also reflected a notion about the making of honest and simple theatre that was in keeping with the landscape and environment of the Rose Valley.

The theatre grew. The repertory expanded each year by a half dozen new productions. Audiences from Philadelphia drove the 15 miles or rode the commuter trains to the Moylan Station. They played five nights a week and never canceled, no matter how small the house. In January 1933, they played *Misalliance* for eight people at fifty cents per head and sent Shaw his royalty check for twenty cents. Later they played for an audience of two student reviewers from Swarthmore College. The work was crucial but there was always a crisis at hand. The Depression threatened their box office; sudden snowstorms iced the roads in the suburbs; wartime rationing limited gas and food supplies, and the draft threatened to rob their company of important actors. But Deeter was resolute and fierce. He frequently

Introduction   9

assembled and addressed the company, assaulting their fears and recalling the threats they had endured.

"Everything used to be a national emergency," he reminded them in 1942.

When we played only on Thursday and Saturday nights there was close cooperation between finance, public relations and the production departments. It was very simple; if we had one ton of coal we sent post cards announcing two performances, if we had two tons of coal we announced four performances and if we had a reasonable expectancy that more coal could be bought we became revolutionary and inserted a Friday performance in between Thursday and Saturday... When the thermometer went down we did too... It would sometimes be obvious that the hand-stoked furnace plus an open grate of coals in the auditorium fireplace, coal oil stoves in the dressing rooms and the eggstove red hot in the green room could not provide comfort for the 20 or 30 people who might be willing to see a play. On those occasions we went into concentrated periods of concentrated preparation... Our best work was prepared in this way.[16]

Jasper Deeter was determined that Hedgerow would survive and prosper. He was charismatic and inspirational. He was also difficult, tireless, and stubborn. Paul Green, for whom he had secured a Pulitzer Prize by directing *In Abraham's Bosom* in 1922, referred to him as "a snaggled-toothed, coarsed-voiced character,"[17] and Theodore Dreiser pleaded with him at one time to be nice to the Shuberts, "because they think you are difficult and rehearse too long."[18] He was uncomfortable with celebrity and impatient with pretenders and fools. Visitors to Hedgerow commented on his casual appearance and dress, and he frequently disappeared after an evening performance rather than meet with people who had made the sometimes difficult journey from New York or Philadelphia.

Deeter was often preoccupied because he had to resolve the contradictions of running a theatre that was both sustainable and survivable. They always needed money because the box office alone could not support them. The company took part-time jobs when times were tough. He wrote grant applications, appealed to philanthropic organizations, and begged from friends and former students. He also began accepting apprentices who paid for the privilege of working at Hedgerow. It all helped, but also raised a larger concern. How could he continue as the absolute master craftsman and retain the support and cooperation of the entire company? Like many others in the Arts and Crafts movement, he wanted to live as part of a genuine community while exercising the singular artistry that would make life truly meaningful. But the mixture of strong personalities, long hours, and disagreeable chores was sometimes explosive. He was haunted by the fear that "the important truth of this place will be lost under the reiterative power of a funny name—Jasper Deeter."[19]

By the force of his personality, however, and an unwavering commitment to the idea of theatre as a sustainable and dignified way of life, he made Hedgerow into one of the most provocative experiments of the twentieth century. For three decades, they maintained a repertory of plays unmatched by any other theatre. Between 1923 and 1937 they built 125 productions, many of which were American or world premieres, and by 1956 they had 199 in their repertoire.[20] They played in true rotating repertory with a different title most evenings as well as two to three matinees. Deeter's goal was to create a living library of plays, and the titles reflect his appreciation of world drama; Russia, Canada, France, Germany, Italy, Ireland, and others were all represented in their canon. Of their 45 world premieres, 12 were presented for the first time in English, and for two years in the mid-1930s they did extensive bus and car tours of the United States. Deeter was the driving force in the organization—acting in exactly half of their plays—but he also encouraged Rose Schulman, Miriam Phillips, Dolores Tanner, and others to assume a more active part in the creation of the work. Schulman, in fact, would become an important teacher and director at Hedgerow and eventually join the theatre department at Boston University. The Hedgerow legacy is vast. From the glamour of Ann Harding and the celebrity of Richard Basehart to the vision of more recent alumni, Deeter's teaching and philosophy resonated in dozens of theatres and schools: Louis Lippa at People's Light and Theatre in Philadelphia, David Ralphe at the Simi Valley Repertory in Ventura County, Kevin Hughes at the Empty Space in Seattle. Actors Tom McCarthy in Philadelphia, Richard Wright in Washington, DC, and dozens of others attest to the influence that "Jap" still has on their work, and most importantly at Hedgerow itself where Penny Reed, who studied acting with Jasper as a teenager, has returned to the Rose Valley as artistic director.

In preparing this work I have spoken with many of them, and their reverence for, and admiration of, Jasper Deeter is generous and genuine. In telling a story of Hedgerow, I have focused on Deeter because he was the spirit and the core of the enterprise, and I have tried to invoke him by talking about the *ideas* that intrigued and propelled him and the people around him. Deeter loved the theatre, and he believed deeply in its power to heal wounds and create beauty. "Pretend," he would say, and "be saved." Hedgerow began as an idea—repertory theatre as a way of life—and it was nourished by a variety of other ideas—civil rights, pacifism, homesteading, conscientious objecting, harmony with nature and truth. In each of the following chapters, I discuss a specific production at Hedgerow and then use that as a platform to describe how the plays embodied ideas that made the theatre unique and helped to sustain it through three turbulent decades. There are many players in the story; Eugene O'Neill, Susan Glaspell, Bernard Shaw, Sherwood Anderson, Theodore Dreiser, Wharton Esherick, and Scott Nearing are some of the more prominent ones, but it was Jasper Deeter who willed the theatre to birth and success. Therefore, it is impossible to appreciate Hedgerow without what Dolores Tanner called "the terrific fire that was Jasper at 30!"[21]

1. *Inheritors*: Growing a Theatre

The Hedgerow produced Susan Glaspell's "American play" every Memorial Day and every Independence Day for nearly 30 years. It was, in many ways, their signature piece. She had written the powerful drama about democracy and individual conscience in 1920 against the background of the Palmer Raids, the Sedition Act, and a wave of "true Americanism," which swept up aliens and suspected "reds" for prison sentences or deportation. *Inheritors* also drew deeply upon Glaspell's Midwestern roots, the pioneering adventures of her Iowa family, and the stories that she had heard as a girl about the bravery and despair of Blackhawk, Chief of the Sauk. While the play resonated clearly with a post–World War I generation, it also invoked the cruelty and injustice of the Indian Wars that resulted in the expulsion of the Sauk and Fox from their Midwest tribal lands in the 1830s.

Jasper Deeter directed the premiere production in New York at The Playwright's Theatre in 1921. He was 28 and had had a checkered career in vaudeville and theatre before attaching himself to the young rebels and iconoclasts at Provincetown in 1919. Like his contemporaries there—Edna St. Vincent Millay, Djuna Barnes, and Ida Rauh—Deeter was attracted to the bohemianism of Greenwich Village and to progressive ideas about sexual identity, race relations, and gender equality.[1] He was also intrigued with the dedication and the mission of Provincetown, especially their commitment to producing new American plays in a noncommercial repertory system.

There was little in Deeter's background, however, which suggested the impact that he would have at Provincetown or in the creation of Hedgerow. He had failed at two colleges, Lafayette (1912) and Dickinson (1915), at newspaper reporting, and after finally landing a New York part in Charles Coburn's *The Better Ole* in 1918, was fired for excessive ad-libbing and "improper care of costumes."[2] Along the way he had tried his hand at

14 A Sustainable Theatre

Figure 1.1 *Inheritors* at Hedgerow, 1932. Courtesy of the Hedgerow Theatre.

vaudeville, Chautauqua performances, and stock at the Little Theatre in Philadelphia. All without particular distinction. But he was passionate about acting and performing. His mother, who aspired to a singing career, had given him vocal training and he performed as a choir boy at St. Luke's Episcopal Church in Mechanicsburg, Pennsylvania, where he grew up. She also encouraged him to attend acting classes taught by Silas Clark—Barrett Clark's father—at Chautauqua, New York, where he deferred part of his tuition by working as a cook's assistant. Just prior to joining Provincetown he had secured a small role as "2nd Policeman" in Frank Conroy's production of *Shakuntala,* the classic Sanskrit Hindu drama, which was performing at the Greenwich Village Theatre.

In spite of his limited resume, contemporaries often remarked about Jasper Deeter's magnetic presence: his "riveting eyes," chiseled features, and an electrifying effect offstage and on. Dorothy Haworth remembered the "comber of black hair which broke over his forehead, his piercing eyes and the aquiline nose which thrust forward like a prow breaking into stormy and untried waters."[3] Mordecai Gorelik, who met him in Greenwich Village and later designed at Hedgerow, was fascinated by his personal magnetism. "A true leader but also the most baffling and dangerous man I have ever come across."[4] He found him "brilliant and erratic," but with typical Gorelik paranoia also accused Deeter of deceit: "taking orders with great meekness then going off in a corner and spitefully and maliciously causing trouble."[5] Henry Miller called him "a man without dross. A man who has been through the fires. No artifice, no conventionality, no histrionics." And he was effusive about Deeter's impact: "communicating through his beautiful brown eyes a magnetic ray which bathed one in an electric effluvium."[6]

It was a heady time to be an ambitious actor in Greenwich Village. The Washington Square Players were reforming themselves into what would become the Theatre Guild, and talk of an actors' union monopolized the discussions at the Sheridan Square saloons. Some railed against the Theatrical Syndicate and the power and excesses of the Shuberts and the Producing Managers Association. Others called for a return to the repertory system that, in spite of its failure eight years earlier at the New Theatre, still held a fascination for those seeking a better life in the theatre. Actors' Equity, fighting for a legitimate existence, finally called a general strike in August and dozens of actors were out of work. Tempers flared as the managers threatened retaliation, but the so-called white way went dark. Youngsters at the Theatre Guild were allowed to continue playing *John Ferguson* because they were legally a private organization and not a commercial theatre, and they had a captive audience of summer tourists. Provincetowners were struggling to clarify their own goals, as a younger generation pushed for more "professionalism" against the will of their founder and philosopher, Jig Cook, who believed that their success and destiny was rooted in their untarnished amateur status. Deeter saw the plays on MacDougal Street and found the work promising and erratic. But he was excited by the idea of Provincetown and eager to join the ranks of a group who seemed to embody his idea of a company of actors working together to make a better theatre.[7]

His success was immediate although not spectacular. The competing egos on MacDougal Street were foreboding even for someone as "cantankerous" as Jasper Deeter. Cook and Susan Glaspell were technically on a writing sabbatical in 1919, and the theatre was being overseen by Ida Rauh and James Light who were charged with identifying the season's work as well as mounting the productions. Deeter made his debut in December 1919 in a play by Lewis Beach called *Brothers*, directed by Light, and was subsequently cast in all the remaining programs in the sixth season. He played "Al" in Edna Ferber's *The Eldest* in January and had a substantial role as "Town Crier" in *Vote for the New Moon*. He met and bonded with Eugene O'Neill, and in February 1920, Deeter played Ned Malloy, the self-absorbed and suicidal lead in O'Neill's lost, autobiographical drama, *Exorcism*.[8] Nine months later, his career found sudden traction when Jig Cook, back from his writing retreat, poured all of Provincetown's resources into producing O'Neill's stunning new play, *The Emperor Jones*. Deeter was cast as the craggy Cockney, Smithers, a role that was tailored to his ability to play distinctive character parts, and he vaulted to prominence at Provincetown.

The enormous success of *The Emperor Jones* split the ever-squabbling players into two sharp camps: those who wanted to capitalize on the notoriety of the production and go uptown, and those who wanted to add it to their list of accomplishments and continue their quest for excellence in the village. Deeter was a strong spokesman for the latter and in the ensuing weeks—while commuting uptown for *Jones*—he became an articulate spokesman for the artistry of the group. He'd learned some directing from Light and Edmund Goodman and developed his skills of observation and his sense of how actors could be coaxed into truthful choices. When Goodman recommended him to codirect the new play that Jig had been working on during his sabbatical year, Deeter was delighted with the opportunity.

The Spring, in Cook's fervent imagination, demonstrated the presence and the power of a universal consciousness through the "gift" of a young woman who could communicate with Native Americans and record their rituals in her automatic writing. Set in modern times among the Sac nation in Illinois, the play was a poetic attempt to endow the modern drama with a true Dionysian spirit. But its language was stilted and its philosophical musings strained credibility. Deeter struggled to make the relationships believable, but the tension between character behavior and Cook's desire for a Dionysian revival confused or bored small audiences. While there were some positive notices, the play faced diminishing crowds in the village, and Cook moved the production uptown where it played briefly and closed.[9] Glaspell, however, was intrigued with Deeter's work on the play, and when the players scheduled her dramatic story of the Blackhawk legacy for production in 1921, Jasper Deeter was invited to direct.

Inheritors unfolds over a sprawling map of ideas, identity, and politics.[10] It invokes racial tolerance, conscientious objecting, and personal commitment and integrity. But at its heart it's about the *land:* who possesses it and for what purpose? The first act takes place in a rural Iowa farmhouse in 1879 on the anniversary of the end of the American Civil War.

But to Grandmother Morton the festivities recall an earlier conflict—the Blackhawk War of 1832—which sealed the fate of native nations and conveyed 15 million acres of the Missouri Valley to the white settlers for $22,000. Now in 1879, that land has become the target of developers and speculators who want to convert it into valuable properties for their emerging Midwest empires.

But Silas Morton, who owns the farm and the magnificent hill that overlooks it, refuses to sell to the "rich and fat" because he has a dream that one day a college will grow in the cornfields and provide the aspiration and joy that was lost when the land was taken. "Look at the land we walked in and took! Was there ever such a chance to make life more? God damn us if we sit here rich and fat and forget that man's in the makin'."[11] For Silas, the idea of a thinking man aspiring to make life better for all is embodied in his future college, and at the end of the act he gives the deed away so that Morton College can be born.

The next three acts take place in the present (1920) on the fortieth anniversary of the college. From the interior of the library on the dramatic hill where Silas Morton made his peace with Blackhawk, you can look down on the campus that has become the legacy of Silas's dream. His portrait overlooks the playing area, and the stage is populated with his heirs and friends. Felix Fejevary, the son of his neighbor and closest friend, is now a prominent trustee of the college, and his granddaughter, Madeline, is a student. But the ideals that nourished both the foundation of the college and its populist mission is under attack in the aftermath of a world war and an America bent on enacting a reactionary ideological vision.

The freedom to search for truth and the commitment to a just society are now in danger of compromise in a world where corporate profits have become the lubricant for the social machine, and where Emerson and Whitman are suspected as "radicals." Morton needs the financial support of the steel mill down the hill, and many of its students are proud to serve as strikebreakers in the name of corporate profits. Hindu students who march and advocate for an India free from British rule are denounced by "American" students who are suspicious of any red taint of radical politics. In addition, a truly gifted professor is threatened with dismissal unless he repudiates his defense of a student who has been imprisoned for advocating conscientious objecting.

Glaspell filled *Inheritors* with her loathing for those who, under the guise of patriotism, advocate intolerance and racism and who imagine success in terms of accumulating wealth. Professor Holden, who came to the college 40 years earlier at the express urgings of Silas Morton, is clearly modeled on Jig Cook with his love of the Greeks and an imagined idea of beauty in life.

> I spoke of the tenth anniversary. I was a young man then, just home from Athens. I don't know why I felt I had to go to Greece. I knew then that I was going to teach something within sociology, and I didn't want anything that I felt about beauty to be left out of what I formulated about society...Not so much because they created beauty, but because they were able to let beauty flow into their lives—to create themselves in beauty.[12]

But Holden does not emerge unscathed in *Inheritors*. Because of his wife's ill health and his own need for security, he allows himself to be silenced. Unlike Jig Cook who could make the grand gesture, Holden agrees to the pragmatic compromise—"You don't sell your soul. You persuade yourself to wait."[13]

For Madeline, however, Holden's best student, Silas Morton's granddaughter, and one of Glaspell's most compelling heroines, there is no thought of compromise. Stunned by the police response to the Hindu demonstration and the thuggery of her cousin and other students, Madeline slams a policeman with her tennis racket and ends up in jail on the eve of her twenty-first birthday. When she is released by her influential uncle she discovers that the Hindu students remain imprisoned and confronts her family about the injustice of American democracy. In a dramatic coup de théâtre, Madeline chalks out the dimension of a prison cell and then confines herself to that imaginary space dramatizing the dream of freedom. Invoking her fellow classmate Fred Jordan, who is currently in prison for resisting the draft, Madeline refuses the special treatment offered to those who have acquired money and power and opts to return to prison. For her—like Thoreau and others—courage to pursue the true American dream is the only path to peace with herself.

Madeline Fejevary was one of Glaspell's most vivid creations and casting the part was critical to the success of *Inheritors*. Accounts vary about who actually chose the amateur and untrained Ann Harding, but the decision had enormous consequences for the play, for Jasper Deeter's career, and for Hedgerow. Harding, at the time, was nearly the same age as Madeline, a stagestruck amateur whose stern, military father was opposed to anything having to do with the theatre. Christened Dorothy Gatley, she had been raised on army bases and loved horseback riding and entertaining young officers at tea parties supervised by her father, then colonel, but eventually general George Grant Gatley. She had performed in school plays and had some vague fantasies of being a writer but was working at an insurance company in Manhattan and living with her mother in the fall of 1920. She was a strikingly beautiful young woman who had also managed to secure a part-time position reading manuscripts for Lasky pictures, and had a vague sense of having an "adventure" when she answered an ad to audition for a role at Provincetown. Glaspell and Deeter were both taken by her youthful enthusiasm, wholesome beauty, and stunningly blonde hair. Provincetown recorder Edna Kenton thought that Deeter believed she might do for one of the "giggling girl" parts, but, in reality, Glaspell was so awed by her surface resemblance to the blonde, Midwestern Madeline that she urged Deeter to read her for the leading role.[14] In his biography of Harding, Scott O'Brien recounts Harding's version, which is that they both asked her to come back the next day, and that Deeter interviewed her and suggested that she read several of Madeline's speeches.[15] Her blond hair—natural and multishaded—turned a lot of heads over the next two decades and led to a very successful stage and film career. Her devotion to Deeter ("my guru") and to Hedgerow ("my church") was legendary, and their correspondence over three decades resonates with the respect that she felt for him as director and teacher. Forty years later, Deeter would still recall her enormous talent as well as the striking color of her hair—"two different colors of natural blonde—half of her head albino and the other golden"[16]—which enamored Broadway producers, Hollywood moguls, and prominent suitors and endeared her to the entire Hedgerow community.

With Deeter directing and Jig playing Silas Morton, Harding made a celebrated debut in *Inheritors*. The production was a success for Provincetown and earned an immediate following for Harding, generous praise for Glaspell, and a good directing notice for Deeter. Critics were divided about its merits as propaganda but were supportive of Glaspell's courage in speaking out about the corruption of American democracy and the reign of terror unleashed by "patriots" on radicals, individual thinkers, and university professors. The production was extended twice and, in spite of its playing time (nearly four hours), was judged a success for the frequently squabbling players. But its success did not wallpaper the schisms that were overtaking the company. Shortly after, Jig and Glaspell left for his long promised pilgrimage to Greece, and Deeter accompanied Charles Gilpin on a tour of *The Emperor Jones*. O'Neill's highly anticipated *The Hairy Ape* caused still more controversy when he bypassed Jimmy Light as director, and the Provincetown experiment morphed into the Experimental Theatre overseen by the triumvirate of O'Neill, Robert Edmond Jones, and Kenneth Macgowan.

For Deeter, however, *Inheritors* was an incredible glimpse into what a life in the theatre might be. His work directing the company through the *politics* of the play was always rooted in terms of their human needs, and he worked patiently with the untrained Harding to help her understand her mission of bringing Madeline to life within the given circumstances. Deeter was particularly struck by the correspondences that emerged in the rehearsal room. Madeline first appears as a tennis-playing, carefree young woman who awakens to the discrepancies in her idealistic world and matures into the social conscience of the play. Similarly, Harding began as an enthusiastic, but amateur, mimic whom Deeter was able to coach into giving a moving and truthful performance. For him it was a memorable achievement. He also played her father, the deranged and despairing Ira who lost his wife to diphtheria and his son to the war, and who in the last act of *Inheritor,* despairs that all that remains of the land is his beloved corn whose seeds will fly away on the wind. It remains for Madeline to deal with the demise of her family while struggling for the ideal of an ever-changing but honest America. Deeter was deeply moved by the play and confided to Glaspell 15 years later, "I cannot tell the story of how *Inheritors* made possible a new kind of theater and even if I could people are not interested, they just don't care. But the story of what life might be if people could bring their caring directly to bear upon their ways of doing can best be told by you."[17]

Inheritors also stirred in Deeter that dream that a life in the theatre could also be about *ideas*. He never spoke of himself as a theorist or an intellectual, for him it was always about understanding the play and making it work. But he had the ability to distill and articulate a play's ideas and find ways for actors to embody them. Unlike some in the "Art" theatre movement, he resisted the temptation to be elitist in his tastes. He knew that all theatre had to fulfill the primary mission of entertainment. (His subsequent devotion to Shaw was fueled by what he saw as an elegant combination of ideas and comedy.) But he was also delighted in the hilarity of Lynn Riggs's *Roadside* or the whacky farce of Sam and Bella Spewack. "There is good box office in truth," he was fond of remarking "and there is truth in all good plays." Even in the lightest comedy, "whether Miss X chooses A, B, or C depends on how the play propagandizes for her to make that choice."[18]

Finally, his experience with Glaspell's play confirmed his notion that a community of artists working together in repertory was the only way to truly imagine a life in the theatre. He had had this conversation many times in the electric Greenwich Village of the early 1920s and with many people, and he had nursed hopes for Provincetown. But more and more the moment seemed to have past, and back on the road with Gilpin in

The Emperor, Deeter despaired at what a career in this theatre truly offered. He admired Gilpin and was saddened by the increasing alcoholism that would soon erode his talent and end his career. In Chicago, Deeter conspired with the Provincetown Board and Gilpin's wife to keep him on the wagon, but Deeter was eventually replaced on the tour when the battles over the pro- and anti-Jig forces escalated in New York. Deeter returned briefly to Provincetown to plan and execute a sound plot for *The Hairy Ape,* but his dream of a "beautiful theatre" was stymied after he left *The Emperor Jones.*

He scrambled for a time trying to pay the bills and keep a career alive. He toured in the Midwest with Madame Bourgny Manner's Ibsen repertory, went home to play summer stock in Harrisburg, and then returned back to New York to do a role in Owen Davis's adaptation of Ĉapek's *The World We Live In.* He doubled in a small part in *Rain* and put some money aside, but knew that this was not the life that he wanted. The idea of making a repertory company free to pursue art and of making a life in the theatre was persistent and provocative. In addition, a field of forces—internal and external—as well as events of chance and desire were accumulating to push him to a point of choice and commitment. The impossible is always tempting, but when chance provides the means it requires immense courage to make the leap of faith.

How is a theatre born? There is usually a master—and often mythologized—story. But frequently there are many threads that taken together offer a more nuanced understanding. Or as one critic mused in reflecting on the enormous international success of Jerzy Grotowski's Polish Laboratory Theatre and their reputation as "poor": "What might you think having graduated from the renowned Moscow Directing Academy to find yourself relegated to a poor, tiny theater in the drab Polish boondock of Opole? If you can't afford scenery, get rid of it. If you can't afford food, eat stone soup."[19] How might one turn this shabby circumstance into something much better? Hedgerow was born because Jasper Deeter had a dream about making a theatre that was a *life.* As Henry Miller later stated so eloquently after visiting the Rose Valley, "It is not the theater which interests him but life manifesting itself as drama."[20] But Hedgerow *started* because Deeter's sister lived close to Moylan, Pennsylvania, and he walked there one day smarting from a failed Chautauqua event at Swarthmore College. He found her rehearsing a play in the old mill that had been fashioned into a theatre by William Price, and being "at liberty" for the summer he asked her if she and some of her friends would help him produce a play. Hedgerow was born because Deeter had a fantasy of a company of artists, but it started because he found a *space*; a workable theatre in an old mill, that most critical ingredient for any fledgling company. Hedgerow was born because Deeter had a vision about the power of theatre but it started because he had *product*; plays that he loved and that he knew he could cast and sell. He would do *Candida* because its beautiful and iconoclastic heroine was another version of the fabled Madeline, and he would bring Harding here to channel her. He would do *Inheritors* in this bucolic wooded landscape and invoke all the American dreams that it promised. He would also do *The Emperor Jones* that he knew better than any other play and would reprise his role as Smithers. Finally, he had the *players*. Harding would surely come and his current companion Sydney Machet, whom Deeter believed possessed enormous talent, would make an extraordinary emperor, (even though he would have to do the role in blackface). And those with whom he had discussed so ardently the joys of repertory—Eva Le Gallienne, Morris Carnovsky, Allan Joslyn, Alexander Kirkland—might also be coaxed to Moylan where they could live cheaply and be free of the distractions and excesses of urban America.

It was all improbable but Deeter persisted. *Candida* became a "season" along with *Inheritors, The Emperor Jones, Androcles and the Lion* and several one-acts. Many did come, and when autumn summoned them back to New York, Deeter declined because now he believed it might work. There was no one thing that made it work, not even Deeter's "fire." And he was clear later in denouncing some of the romantic mythology that had grown up about Hedgerow.[21] But a climate evolved and a kind of zeitgeist that was peculiar to the Rose Valley nurtured the infant experiment. Part of that zeitgeist was the way that *Inheritors* became entwined with the legends of the theatre.

In a superb article articulating the similarities between the founding of Hedgerow and Glaspell's fictional Morton College, Jonathan Shandell observes that "Jasper Deeter's vision to build a world-class repertory theater in a rural gristmill clearly evokes Silas Morton's ambition to climb a hill and plant a college amid the cornfields of the Midwest."[22] He further stated that "like Morton College, the Hedgerow Theatre sprang directly from the mind of an anti-commercial dreamer into the American countryside."[23] In many ways Hedgerow did inherit *Inheritors*. Deeter's respect for Glaspell was foundational and manifests itself in the theatre's commitment to civil rights, nonviolence, participatory democracy, and conscientious objections to war. The notion of seeking truth in harmony with a rural America is a concept that not only flowed from Glaspell's play but also reinforced the Arts and Crafts credo that Deeter found in the Rose

Valley. Susan Glaspell was certainly a potent force at the moment of origin, and remained so throughout Deeter's life, but it was Wharton Esherick and others who helped to sustain him as he turned that first tentative summer into a celebrated repertory theatre. And it was Esherick, still largely unsung, who was vital to the success of Hedgerow.

Wharton Esherick, hailed today as a major figure in American wood sculpture, was a solitary and obscure artist who lived with his family in a rural remodeled farmhouse in Paoli, Pennsylvania, a few miles from Moylan. He read Thoreau and believed that *Walden* spoke truths about the simplicity of existence and respect for the land, and the book became a cornerstone of Esherick's life and art. Like many others in the "Crafts" movement, he turned away from the city and the tastemakers of the commercialized art world. And like Thoreau he began to seek what it meant to be human, to be in touch with the natural world, and to live by personal values, not those constructed by church, state, or political ideology.

It was not an easy life. He and his wife, Letty, grew their own vegetables, and he spent many hours repairing and renovating the stone house and barn, which was also his studio. He had tried to sell some paintings in the early years of their marriage, but his avant-garde swirls and color masses attracted little interest, especially among Philadelphia gallery owners. He made most of the furniture for their home, and his increasing skill with chisels, as well as his new knowledge about local trees and wood led him to abandon painting in favor of crafting furniture. At one point, with money running out, he accepted a teaching position in the utopian community of Fairhope, Alabama, where he and Letty felt comfortable with the progressive lifestyle. There they formed a lasting friendship with a young Chicago writer named Sherwood Anderson who would eventually play a pivotal role in their lives and the theatre of the Rose Valley.

Wharton is credited by many as being one of the architects of American "modernism" because of his fascination with a variety of the arts. His wood cuts and sculptures, for which he became famous, were all influenced by dance and music and drama. And his avocation of the Crafts movement made him one of the most respected artists in the Rose Valley. His passion for the land and for the sustainability of the environment were inspired by Thoreau—he is said to have kept a copy of *Walden* by his bedside— and his rejection of urban landscapes as corrupting resonated with Jasper Deeter. Esherick was introduced to Hedgerow by Deeter's sister who was an osteopath and friend to Wharton's wife, Letty. They were both immediately supportive of the notion of a truly sustainable theatre, playing not for profit but for a creative life, and over the years became active members of the community. Both of their daughters grew up as company members at Hedgerow, and Wharton eventually formed a lasting relationship with Miriam Phillips, an acclaimed member of the company, after separating from Letty. He attended rehearsals frequently and made sketches that later became celebrated sculptures or museum-quality drawings. Esherick designed and built scenery and props as well as furniture for the green room and lobby, a dramatic staircase, and numerous wood cuts, carvings, and freestanding sculptures. He also mended cracks in the theatre, reinforced old beams, and kept the ancient mill functioning as a playhouse.

Like Deeter he was an iconoclast, a free thinker, and scornful of numerous social conventions. He, like Deeter, also believed passionately in the notion that the earth had to be respected and maintained in harmony with human life. He adored *Inheritors* with its rejection of the land as a resource to be exploited by developers and corporate enterprises, especially as the Philadelphia suburbs pushed out into the enclaves of the Delaware Valley. Glaspell's play became even more resonant in Hedgerow mythology as Deeter sought to acquire land and buildings to preserve the landscape, but it was Esherick who provided the grandest gesture when he borrowed money to acquire several acres of land above his property that was scheduled to be blasted into a stone quarry. There

> he began laying the stone foundation for a woodworking studio on the very crest of the mountaintop above his farmhouse—a site that visually evoked Thoreau's notion that "there are none so happy in the world but beings who enjoy freely a vast horizon." The spot provided a panoramic of the surrounding hills carpeted in oak and evergreen, dogwood and laurel. Below birds glided in languid formations or hung themselves stationary like individual kites, in the updrafts. Lush green farmlands, laced with rivers and often tufted with morning mists, stretched as far south as the eye could see... It was on this mountaintop, amidst saws, planes, wood shavings and his well-thumbed copy of *Walden* that Wharton Esherick finally found himself as an artist.[24]

Esherick was inspiration, but the hard work of making a theatre that could support them in a totally rural area was daunting. In their first "season," they earned $3,767 at the box office. Deeter also made a special appeal to the Philadelphia Art Alliance that netted them another $3,200 and they were able to survive.[25] But he was determined and ready to make a total commitment to the dream. He wrote to Eleanor Price Mather that "they could have the finest repertoire theater in the country in R[ose] V[alley] next year."[26] In April 1924, they began a second season and their box office improved to $13,981.87 largely because Deeter, who had been critical of

Eva Le Gallienne's production of Ibsen's *The Master Builder,* invited her to Hedgerow that summer to stage "dueling" productions. He directed Will Price and Ann Harding in one version, and Le Gallienne played Hilda Wangel and directed herself and Sydney Machet in the alternating version. Although there was some tension between the two casts the production was a terrific success, and the Philadelphia papers began to extend their theatrical coverage to Hedgerow.

Things did not always go smoothly; there was tension about whether they were really welcomed in the old gristmill, living quarters were difficult to find in the tiny community, and many viewed them as undesirable. They were perceived as "bohemians" who often walked around in their bare feet, and their clothing was a subject of discussion among the more conservative natives. Townsfolk looked with particular askance on "the woomus, an all-embracing purple garment worn by Deeter over his overcoat in cold weather."[27] But Deeter persisted and after establishing stronger links to the Davis family and the local artist's community, they became Hedgerow.[28]

An early clue to how committed Deeter was to the notion of a theatre without stars or the trappings of careerism and individual achievement can be seen in the programs of those first few years. Unlike other companies who would occasionally break away from the traditional star billing—the Group Theatre, for example, advertised their productions by listing the casts alphabetically—Deeter wanted to foreground the play and not the players. The theatre programs at Hedgerow listed only the character names. If you wanted to find out who was actually playing the part, that list was posted in the lobby.

Like Morton College in the cornfields of the Midwest, Hedgerow was founded with noble ideas and ideals. They would all be tested, sometimes ferociously, in the years ahead. Is it really possible, for example, for an actor to play all kinds of roles as Deeter proposed? Or is there a limit to how far even the most supple performers can be stretched? Deeter preached that the actor grows by the roles he or she plays, but in the company this often caused strife and resentment. And in the performances, critics sometimes winced at the results. Looking back, Rose Schluman reflected on what was one of their major growing pains.

> By the mid-twenties the company was having difficulties, for Jasper's desire to teach—to play God, often led to atrocious casting which accomplished nothing for the play and often threw the centers of the plays off base. Most of his best actors left because they were promised casting which they deserved and were able to handle, but someone else would get the part.[29]

Deeter understood the frustrations and would make occasional concessions, but he was also deeply committed to the notion that learning only proceeds from error and experiment, and he was not willing to compromise his central notion that Hedgerow is not a theatrical platform for some other pursuit, but a way of life. Many actors did leave but many others wanted to come, and they did. Learning first that they were not "actors" but aspirants to a way of life who were expected to embrace every aspect of this new and strange community.

2. *The Emperor Jones*: A Passion for Equality

In the first scene of Eugene O'Neill's stunning play, Brutus Jones, the powerful and self-elected emperor of an island empire, looks down from his scarlet throne at the Cockney trader, Smithers, and reminds him who has the power in this kingdom.

> JONES (*His hand going to his revolver like a flash—menacingly*): Talk polite, white man! Talk polite, you heah me! I'm boss heah now, is you fergettin'? (*The Cockney seems about to challenge this last statement with the facts but something in the other's eyes holds and cows him.*)
> SMITHERS (*in a cowardly whine*): No 'arm meant, old top.
> JONES (*condescendingly*): I accepts yo' apology. (*Lets his hand fall from his revolver*) No use'n you rakin' up ole times.[1]

The impact of a black man speaking to a white man—even a slimy beachcomber like Smithers—in such terms was still shocking to a lot of theatregoers in 1920s America. Jasper Deeter recalls how he and Charles Gilpin weathered the audience storms.

> We always had to watch our timing in the first scene... usually from the orchestra floor from eight to fourteen people would leave the auditorium. Sometimes they would leave noisily enough so that we could get away with a little sotto voce dirty talk on the stage. Sometimes maybe we were heard but it didn't matter at that time.[2]

The play was a huge hit off and on Broadway and then in its road tours. Gilpin's performance was powerful, often erratic, and compelling in its conception and delivery. The sight of this black, masculine figure driving the action of the play and yet succumbing to powerful psychological forces was thrilling to experience. And the theatricality of its beating drums, ghostly scenes, and vocal chants all contributed to the impact of

28 A Sustainable Theatre

Figure 2.1 Arthur Rich and Jasper Deeter in *The Emperor Jones*. Courtesy of the Hedgerow Theatre.

the production. O'Neill, who had a fierce commitment to racial justice and who was intent on using the stage to address adult concerns, was fascinated by the landscape of human behavior in *The Emperor Jones*. He was reading widely in Freud and Jung, and the play was infused with notions of how fear can grow from the almost benign appearance of "little formless fears" to the absolute terror of confronting the subconscious. It was both a literal journey through the jungle as well as a psychological journey through Jones's mind as he regresses into his personal and collective past. The accompanying drum beats, which start at the exact tempo of the human heart, escalate as Jones's fear blossoms into hysteria and drives him into the waiting arms of the natives whom he has duped and fleeced.

Gilpin was a seasoned performer when Jig Cook cast him in the central role at Provincetown. Born in Richmond, Virginia, in 1878, he had worked with a variety of vaudeville and minstrel troupes before joining the Anita Bush Company in 1915 and subsequently became a featured star at the Lafayette Theatre in Harlem. His success there led to his Broadway debut as Reverend Curtis in John Drinkwater's 1919 production of *Abraham Lincoln*. O'Neill and Deeter had heard of his performance and both were committed to challenging the color bar that segregated the American theatre. It is not entirely clear who insisted that Gilpin be cast as the emperor. O'Neill's preference for a black actor has been widely documented, but Deeter claimed repeatedly that he lobbied for Gilpin rather than a more seasoned white actor—Charles Ellis—who would do the demanding role in blackface as was the custom. Deeter wrote to Shaw, "I put up a fight which resulted in Charles Gilpin being permitted to bring the negro into drama for the first time in our present American scene."[3]

Deeter and Gilpin became good friends through the Broadway run and subsequent tour, and Deeter was often in awe of the power and presence that Gilpin brought to the role. He watched *The Emperor Jones* dozens of times from backstage before making an appearance in the last scene when the scheming Smithers watches the natives drag the dead emperor out of the forest. Deeter was very fond of the play and would never tire of reprising it at Hedgerow where he played Smithers to a variety of Joneses. He was aware of the intellectual landscape that O'Neill was exploring, but in typical Deeter fashion he also saw the play in terms of box office potential. "*The Emperor Jones* still makes money...People like stories of fear, it enables them to feel brave and to find *truth*."[4]

It is ironic, of course, that in struggling to establish Hedgerow in 1923 he selected a white man, Sidney Machet, to play the title role. He quite likely had no other choice among the small company who were the nucleus of the experiment, and from all accounts Machet was a very talented performer who was quite remarkable in the role. An undated clipping from the Philadelphia *Record* hails both Deeter's direction and the performance of the young leading man.

> Sydney Machet, a youth of nineteen years, is a Deeter discovery and Machet gives notice of being an actor of renown. His work as Emperor Jones has already indicated a genius for the histrionic art. The role is lengthy and by no means easy. The colored actor, Gilpin, was acclaimed for his interpretation of the part, but Machet has developed some features of the role not touched by Gilpin, and is surely as effective in portrayal, holding a theater audience tense and in thrall. Some day he ought to be one of the big players of the land.[5]

Sadly this promise was not fulfilled. Machet, like many others who followed Deeter to the countryside, was unable to adjust to the communal lifestyle and returned to Provincetown and hopes of a New York career. He was deeply influenced by his friendship with Deeter, however, and with the notion of repertory. He eventually became a member of Eva Le Gallienne's company at the Civic Theatre in New York and was in rehearsal for a revival of *Inheritors* in 1926 when his manic behavior and depression alarmed members of the company. He was rehearsing the dual roles of the young and old Silas, a hallmark of Deeter's own repertoire, but was repeatedly late for calls. Shortly before opening, Machet suffered a nervous breakdown, therefore, Le Gallienne was forced to release him from the company. However, she admired him enormously and spoke often of his performance opposite her in *The Master Builder* at Hedgerow. When he appeared to be cured she allowed him to rejoin the company, and he took up his old role in the Glaspell play. But prior to opening he disappeared again, and LeGallienne was shocked to learn that he had committed suicide.[6]

The Emperor Jones became a staple at Hedgerow, their most performed play, and the backbone of several successful seasons. Not only was its prominence in the repertory linked to its box office success or Deeter's prominence as the original Smithers, but it was also emblematic of a commitment to racial equality that Deeter and others in the Rose Valley community actively embraced. In spite of its "racist" language and its problematic assumptions about a racial collective unconscience, *The Emperor Jones* and other "Negro productions" made Hedgerow one of the most progressive and remarkable of American theatres. Years before the "Great White Way" submitted to equality in seating and staging, the audiences and the casts in the Rose Valley were integrated.

Deeter's commitment to racial equality had many sources, but it was certainly stimulated by the progressive nature of his own politics and the bohemian socialism that was rampant in Greenwich Village during and after the war. Like others at Provincetown, he was deeply opposed to the Jim Crow mentality that excluded blacks from most white institutions, and like James Light and O'Neill, he found the color barriers of the American theatre unacceptable. Deeter was aware of the literary and artistic explosion in Harlem and of the disgrace of young black men and women being thrown out of jobs when the white soldiers came home from the war in Europe. He read and discussed Carl Van Vecheten's explosive *Nigger Heaven* when it was published in 1926 and was sympathetic to the controversies about how to represent black experience on the stage. He had talked with Gilpin frequently about the actor's growing dissatisfaction with the language in *The Emperor Jones* and Gilpin's tendency to improvise with O'Neill's text or substitute "Negro" for "Nigger" or even "black baby" in performance.[7]

The communal nature of the Rose Valley also encouraged a healthy distrust of corporate capitalism and its tendency to reduce human beings to capital and labor. Media and Moylan were both historical shelters on the underground railway, and the old snuff mill had employed both white and black laborers. Among the many bonds that Deeter shared with the visionary Wharton Esherick was a disgust for the way that Negroes were marginalized and segregated in opportunity and education. Mansfield Bascom relates how Esherick aroused the anger of his southern colleagues when he tried to extend the principles of utopian socialism outside the geographical confines of Fairhope, Alabama.

> He also volunteered to teach at the school in the black neighborhood, just beyond the edge of town, where the sidewalks ended... The white community wasn't entirely accepting of Wharton's liberal, non-prejudicial sense of inclusiveness. A lawyer there in Fairhope said, "Mr. Esherick, you're going to be chased out of town. The people are very much disturbed by you. They know you are going out and teaching at that colored school and they don't like it. They're real Southerners and they'll have nothing to do with Negroes." The lawyer suggested that Wharton take a detour to disguise his destination. "I used to go maybe two miles out of my way so I could dodge those people and not let them know I was going over to the Negro school."[8]

Wharton and Jasper had many conversations about the contradictions in American racial attitudes that led to a deepening friendship as the Eshericks became more entwined with life at Hedgerow. They shared similar views about individual freedom, respect for the environment, and collaboration in the arts. For the premiere of their second full season in the Rose Valley, Jasper invited Wharton to design the sets, costumes, and lights for an original play on "myth and beauty" by Hermann Hagedorn called *The Heart of Youth*. Although they were both disappointed with the production, they enjoyed the process of the work, and it became the basis for several future productions including a stunning expressionistic design for Ibsen's *When We Dead Awaken* in 1930. Esherick had great respect for Deeter's determination to realize his idealistic vision, and his influence at Hedgerow was manifest in a number of lobby exhibitions and in two wooden horse sculptures ("Cheeter" and "Deeter") that stood outside the front entrance of the theatre for 20 years and became important landmarks for neighborhood and visiting children.

The impact that Deeter's liberalism had on colleagues, actors, playwrights, and many others is legendary, and his commitment to civil rights was hailed in a wonderful piece in the *Chicago Defender* in 1932 pointing out that prejudice has no place there and praising the Hedgerow Theatre as "an experiment in democracy."[9] In 1926, his protégée, and budding

Hollywood star, Ann Harding became a celebrity spectator at the infamous Sweet trials in Detroit where a prominent Negro doctor and his son were charged with murder after a mob attacked their home in a previously white suburb. Harding, who was infatuated with the presiding judge in the case, was shocked by the open racism in the community, and at the conclusion of Clarence Darrow's seven-hour defense summation she caused a sensation by leaping up and embracing him. In both this outburst and in her subsequent decision to join the National Association for the Advancement of Colored People (NAACP), Harding was acting out the commitment to Negro rights that she had been tutored in at Hedgerow.[10]

While *The Emperor Jones* signified the importance of dramatizing racial relations at Hedgerow, it was another play about black and white issues that was the catalyst for both their integrationist agenda and for resuscitating their lagging box office. Midway though their fourth season, Deeter believed that they could capitalize on the celebrations surrounding the Sesqui-Centennial International Exposition in Philadelphia by playing a six-week summer season at the Broad Street Theatre. The increased income generated by visiting tourists and the chance to expose their repertory to mainstream Philadelphians seemed like a good gamble. Unfortunately, it was a mistake. The high rent, sparse attendance, and transportation costs left them with a $19,000 debt at the end of August, and in desperation Deeter announced that Hedgerow would have to suspend operations while the four principle company members figured out ways to pay off their debts.[11]

Back in New York, he landed a part in *Princess Turandot* and then was approached by Eleanor Fitzgerald and Kenneth Macgowan at Provincetown for directing a new play by Paul Green called *In Abraham's Bosom*. Green, who had an established reputation in the south and some modest success with one-acts about Negro life, was anxious to break into Broadway, but commercial producers were either reluctant or opposed to producing a "Negro play." Provincetown, however, was anxious to sponsor him and to return to the lagging experimental theatre some of the charisma that had once typified their offerings. The play has some remarkable similarities to *The Emperor Jones*, especially in the long monologues by the terrified Abe after he has been assaulted by a white mob and in the appalling ways in which black people are threatened and humiliated. Deeter was intrigued. Working with the new management at the theatre where he had earned his initial directing credits, Deeter was able to assemble an outstanding cast of Negro performers. Jules Bledsoe, who did a stint as Joe in *Showboat*, was a powerful actor with great vocal range. His portrayal of the title role Abe McCranie, who sacrifices all trying to bring education to his people, was the powerful centerpiece of the production, and the talented Rose McClendon as his long suffering wife, Goldie, and Abbie Mitchell as his aunt, Muh Mack, rounded out a superb cast. The play is deeply rooted in southern Negro life: collecting turpentine, enduring poverty, and denying white parentage. It unfolds over several years and is rife with whippings, mob violence, and sexuality. Deeter was inexperienced in the customs of sharecropper livelihood, but he worked through the emotional peaks in the play by focusing on the dramatic action, and the company responded to his method. Paul Green was absent for most of the rehearsals, but as opening night loomed he came to New York for his debut.

It's impossible, of course, to recreate what he saw or to recapture the tension that accompanied that historic opening, but we do know that Green was deeply upset with much of what he saw and recorded that anxiety in a written note to Deeter.

1. It's too slow; speed it up.
2. too much mumbling especially Bledsoe in prayer scene, road scene and final scene.
3. the whipping is ridiculous.
4. Douglass is dead.
5. the girl "Lanie" hogs the stage.
6. and, mispronouncements are awful.[12]

There's no record of Deeter's response, but on December 30, 1926, the play opened and ran with enormous success for 123 performances. After it moved uptown to the Garrick Theatre, it was honored with the Pulitzer Prize in Drama. Green subsequently wrote to Deeter that "I feel honored having you set me forth in the theater. Thank You!"[13] Deeter posted the letter on the call board for the company to read. Provincetown and Green were both bathed in celebrity, and Deeter was determined to capitalize on the prestige of the production by reopening his suspended Hedgerow with *In Abraham's Bosom*.

The entire company traveled to Philadelphia and the Rose Valley for a special performance on June 16, 1927, and then went back to New York where the play was still running. A second Hedgerow performance was given two weeks later to a sold out house. Although the theatre continued to struggle (1928 would be their lowest year at the box office) Deeter's work with the cast of *In Abraham's Bosom* had a huge impact on him, and he was determined to make plays and performances about the Negro experience a part of the Hedgerow mission.

It was a daunting task. Hedgerow didn't even pay salaries to its "resident" actors, so the thought of assembling enough Negro actors to perform in repertory seemed utterly idealistic. But Deeter had connections in New York and in Philadelphia, and in the summer of 1929, he coaxed the cast of *Abe* back to Hedgerow for a revival that alternated with *The Emperor Jones* and an evening of Paul Green one-act plays (*White Dresses, No Account Boy, The Man Who Died at Twelve O'Clock*). The leading roles in both *Abe* and *The Emperor Jones* were played by Wayland Rudd, a talented young black actor who returned the next season to play Othello for Deeter in what is believed to be the first instance of a black man playing the part in America supported by a white company. Rudd had worked with Rose McClendon and Richard Huey in the revival of *Porgy* in 1929 and would appear on Broadway with Frank Wilson in *Bloodstream* in 1932. He was a remarkable actor and singer and was on the verge of carving out a distinctive presence in the heavily segregated theatre. Like Paul Robeson, he was pursuing a variety of stage opportunities and received strong notices for the narrative voice that he provided for the Stravinski-Stokowski *Oedipus Rex* that premiered in Philadelphia in April 1931. Like Robeson, he too was deeply offended by the racism in the United States. He looked to the Soviet Union, as did many Negro actors and artists, as a site where equality was guaranteed for all, and in 1932 he traveled to Russia with Langston Hughes and several others in an ill-fated attempt to make a film about American racism.[14] Following the collapse of that project, Rudd—disgusted with race riots, lynchings, and a totally segregated stage—elected to stay in Russia where he lived and performed until his death in 1952. He played a leading role in a Russian film version of *Tom Sawyer* in 1937 and two years later wrote a play about the barbaric work conditions in an Alabama coal mine called *Andy Jones*, which was based on Rudd's reading of Angelo Herndon's autobiography, *Let Me Live*.[15] Unlike other pilgrims who recognized the Stalinist threat behind the Bolshevik facade, Rudd returned to America only once. In 1934, he came home for a short visit and spent time at Hedgerow visiting with Deeter and his former colleagues. The *Philadelphia Independent* reported that the man "who rose from Washington news correspondent to star" was at Hedgerow watching rehearsals and later noted that he had now worked for the Russian director Meyerhold and "praised the Russian theater."[16] Although marginalized in many accounts of the American theatre, Wayland Rudd, in the summer of 1929, was the centerpiece of a remarkable theatre event in the Rose Valley. Deeter wrote to Paul Green about the productions of his one act plays and noted that, "With these three bills we did the first week of Negro repertory that we know anything about."[17]

Wayland Rudd's story echoes with several others at Hedgerow and is emblematic of the respect that actors developed for Deeter and the determination that he had for finding outstanding performers regardless of race. Deeter continually referred to Hedgerow as "rooted growth," and among other things he felt that developing local actors was as much a product of his vision as being compatible with the natural world. After Rudd left for Russia, Deeter recruited a local Negro chauffeur, Arthur Rich, who joined the part-time company in 1931 and throughout the decade had a storied career at Hedgerow. Under Deeter's tutelage and direction, Rich played the leading role in *The Emperor Jones* and became an important member of the Negro unit. Rich developed a passion for performing and a desire to learn as much as possible about Deeter's belief in the power of acting to discover and reveal truth. Over the years he became one of the most celebrated of the Hedgerow "Emperors" as well as playing Enos in *No Count Boy*, Uncle January in *The Man Who Died at Twelve O'Clock*, and Hunnycutt *In Abraham's Bosom*.

Arthur Rich was born and raised in Cheyney, Pennsylvania, and was 35 years old when Deeter coaxed him into the Hedgerow family in 1931. His father was a chef at Cheltenham Military Academy in Philadelphia, and Arthur, after attending public schools, secured a position as valet for Maurice Bower Saul, a prominent lawyer in Media, Pennsylvania. With the outbreak of World War I, he enlisted in the all Negro 325 Field Signal Battalion and was promoted to sergeant after combat in the Argonne Forest. Following the armistice, Rich returned to Media and became the chauffeur for his former employer as well as "Assistant Constable" for the tiny Media-Rose Valley community.[18] He married and was raising four children when Jasper Deeter convinced him to read for the role of the Emperor Jones in 1930. Deeter knew and liked Rich and was convinced that he could become an important part of the Negro company that he wanted to build.

While he was not nearly as powerful as either Gilpin or Rudd in the demanding role, Rich received dozens of good notices over the years and played the role in New York when Deeter took the Hedgerow company for an extended residence at the Phoenix Theatre in 1945. Ruth Esherick, who sometimes stage managed *The Emperor Jones* as a youngster at Hedgerow, recalls that he was fascinating in the role but was sometimes erratic from night to night. He occasionally drank a bit before the show, and she kept an extra prop pistol backstage that she would fire in case he nodded off. She also remembers with great fondness when he took her to a matinee film at the Media movie theatre, and they had to use a special entrance reserved for the coloreds. "I suppose I should have known but I had no idea."[19]

The audacity of Jasper Deeter integrating both the stage and the audience at Hedgerow was courageous and controversial. Pennsylvania at the end of the 1920s, like many northern states, was deeply segregated in its public facilities, and Negroes were simply not allowed in the best hotels, restaurants, amusement parks, or swimming pools. They were routinely denied admission to Pennsylvania colleges and universities, and theatres relied deeply on the balconies and segregated sections that Van Vechten had popularized as "nigger heaven." In 1935, when the Pennsylvania legislature passed a law granting integrated admission to all public gathering places, the outcry was enormous. In September, *The Literary Digest* interviewed several proprietors who were articulate and outraged about the legislation. The manager of a prominent hotel said he would never allow a Negro in his establishment. "A white jury would never convict a white man for refusing to let a Negro in his place."[20] Another manager commented, "This bill is a terrible thing. It was passed for purely political reasons. We will positively not allow Negroes to enter our dance halls or our swimming pools except when there are Negro picnics... I don't think there is a jury that will find us guilty."[21] Well before the uproar over this threatening legislation, a young black actress named Frances Williams recalls Jasper Deeter pausing in the midst of a play at Hedgerow to confront a patron who objected to rubbing shoulders with Negroes, "We have plenty of time to wait for that man to get up and go out if he doesn't like my friends who are here."[22]

Deeter's hope following the first Negro season was that he could form a company of local black performers who would be featured in the summer repertory along with some other prominent names who might be induced to be in residence at Hedgerow for six to eight weeks. The bait, as always at Hedgerow, was not salary but a chance to work with like-minded artists on plays of merit and substance. Deeter was always on the lookout for scripts in which he could feature the Negro performers because available plays were limited. He corresponded frequently with agents and producers to see if he could get special royalty rates and thus reduce the overhead drain. Typical is the following letter to Frank Sheils at Samuel French requesting a special reduced fee to present *In Abraham's Bosom* "at Hedgerow only."

> Our present Negro Company has made three tries: They did Countee Cullen's *One Way to Heaven* to average grosses of about forty dollars, while the rest of the list stood at about eighty-five. Then they did three of Paul's one-acters,

doing splendid work to an average of about thirty-two dollars while the rest of the list stood at ninety. Their present averages in *Abe* are second only to *Beloved Leader* in this year's list.

These facts naturally encourage our whole theater and make it easier for our colored part time group to make the personal satisfaction necessary for the development of a solidarity of their own. I have hopes of a comedy from the Gilpin Players but failing that I have no other option to lay before them at this time. I give you these facts to show you how difficult it will be for me if we must take away from them the vehicle of their first success in three years.[23]

It might have been convenient to give up on the idea of having plays about Negro life performed by Negroes as part of the Hedgerow repertory, but Deeter was committed to the *idea*. The 1930s seethed with the rising discontent of America's beleaguered and formerly enslaved population. Scottsboro was in the news and on the lips of many blacks and whites throughout the decade. Lynchings embodied both the popularity of white southerners in celebrating their way of life and the barbarity meted out to those who had the courage to oppose the system. Race riots in Harlem and other American communities foreshadowed the ferocity that both northerners and southerners would display in refusing to accommodate Negro participation in the American "dream."

The American Communist Party appealed to a great number of Negro intellectuals and artists because of its avowed support of civil rights and its frequent denunciations of racism. In spite of the party's own significant shortcomings and its frequent fealty to a Russian-led Comintern, which seemed ignorant of the realities of day-to-day life south of the Mason-Dixon Line, the Communists exhibited enormous courage in defense of American Negro rights. They sent union organizers into the teeth of the sharecropping south and rushed legal aid to the Scottsboro boys while the NAACP delayed, trying to anticipate the public relations consequences. Robeson, Rudd, Hughes, and others were attracted and often seduced by their ideology of classless equality and freedom.

White, progressive Americans joined with their black colleagues in a variety of attempts to combat the racism that was threatening civil order. Liberal democrats introduced antilynching legislation in congress after congress but were unable to overcome the New Deal's reliance on its southern politicians. American labor, particularly the emerging and powerful Congress of Industrial Organizations (CIO), opened their rolls to Negro workers who had been routinely barred from the American Federation of Labor (AFL). In addition, American stage, dance, and film artists responded with works like *Stevedore; We, the People;* and *Marching Song.* In 1936, the Works Progress Administration (WPA) Federal Theatre Project established a network of nationwide black theatres that began producing groundbreaking performances of *Haiti, Black Empire,* and *The Trial of Dr. Beck* to integrated audiences.

In the Rose Valley, Jasper Deeter, unheralded and largely unremembered, carried on his own very personal and quiet crusade. To keep the players together throughout the decade required persistence and patience and discipline. Most of them commuted from Philadelphia or nearby communities for rehearsals and performances, often at their own expense. Most had jobs and/or families that could interfere with their scheduling and professional theatre. But connections to the black theatre community in Philadelphia and the growing reputation of Hedgerow as a place that was sympathetic to Negro performers encouraged a stream of volunteers. Deeter's former Provincetown colleague, James Light, had been appointed director of a Philadelphia Black Unit of the newly organized Federal Theatre Project and was utilizing both newcomers to the theatre as well as some who had experience at Hedgerow. Together they provided opportunities for Negro performers who had been systematically excluded from most American theatre.

Faced with limited options and anxious to celebrate Hedgerow's commitment to civil rights, Deeter, in 1936, undertook a production of Countee Cullen's dramatized novel *One Way to Heaven.* It was a provocative and challenging choice. Cullen had been a star of the Harlem Renaissance, one of the finest of an emerging coterie of Negro poets and a lightening rod of artistic and personal controversy. He believed that art and poetry could transcend race and young writers should look to aesthetic models, like Keats and Housman, regardless of their lineage. He often disagreed with colleagues, like Langston Hughes and others, about depictions of the black experience, preferring not to dwell on the sensational aspects of underworld life or clichés of dope, pimps, and violence. His artistic prominence had won him wide respect in the intellectual communities of the 1920s, and his marriage to the daughter of W. E. B. Du Bois was a major event of the Harlem Renaissance, although it too was engulfed in gossip and scandal.[24]

By the early 1930s, Cullen had turned away from poetry and was exploring dramatic writing. He undertook a dramatization of *One Way to Heaven* and upon the advice of Rose McClendon sent it to Jasper Deeter. On June 13, 1933, he wrote, "My Dear Mr. Deeter, Would you like to look at my play of Negro Life?"[25] Deeter was very interested and invited Cullen and

McClendon to the Rose Valley to talk about the script and design possibilities. Cullen was impressed by Deeter's reaction to the play and later wrote "if you are interested, I should be totally amenable to any changes you wish to make."[26] Deeter was committed to producing, but the script presented huge casting demands and he wanted to slot it into the repertory at a time when he'd have the most black actors available. In the interim, Cullen arranged with the writer Harry Hamilton to create a new version that Cullen's agent sent to Hedgerow. Jasper, however, liked the original and did not want to collaborate on a new version. In addition, he wanted Cullen to understand that if they produced it, it would remain in the repertory and not be pulled for other (New York) productions. He wrote to agent Leah Salisbury that he wished to produce the original dramatization and that "we can cast it but want to make sure that we'll continue to play it."[27]

One Way to Heaven features a black con man who pretends to find religion and ingratiates himself into a church community in order to pursue his real goals—lust and money. He seduces a young woman, Lottie, who is a servant to Constancia Brandon, a Negro aristocrat who conducts a salon for the betterment of Negro intellectuals in her Stivers Row home. This salon brings the two plot lines together when Constancia insists on hosting Lottie's marriage and then discovers that due to a scheduling mistake her guests will listen to a distinguished white professor read his paper on *The Menace of the Negro to our American Civilization*. The blending of the two Negro lifestyles made it an appealing and controversial choice for Deeter, and the characterizations of the upper-class, cultured Negroes reflected Cullen's ongoing agenda to represent the aristocratic "New Negro." The script has never been published, but the stage directions describing the salon in the manuscript serve to situate the intent of the production. "Home of Dr. and Mrs. (Constancia) George Brandon. The scene is a large living room furnished with taste. The house is in a section once inhabited by fairly well-to-do whites. Now that it is inhabited by fairly well-to-do blacks there is little change except in the complexion of the inhabitants."[28]

Constancia is a regal, thoughtful, and formidable hostess who sponsors parties and lectures in her salon that are attended by the Harlem elite. She is kind to her servants and generous with her wealth. In Act III she gives an hilarious "As Others See Us" evening where the guests are costumed as Toms, Mammies, Jungle people, and Topsy. But she also mistakenly mixes up her invitations allowing a celebrated, white professor to lecture to a salon gathering on the menace of the Negro race. Constancia and her guests listen with patience as the flabbergasted Professor Calhoun enumerates his hateful screed culminating in the charge that the Negro's worst failing is their horrendous smell. At the conclusion of his talk, Constancia shrewdly intimates that she will never betray the fact to his southern friends that he attended a Negro salon and then offers him his fee. "You must forgive me Professor," she coos, drawing his check out of her bosom, "but I had no advance notice of your ideas on our racial fragrances or I would have put your check in a less aromatic place of concealment." Striving to exit and save some composure Calhoun stammers, "Madame, I have long ago learned that money never smells."[29]

Deeter persuaded two Philadelphia "socialites" (who aspired to become actors) to play the critical roles of Lottie and Constancia and filled the cast out with his fledgling Negro company. But the rehearsals were fraught with problems of attendance and confusion. Deeter, who insisted on discipline and a total commitment to the rehearsal process, was frustrated by people not showing up and with a general lack of theatre etiquette. Not wishing to play the role of paternal overseer, however, and anxious to preserve the integrity of the Negro unit, he asked that they hold a company meeting to clarify the issues and the problems of rehearsing and performing. The minutes of that meeting make a fascinating record of the dilemmas that Deeter wrestled with in his quest for an integrated theatre.

> The meeting of the Negro actors of the Hedgerow Theatre was opened by Miss Goldie Ervin and she explained a series of "unpleasant happenings" as follows—the leaving of Mrs. Marquess and Casco Alston; Guernsey Booth's inability to report to every show also Lester Harris and Ruth Jackson; the unpleasantness of Bob Watson and also his leaving the company in a most abrupt manner.
>
> Then Miss Ervin related her interview with Mr. Deeter in which he stated that he could not go on with the production *One Way to Heaven* on account of the foregoing reasons, and also for the lack of discipline the group has shown.
>
> Miss Ervin then asked Mr. Arthur Rich to explain from his experience how the Hedgerow actors discipline themselves during a performance. He brought forth the talking "off stage," "on stage," and "down in the basement and during a performance." He stated an actor cannot give a good performance unless he or she is in character from the beginning of a show to the end.
>
> After a very lengthy discussion by the entire group an "Advisory Board" was elected composed of (3) three persons. The motion was amended to add two (2) more if the company became larger. The members of the Advisory Board are—Arthur Rich, Goldie Ervin, and Betty Howard. It was decided that the Advisory Board be responsible for the discipline of the group. Other duties of the Board will be discussed with Mr. Deeter, especially maters related to "application" and "expulsion."[30]

The production did proceed, and while not a great success at the box office, Deeter was pleased with the dialogue that it stirred and the way that it participated in the race debate. A reviewer from the *Philadelphia Independent* wrote that "Cullen has written a strange mixture of satire and faith, love and comedy, into the ten scenes of his script, which is believed to bring a group of upper class Negroes to the stage for the first time."[31] Deeter told Glaspell that "the social scenes are a grand answer to the Carl Van Vechten kind of Nigger Heaven thing. Our white audience literally can't understand them and our Negro audiences are entirely at home with them so for this reason I think the play of great importance as the first statement of a subject of great interest to the civilized Negro."[32]

The production was introduced on September 28, 1936, and was repeated, as was frequently Hedgerow custom with new works, the next night. It played five times in October and an additional two in November. Deeter then played it in February, June, July, and December of 1937. Its grosses ranged from $100.00 to $18.00 over a two-year period, and Deeter was pleased with the stir that it caused and its modest income. But he had difficulty in keeping the large cast in line and eventually removed it from the active repertory.[33]

Jasper Deeter was not able to sustain a Negro company at Hedgerow in the manner that he had originally envisioned, but it was a constant theme in his correspondence and his conversation. He continued to schedule *The Emperor Jones* and to cast black actors in some traditional white roles. But it was always a difficult dance. O'Neill had given him the rights to the play and it always made money, but Deeter sometimes used white actors like David Terry Martin before finally recruiting Arthur Rich and the splendid Stanley Greene. In 1940, Deeter tried to convince David Stevens at the Rockefeller Foundation that Hedgerow would be a wonderful target for their largesse and suggested among other things that they might help fund the Negro company. Stevens was gracious in his reply but essentially said that they are unable to fund a grant to Hedgerow at this time.[34]

The record of Deeter's commitment to equal rights is laudatory but still fragmentary in the written record. A film of the Hedgerow company in 1947 (see chapter 9) has only one black man. In addition, Deeter's public speeches on Negro actors sometimes betray an unintended paternalism or racial clichés.[35] However, it is clear that in the black community Hedgerow was widely known and respected. In addition to the praise heaped upon them by the *Chicago Defender,* the archives of the theatre contain letters of inquiry from many Negro artists and actors. Thomas Richardson, who directed at Langston Hughes's Suitcase Theatre and later founded the Richmond Virginia Community Theatre, inquired about working at Hedgerow in 1935,[36] and Abram Hill, a founding member of the American Negro Theatre, urged Deeter to come to New York and direct *Anna Lucasta* for them.[37] But perhaps the most touching inquiry is from a 20-year-old Loften Mitchell, who would later become one of America's most gifted historians of the Negro theatre as well as a successful playwright and essayist. Mitchell, who also won a Guggenheim award and was a respected college professor, wrote to Deeter in 1939 that he was already working and writing but at Hedgerow he would be willing to do almost anything including "sweep the stage."[38]

3. *Winesburg, Ohio*: Democracy between the Hedgerows

The economic collapse that shattered American prosperity in the fall of 1929 had devastating consequences for the theatre. Producers were bankrupted, theatres were closed, and hundreds of actors, designers, dancers, and others, lost their jobs. Provincetown was closed, and in the ensuing Depression of the early 1930s, Eva Le Gallienne's Civic Repertory was also forced to shut down. Deeter was depressed about the misfortune befalling so many of his friends and colleagues, but the "crash" reaffirmed his belief that professional theatres were the factories of American culture, chasing profits rather than a way of life, and hence as vulnerable as the factories that made steel, automobiles, or rubber tires. "The Civic Repertory was founded on the basis of a large contribution of one person and forty persons with a thousand dollars each," he remarked, and "when the market crashed, those people were busy learning how to do their own cooking and getting rid of at least all the servants but one, and they had no dollars."[1]

At Hedgerow, the dollars too were down, but the company was determined to keep producing the repertory they had promised. "Thank God, we never depended on 'mainliners' to keep the place alive. We never did. Our gross was always from the ground up," said Deeter, as he remembered the hardships of the early 1930s.[2] The permanent company—those who lived on the grounds or in the community—now numbered 24, and they all worked in the gardens picking squash and carrots and onions and in the theatre rehearsing, building, and performing the repertory. This sense of being linked to the earth was fundamental to Deeter's belief in Hedgerow and enabled them to focus their meager income on the productions. In 1929, they did a full season of nightly repertory including productions of *Thunder on the Left, A Doll's House, Misalliance, The Stronger,* and several others on a production budget of $4,000. They projected an income of $12, 500 and actually took in $13,703.30.[3]

44   A Sustainable Theatre

Figure 3.1   Sherwood Anderson and Jasper Deeter on the set of *Winesburg, Ohio*, 1934. From the Hedgerow Theatre Collection, Howard Gotlieb Archival Research Center at Boston University.

The lifestyle at the theatre was a constant subject of speculation by the press and the local townspeople. Rumors of bohemianism and communism were frequent topics of discussion in the Rose Valley, and some youngsters were cautioned by their parents to be wary of the colony.[4] Many young actors came to the Rose Valley in the early 1930s to learn from the Hedgerovians, but most of them left when they discovered the nature of the commitment. Hedgerow was a mysterious commune in the eyes of many young professionals who were leery of the work but wanted the patina of its approval as a way of insuring their pathways to commercial success. But Deeter never wavered in his stubborn crusade to create a theatre that was not based on the starring system and which showcased a repertory of carefully mounted productions.

They struggled but they kept mounting new work and showcasing some of the audience favorites in their repertoire. Their income stabilized even in the bleak days of the early 1930s. In 1932, they took in $14,307.36 at the box office and the following year they earned $13,632.72.[5] Reporters and drama critics began visiting the Rose Valley when it appeared that the theatre was going to survive the impact of the Depression, and most came away with laudatory, although superficial, accounts of the community. But as the theatre continued to make an impact in the national scene by producing modern masters like Shaw, O'Casey, and Chekhov, along with new and innovative American premieres like Sherwood Anderson's controversial *Winseburg, Ohio,* the demand for coverage surged.

John Guyer had given Jasper a job as a cub reporter at the *Harrisburg Patriot* in 1910 when he was the city editor, and in 1932, he asked if he could come to the Rose Valley and do a feature story about the success of the company. He was intrigued, as were so many others, about why people put up with the often primitive living conditions, worked for virtually no pay, and endured sometimes 14 hour calls. Over several days in 1934, Deeter granted Guyer free rein to live at Hedgerow, talk to whomever he desired, and report whatever he discovered. The result was a fascinating piece called *A Look Behind Scenes at Hedgerow Theatre* that captured the lifestyle in the community as well as made a case for the value of the work.[6]

Guyer followed the company members around on their daily chores, ate meals with them, washed dishes, mowed lawns, drove the bus, and observed their rehearsals and performances. While his account is laudatory and sometimes borders on puffery, it also reveals some of the hard truths of why the company continued to function despite hard times. For example, "Deeter trains everyone, women not exempted, in every department of the theater. They all have knowledge not only of acting, but of stage setting, costuming and general production work."[7] Guyer knew this beforehand but until he saw them close-up he had no idea how vital it was to their work. He watched Ferd Nofer play Feste in *Twelfth Night,* wield a smith's hammer in the shop, operate a cultivator in the garden, and function as treasurer for the entire enterprise.[8] Catherine Rieser played Maria in the same production and also oversaw the costume department, patching and mending the 30 shows in the current repertory and preparing clothes for the monthly opening of a new production. Repertory demanded nightly changeovers, and shortly after the evening's curtain went down the company busied itself installing the next show's settings. And then amazingly Guyer reports that "after that or sometimes before, depending on demands, Deeter may put a group through from two to six hours of rehearsal. And after eight hours of sleep he may have them at it again that afternoon for as many more. They have been at it 14 hours in a stretch, upon occasions, which accounts for their ability to produce such exceptional work, day in and day out."[9]

The work sustained them, but Guyer also offers two other insights that help the reader—and the historian—to understand the complex social nexus that enervated these "Hedgerovians." First, the long hours and hard work sometimes led to conflict, jealousy, disagreement, and a host of other interpersonal dynamics that threatened the solidarity of the community. Guyer seems to recognize this—though not explicitly—and offers up an explanation of sorts.

> There is high character and fine personality in the entire group. No questionable type remains longer than is required to learn his or her true character. Then there is an instant show-down, followed by a resignation, voluntary or otherwise. No unpleasantness, aside from forceful debates over politics or similar topic, mars the conduct of the group. No energy is wasted in futile debate. Everyone is working for Hedgerow. They eat, sleep and work with but one objective, which is to produce plays of merit and set standards that are high and which will endure.[10]

Guyer also testifies to the commitment that they seem to share about the value of living a life in and for the theatre. A life that is Jasper Deeter's creed as well as Hedgerow's belief system.

> So why do they keep at it? Some of them, maybe more than I suspect, believe that their work is doing something for the drama in the United States, if not elsewhere, that hasn't been done. Others like the associations and friendships they find in and out of the group. A few may be in it for the training they get...so that they make money or a name for themselves. But most of them simply enjoy the work and especially the life of freedom from many of the qualms and quirks that beset our shattered civilization.[11]

Guyer's visit came shortly after Hedgerow had opened one of their most publicized offerings, Sherwood Anderson's dramatization of his best-selling and controversial *Winesburg, Ohio*. Anderson, who grew to love and be loved by the company, confirmed many of Guyer's observations about the spirit and the work ethic in a piece for *Esquire* that was subsequently published as an introduction to the script for *Winesburg*. "Deeter has apparently found out a certain secret, that there is a deep and real passion for the theater in many people that goes pretty far. It is obviously his belief that in acting there can be found a way of life too, that if men and women can find work that they love doing they do not too much mind much discomforts."[12] Anderson too was struck by the commitment that he saw among the young people and by the way that they all shared the work of keeping the company thriving in the hard depression times. "The young woman of Pennsylvania Dutch ancestry who last night played a leading role in a play by Shaw, Chekhov or Lynn Riggs may this morning be planting sweet corn or setting out cabbages in the garden."[13] But the thing that impressed him most about Deeter was that he was a superb teacher, and it was this gift that Anderson admired most about the Hedgerow experience and which brought him back numerous times over the years. "Like all good teachers Jasper Deeter is never tyrannical. He is infinitely patient," wrote Anderson, "'Wait' he will say to a criticism of one of his actors. 'He is still trying. He is working.'"[14] Watching the rehearsals of *Winesburg*, Anderson came to understand the talent that was Jasper Deeter as well as the attraction that drew so many hopefuls to the Rose Valley.

Winesburg, Ohio was published in 1919 and remained Sherwood Anderson's most famous story until his untimely death in 1941. It was controversial in its subject matter as well as its format and would eventually be regarded as a milestone in American modernism. Anderson abandoned the plotting structure of the traditional novel and wove his story around the accumulation of knowledge gained from the 26 short stories (or character sketches) that make up the book. In addition, he drew upon his own small town, Midwestern roots in depicting the often grotesque and frequently unpleasant aspects of human nature. The people of Winesburg are often venal and manipulative, narrow-minded in their appraisals of one another, and products of an avaricious capitalism and a puritan sexuality. The central focus is the coming of age of young George Willard who has to negotiate his journey to adulthood through various sexual encounters and the conflicting ambitions of his unhappily married parents. In the climactic scene, George's father discovers that he is not the true parent and that his wife has hidden this fact from him, as well as a substantial amount of money, which now is George's ticket to get out of this poisoned environment and perhaps find his way as a man.

Much of the book is in dialogue form, and Anderson had thought about dramatizing it ever since Jacques Copeau had suggested the idea shortly after the book was published. Copeau was in New York with his Vieux Colombier Company during World War I and had met and admired Anderson. He was impressed with the writing and is reported to have said that "the stories were the first full rich expression of something he, a Frenchman, after living among us, had come to feel about American life."[15] Subsequently, in 1932, Anderson met a promising young playwright, named Arthur Barton, who had had a mild success with a production of *Wonder Boy* and who was very enthusiastic about undertaking collaboration with Anderson to bring *Winesburg* to the stage.¹⁶ Anderson was delighted by the challenge, and shortly after Barton sent him an outline scenario, Anderson began writing dialogue. They signed a contract giving them equal shares in the revenues, but the partnership did not go well, and Anderson became increasingly frustrated with Burton's contributions. They disagreed about several characters in the play, and Anderson did not like the ending that Barton proposed. (Later Anderson discovered that Barton had tried to register the copyright in his name only, and that he had represented himself to agents at the Theatre Guild as the sole dramatizer of the famous novel.) When Barton was reluctant to do any further revisions, Anderson changed the legal documents to a 65–35 arrangement. However, as Barton's behavior became more erratic, Anderson removed him from the partnership and began to rewrite the play by himself.¹⁷

He submitted the finished manuscript to the Theatre Guild, which took a year's option, and Anderson was enthusiastic about the possibilities of a production. Always an avid theatregoer, he began to look at potential casting choices amongst Broadway actors. He saw a production of Maxwell Anderson's *Both Your Houses* and thought the young Sheppard Strudwick would be an ideal George.¹⁸ But the Theatre Guild was nervous about the Barton contract and about the similarity in content to O'Neill's *Ah, Wilderness!* that they had just committed to produce. Frustrated by the pace of the negotiations, Anderson expressed his discomfort to his friend Wharton Esherick, who told him that Jasper Deeter ran the best theatre in the country and he should let him read the play. At Hedgerow, he stressed, it would not only get a professional production but it would get worked on and developed and become part of a repertory that would keep it before the public in the hands of some very skilled performers. Anderson was curious and Esherick introduced him to Deeter who agreed to read the play.

Winesburg went into rehearsal on June 1, 1934, for a month of intensive staging and rewriting. Deeter loved the ideas in the play; its critique of the big business aspects of American culture, its view that the simplicity of rural life was giving way to the lure of the metropolis, and its depiction of the narrow-minded prejudices that undermined the promise of equality. He cast it with a team of his very best players including a newcomer, Libby Holman, who had come to Hedgerow to study with Deeter after a scandal involving the death of her husband, the heir to the R. J. Reynolds tobacco fortune.¹⁹ The talented and trusted Ferd Nofer played George's materialist father, Ted, and Catherine Rieser played his unhappy wife, Elizabeth. Joseph Taulane played George Willard and Holman played Belle Cartwright, the older woman who is George's first sexual partner and mistress to the town banker.

Deeter told them repeatedly that it was among the finest writing that they had worked with, and he counseled Anderson to adapt the play to the strengths of the Hedgerow stage. Because they had a small stage, Deeter wanted the play to move swiftly from scene to scene with a minimum of set changes to give the production flow and to minimize the number of changes. He also—with Anderson's involvement and input—worked to make the transitions as seamless as possible. Thus, they developed a complex sound plot that eased the transition from scene to scene while maintaining the reality of the fictional moment. In his authoritative book on Anderson's life, Walter Rideout attributes these transition moments to Anderson's "recent interest in off-stage sounds...popular tunes, voices and other sounds," to bridge the action, but it certainly seems that the collaboration was equally due to Deeter's intense sense of stagecraft and what would work in the theatre.[20]

In his dissertation study of Hedgerow, John Wentz concluded that the real strength of their work was the intimacy of the performances. The stage was small and the technical effects were limited. Deeter had installed a permanent cyclorama similar to Provincetown that enabled them to create the effect of a larger space and employ imaginative lighting effects. The cyc was concrete and permanently attached to the stage floor. It wrapped around the playing area and had a three-foot crossover space upstage in front of the back wall. Because it was permanent, it limited access to the stage so that in production the sides were frequently masked so that actors could make entrances from deeper in the set. Jack Wade, who designed for the theater in the early 1980s, recalls that the cyc was painted white with bluish undertones, and when you washed it with blue light it created a phenomenal effect.[21]

For *Winesburg*, Deeter used the cyc as a permanent background for the action and then localized the scenes with simple set pieces—a few headstones for the opening funeral scene, a small woodpile for the meeting between George and Belle, or a picket fence. This allowed the action to keep flowing and also enhanced the sound score that played in the blackouts between the scenes. But the emphasis was always on the actor seeking the "truth" of the moment and of the character. *Winesburg* was reduced from a traditional three-act play to one with nine extended scenes and an epilogue that Deeter encouraged Anderson to write. There were crowd scenes, such as at the funeral of Windpeter Winters, that opened the play, and eventually Deeter's cast numbered 26. But the heart of the play was clearly in the two-character scenes that propelled the action: Elizabeth and Ted's long and nuanced struggle over who will determine the future of their son; Belle and Helen's poignant meeting that begins with issues of class and concludes with a revelation of character; and George's attempts to negotiate a future with Helen. Deeter spent extended rehearsal time encouraging his actors to explore the personal landscapes that Anderson had provided as well as the emotional life that they themselves brought to each moment.

The opening night was festive with several out-of-town friends, including Theodore Dreiser, in attendance, as well as a number of Philadelphia and New York critics. Deeter and Anderson were apprehensive about the frank sexuality, which had been one of the criticisms of the novel, and one line in particular did cause an audience stir and was subsequently cut in later performances.[22] The theatre was hot and even with the excellent performances and the rapid transitions between scenes it was by nearly all the accounts a long evening in the theatre. The reviews ranged from unkind ("Only the intermission served to relieve the tepid tedium") to outrage ("depravity, blasphemy, vulgarity and banality") to mixed ("the cast gave convincing and moving portrayals").[23] Dreiser found it tremendously exciting and was impressed with Deeter's staging and Anderson's dialogue. (A year later Dreiser would have a triumph in the same theatre when Deeter produced his *American Tragedy* with spectacular results.) The Eshericks hosted an opening night party at their home in Paoli, and Anderson and his devoted wife Eleanor were flattered by the attention and the occasion, but he was surprised and somewhat depressed by the seemingly unanimous verdict that the play was too long and needed to be cut. He wrote Deeter a long letter when he got back to his farm in Ripshin, Virginia. "Jap, the play as a whole stands solid in my mind. I do believe that in a week or two I can do some effective cutting that will not hurt but will help the movement and the music. I shall be very happy if you and your company feel that they want to go on working with me until we get it absolutely right."[24]

For Deeter, however, the hoopla of the opening night and the wait for the reviews to receive the up or down vote mattered little. He had long since given up on the hit-or-miss mentality that characterized Broadway, and he was intent the next day on continuing to craft and shape the play that they had all devoted the last month to making. Still imbued with the arts and crafts vision that had inspired him to nurture a theatre in the heart of the Rose Valley, he would no more give up on this play than Esherick would on one of his emerging wood sculptures. Making theatre was still above all else a way of life and his art. He had good materials in a strong cast, a thoughtful and iconoclastic play, and an imaginative mise-en-scène.

Monday night was better, and by Tuesday they had shortened the playing time considerably. Deeter planned to offer the new production once a week throughout the season and he kept his word. With Anderson's approval he edited several scenes and then worked with the company to sharpen some of the characterizations so that the relationships were more nuanced. They wanted Dr. Parcival to become more philosophical about his pronouncements on the people in the town and gave him a weary kind of humor to temper his bleak view. They wanted Tom, George's hapless father, to be more sympathetic in his quest for material things and "bigness" so that it captured the ideology of the place and time and not just his individual ambition. And they worked to humanize Belle so that she would be seen more as the victim of an aggressive male world and not just as a "fallen woman."

The sexual subject matter still angered some, and in August an entire row of spectators made a noisy exit when the young men of Winesburg were discussing their conquests. But at that same performance, Walter Rideout quotes a New York critic who had come down to see what was causing such controversy saying "that the play is not to be taken lightly" because out of the production there does emerge the portrait of a whole town "not a pleasant portrait but worthy of study and contemplation."[25]

They played it 22 times that year along with a repertory that featured plays by Shaw, Chekhov, and others. They kept it in the active repertory for three years giving it a total of 41 performances (nine in 1935 and ten in 1936). The average play at Hedgerow between 1923 and 1952 was staged 31 times.[26] The production grossed $3352.41 or an average $81.77 per performance.[27] As such, it was clearly a successful investment in financial terms though somewhat below the average nightly income of $84.70 for all productions that summer. It was never produced in New York though Anderson pursued a number of producers who evinced an interest in the text after Hedgerow. At one point, he was optimistic that Libby Holman might be able to interest a producer based upon her excellent performance as Belle Cartright and the notoriety surrounding her divorce. But nothing came of it.[28]

Sherwood Anderson was utterly enthralled by the Hedgerow experience and community and he returned there often in the years following *Winesburg*. In 1936, he began a new play for the company—working furiously at times—but never finished the project. Like Esherick, he enjoyed Deeter's company and would frequently sit and drink with him after late rehearsals. He was fond of many of the company there, especially the talented Miriam Phillips, who was a remarkable actress and Esherick's companion after his wife, Letty, contracted encephalitis. Phillips is said to have observed of Anderson (who was married four times): "I loved Sherwood. He was the only man who never tried to make me."[29]

But Anderson's commitment to Hedgerow was more than just starstruck author. Like Jasper Deeter, he was deeply concerned with rifts in the American polis and with the function of the artist in an increasingly "big business" world. He shared with Esherick the admiration for the simplicity of rural life and the utopia of the single tax movement. He flirted with radical thought and the Communists, and accompanied his wife Eleanor, who was an activist social worker, to mining camp strikes and labor rallies. But he never could make the total commitment demanded by many radicals because ultimately he believed that the artist was in a different "class," and he valued trying to sort out the nature of the artist's struggle in society. Anderson became an avid reader of the painter Van Gogh's published letters to his brother that detail the artist's anguish and compulsion to create. In 1935, he purchased three volumes of the letters at the Weyhe gallery in New York, and in November he thronged with thousands of others to the big Van Gogh exhibition at the Metropolitan Museum.[30] He was inspired by Van Gogh's empathy for the natural world and for his understanding that the artist has to find his integrity and endure, even if that meant suffering and ridicule. In that light, artists like Deeter and Esherick became heroic for Anderson, and he shared his admiration for them with others and made sure they read Van Gogh.[31]

Anderson had one other impact on Hedgerow that had great consequences for the way that they lived and worked. By 1934, out of enormous industry and careful planning, Deeter had managed to pay off a significant amount of their mortgage debt and was contemplating a restructuring of the way they functioned as a theatre community. The impulse came from many sources, but essentially he wanted to make the company more responsible for the planning and execution of their work, and he wanted to begin to democratize Hedgerow. He was still sensitive—as he always had been—about the tension between a commune of like minds and his own artistic dictatorship. As the company grew and new people flooded to them, Deeter felt compelled to undertake a radical reorganization of the theatre in order to share out more of the responsibilities. It would be a revolution of sorts, but from the top down and it would result in a great experiment involving numerous committees, long and sometimes stormy meetings, and a reevaluation of the power structure. Anderson offered his farms a retreat so that Deeter, Miriam Philips, and Ferd Norfer could map out the manifesto. They called it "The Virginia Plan."

John Guyer's look behind the scenes at Hedgerow is enthusiastically positive but obscures or overlooks many of the tensions that were endemic to a community of aspiring artists. Especially one that demanded that they subvert their own egos for the health of the group, and that they exist in sometimes primitive, if not squalid, conditions. Hundreds of actors came and left Hedgerow over the years because they were unwilling or unable to put up with the demands that Deeter and others imposed on them. Letters in the Hedgerow archive provide some glimpses of the rents in the fabric of artistic community that was vital to the enterprise. Bill Ulrich wrote that he is "sober now" and defends himself from the charges that he "stole twelve dollars and used food budget money to buy booze."[32] Deeter's homosexuality—which was widely acknowledged but nearly invisible in the written record—could also be a source of tension as evidenced by this nasty missile from Mr. Orlovitz who addresses him as "darling, sweetie, Jasperia, precious" and urges him to " tear off your false tits."[33] But the source of most of the tensions had to do with Deeter's authority as the ultimate decision maker, the final voice on repertory and casting.

Although they crafted the document at Anderson's farm in Ripshin, the irony in the title was obvious and intentional, since it clearly invoked the famous "Virginia Plan" of 1787, which had been written by James Madison and which became the basis for creating the "checks and balances" fundamental to the United States Constitution. In fact, the original Virginia Plan gave expansive powers to the citizens through its creation of a legislative branch composed of two elected bodies that would curb executive authority. Hedgerow had both a "dictator" and a core group who lived and worked on the premises, as well as a host of other part-time volunteers who gave their affection and industry to the enterprise. The Virginia Plan created a Policy Group that was made up of "old" members and a New Policy Group that was constituted of the part-time community. The groups were charged with formulating distinctions between residents and nonresidents and between part and full-time participation. But the major focus of the plan was to implement a series of committees who would affect the day-to-day operations of the theatre and replace Deeter's absolute authority with committee decision making.

In retrospect it was a bureaucratic boondoggle, but at the time it seemed both judicious and forward looking. It relieved Deeter of a lot of the administrative wrangling over production details, and it empowered members to become involved actively in the functioning of the theatre. Committees were created to deal with all aspects of Hedgerow life including ushering, parking, scheduling, advertising, selling, and production calendars. Two of the most powerful were personnel relations and direction. Personnel made critical decisions about who and how one might join or leave the company, about misbehavior and internal governance, and about financial arrangements with individual members or interns. Deeter was the chair of this committee and was the titular chair of Direction that was responsible for selecting the annual repertory. In response to members who complained of having no voice in the selection of titles, the Virginia Plan encouraged individuals to make suggestions to Direction. In subsequent discussions two of those titles could be put forward for a vote by the entire company.

The Policy Groups also formalized the distinctions between the resident company who were full-time members and received room, board, medical coverage, and a modest allowance and the nonresidents who participated as actively as their schedules allowed but who received no remuneration from Hedgerow. In addition, the theatre created a designation of guest actor for performers who were essential to making a production work but who assumed no additional duties or obligations.

The Virginia Plan was controversial but probably critical to Hedgerow's continued growth and survival in very difficult times. Deeter was committed to a democratization of the company but he also preserved the principal voice in aesthetic issues that were fundamental to him. Over the years, the plan was modified as members became frustrated with the "committee work" that consumed so much of their time and with many details which seemed like "busy work." Audrey Metcalf, however, who would later become a partner when the Virginia Plan was replaced with a legal partnership in 1942, believed strongly, "Had it not put its affairs in order when it did, the theater would not have survived the problems of the war and the post-war periods."[34] Deeter, too, was pleased with the plan because it represented an attempt at democracy and recognition of dozens of people who had made Hedgerow possible. The Virginia Plan provided a framework for allowing the theatre to function and grow at a time when it had little formal structure and was a genuine compromise between democratic instincts and an aesthetic vision forged by Jasper Deeter. A delightfully dissenting voice, however, was provided by one of Deeter's most famous protégées, Ann Harding, who maintained a steady correspondence with Deeter throughout her career. Writing in response to the reorganization, she chastised her beloved Jap: "another triumvirate...you get weary and try to make others be you. But you can't and you have always come alive in time to save it."[35]

The Personnel Committee was central to the reorganization of the Virginia Plan because it was this group that dealt with one of Hedgerow's most difficult problems: who and under what conditions would someone be admitted to the resident company? And, more importantly, how would the theatre respond when someone chose to leave? Since they operated on a true repertory system, the loss of a single performer could jeopardize the entire system. An actor would have to be replaced in more than one production and his/her other duties would also have to be covered. Opinions varied within the community. Some wanted a year's commitment before new people became full-time members; others argued for a minimum of three years before someone was "allowed" to leave. Deeter, who really did advocate democratic principles, was reluctant to coerce anyone and believed in appealing to human instincts rather than legal contracts. He did not wish to prevent someone from pursuing a professional career in New York or Hollywood. But he always stressed that the training that people received at Hedgerow was virtually "free" compared to the costs that one was charged at any of the professional acting schools or programs. Deeter believed—and told departing actors—that he felt a contribution of 10 percent of their first contract would be a wonderful way of "reimbursing" the theatre for what they had learned there.

With the formal reorganization of the theatre into a legal partnership in 1942, however, the use of contracts became accepted practice. Apprentices—and there were hundreds of them who wanted to be there after the war—signed agreements that not only stipulated certain duties but required them to pay Hedgerow $40 a month *in advance*.[36] The Personnel Committee was replaced by a board of directors who now reported to the partners and handled the details of managing personnel issues. Company meetings were mandated with official minutes taken and then posted so that everyone was aware of the issues affecting their schedules. Actors who wanted to change their contracts or commitments had to petition the board whose word was final on the affairs of the organization.

Of course, Deeter was a full partner and his sense of fairness and decency still had a powerful impact on critical issues. Under the Virginia Plan, actors agreed to be there for extended periods of time, often one to three years, and they were allowed to "teach their way out" if something interrupted their careers or personal lives. In the Carnahan tapes, Deeter describes how that spirit persisted and how he managed the departure of Richard Basehart when it became clear that he would have a major career. "Dick had a six year contract and after four it became obvious that he wanted to move on. I didn't want to stand in his way. He was a wonderful young man and actor. So I told him I'd take *Henry IV* out of the repertory because it wasn't making a lot of money and I couldn't replace him in that. But he would have to teach his way out of the other roles. There isn't time to rehearse every change in our system so I let Dick take that on and we released him from a six year contract in four and a half."[37]

The Hedgerow partnership stabilized a lot of uncertainty about operations, and the company meeting notes are a rich source of information about the interactions of company members. They also reveal how the company tried to deal openly and honestly with difficulties that haunt all theatre production. On one particular long Sunday session, they wrestled with the rumors that if people spoke out about political or personal issues it might affect their casting. The claim was that some people preferred to keep silent rather than betray their thoughts but were then perceived as "sullen" or not collegial. The discussion morphed into an inquiry of whether directors were "prejudiced" in casting based upon "off stage" behavior in the community.

There then follows a long discussion of how casting works and all the variables that are involved. Would this actor look like a member of the family in this family drama? Does this actor need to be stretched beyond what he has shown he can do? Deeter is remarkably articulate about his own "discrimination" that he openly practices. He discriminates in favor of people who are not sullen and silent but who speak up and ask questions and challenge. "To discriminate on behalf of the fluent, the open, the vocal, the musical is our work. This ancient legend of 'what I say will be held against me.' Well, why shouldn't it? So why don't you think first, then open your trap and yell like hell and say 'you stink and this is why.' Is there a life—have we a right to a life in which what I say will not be held against me? What does that mean?"[38] Deeter stresses that the key is for actors to ask when they don't understand. "Individually I am very happy always to explain all the grudges I have about anybody. That is always easy for people who love people. I love people intensely, so all that I think is dreadful about you I can tell you all the time—just get in my way. I do pretty well. I mean pretty thoroughly. Whether I do it well or badly will show in your acting."[39]

Deeter addresses the suspicions about casting by reminding the company that "I think we are all very open on this. I don't know any cases. I haven't seen directors behaving secretively or super-sensitively about him or her or it—I haven't seen it... If anyone catches any director at it, I think there ought to be a great scream, right in the middle of the place."[40] And he is open about his own casting decisions frequently naming actors to make his points and underline his belief in speaking out. "In my own casting, there is often educational purpose. I think these things are pretty clear, but if you asked my why, I'd tell you. I don't think Ann Follman's performance in *Pudding Full of Plums* is particularly good. I don't think it is as good as three or four girls could do on a stage right now. I protected the show by asking Arlene to have a study on the sidelines. But I want to know if this girl, whose class work was so fine, was soft and gentle, and so on, can come through and play this hard."[41]

It's clear in the minutes of the Hedgerow company why actors were devoted to him and why many stayed for years longer than they intended. Some never left. Others came back because the experience in the Rose Valley could not be duplicated elsewhere. Sherwood Anderson, in spite of the fact that *Winesburg, Ohio* was not the big success that he hoped for, came every October to spend a month before moving south for the winter. Henry Murdock wrote, "Hedgerow actors have forgone the rewards which might follow twenty-nine years of such dedicated labor in another enterprise. Their professional ambitions are concentrated in two efforts—making Hedgerow an artistic success and dodging worries about personal security."[42] The minutes of the theatre's company meeting provide valuable insights into the way Hedgerow functioned, and how a certain camaraderie and frank discussion informed a community where they were very seldom off-stage. But the minutes also reveal how the company was often isolated from the mainstream of American life and theatre. Moylan was a tiny and remote township that nurtured their work but which also fostered a neglect of their accomplishments and their marginalization in the historical record. A long and meandering Sunday meeting—the minutes run to 65 pages—concentrates on the frustrations of implementing contracts and disputes about how departing actors should be honored, but makes no mention of events outside the Rose Valley. The minutes are dated December 7, 1941.[43]

4. *An American Tragedy*: Whose Social Conscience? ❧

"Find time to help the workers theaters, cut the synthetic, don't use your talent on pap...Cut your repertory and join the revolution...It's been a month since I left and YOU ARE NEEDED."¹ This open letter to Jasper Deeter from actor Curt Conway was symptomatic of the emerging Left sensibilities in the 1930s as well as the pressure on many prominent artists to join the crusade. Conway was not the only voice urging Deeter to abandon his exile in the Pennsylvania countryside. Reviewing Hedgerow's stunning production of *An American Tragedy* for *New Masses*, Herb Kline remarked:

> This is an American tragedy that will not be remedied until Jasper Deeter leaves the isolation of Hedgerow and identifies himself completely with the great revolutionary audience that has never heard of him but is waiting nevertheless to welcome his work...*An American Tragedy* is a class war set upon the stage by a first-rate artist who belongs to the theater of the working class.²

It was not the first "class war" to grace the Hedgerow stage and raise the expectations of the radical left. Four years earlier Deeter had produced the initial professional production of Hallie Flanagan's controversial *Can You Hear Their Voices?* following its debut at Vassar College. Emmet Lavery, a young playwright who later worked with Flanagan on the Federal Theatre Project, had seen the production and written a letter to the *New York Times* that had caught the attention of Deeter and others in the theatrical community.

> This is to advise that something new has been done about the drought relief. The Experimental Theatre of Vassar College has done about it what the Russian propaganda theaters do about similar tragedies. It has written and produced a searing, biting, smashing piece of propaganda called *Can You Hear Their Voices?* and there is tumult in the air as a result.³

60 A Sustainable Theatre

Figure 4.1 "Scene from original Hedgerow Theatre production of *An American Tragedy*." Photograph 1935. Hedgerow Theatre Photograph Collection, Rare Book & Manuscript Library, University of Pennsylvania.

Much of the notoriety surrounding the play was fueled by the controversy of its source. *Voices* was not an original work but a dramatization of a powerful story that was published in *New Masses* and written by a communist sympathizer named Whittaker Chambers, who was also destined like Flanagan to play a significant role in the turbulent American politics of the 1930s. Chambers had crafted a deeply moving tale about the plight of Arkansas farmers as they watched the sun burn the crops, the cattle die, and the ineptness of relief agencies like the Red Cross dealing with their desperation and starvation. Ultimately they are led by a courageous farmer, Jim Wardell, into open and violent revolt, breaking windows and bearing arms to gain food and milk for their families. They realize, of course, that there will be consequences for their lawbreaking, and as the story concludes the embattled farmers are awaiting the arrival of the militia and state police. A class war is imminent and only the communist comrades seem to be capable of crafting a solution to America's inequity and depression.

Flanagan saw immediately the dramatic possibilities in Chambers's story, and she and Clifford conceived a production that was reflective of the new stagecraft that characterized much of the work that she had seen in Europe. They reduced the story to seven dramatic scenes depicting both the conspicuous consumption of the Washington, DC aristocracy and the desperate poverty of the farmers. They expanded Chambers's characters to include a wealthy young woman (Harriet) who provides a critique for the federal neglect of the drought conditions and added two Russian characters to suggest alternative solutions to the charity handed out by the Red Cross. They incorporated a number of theatricalist techniques—graphs, projections, lighting effects—that would later become associated with the Living Newspapers of the Federal Theatre Project. Less than two months after its publication in *New Masses*, the play was on stage at Vassar.

Jasper Deeter was intrigued. Like others in the noncommercial, professional theatre, he was aware of Flanagan's work and her interest in the "new" theatre of the Soviet Union. He also had read with interest about her travels to Russia when she had become the first woman to win a coveted Guggenheim fellowship. They corresponded and Flanagan was thrilled when he offered to add *Voices* to their current season with a first performance scheduled for September 1931. He also asked her to come to Hedgerow and direct the production.

But Flanagan was preoccupied that summer with her mother's health, an eye operation, and "subsequent blindness," and felt that the play would be better directed by Deeter. In an undated letter from the Detroit home where she often visited her aunt and uncle, Flanagan told Deeter that she had been depressed but "now feels much better" with the news that the production will go forward with Jasper directing.[4] They agreed that in lieu of a royalty Flanagan and Clifford would receive 10 percent of the gross.

Can You Hear Their Voices? opened at Hedgerow on September 5, 1931, on a double bill with curtain raiser *Champagne* by Isaac Loeb Perex. The reception was mixed. Reviewers praised the acting and singled out several of the performers, but the play was criticized for its lack of formal dramatic structure and for its "propaganda." And in 1931 that was clearly a damning charge. Here is how one critic described the evening.

> The little stage of the Hedgerow Theatre on Saturday night assumed the appearance of a large soapbox. Across its worn and weary boards strode actors whose countenances were bright with a burning crusading spirit. From their lips dropped hot words of denunciation and rebellion against their government and its political and charitable agencies... the concoction overflows with propaganda and youthful indignation. Its argument is unconvincing, however, due partly to the author's lack of skill, and partly because they allowed their pens to become so clogged with facts (gleaned chiefly from newspapers and periodicals) that they were unable to set down their message with any clarity.[5]

Another viewer commented, "Propaganda, for and against the Communists, President Hoover and the Red Cross runs riot through the play," but concluded that "there is hardly a beginning or an end. When the play opens the farmers are suffering from a drought and when it ends they are in the same fix."[6]

It is difficult, of course, to reconstruct this distant and obscured performance, but from documents available in the Hedgerow archives it does seem clear that Deeter made a critical production decision that worked against much of what Flanagan intended. Instead of employing the various slides and projections, he apparently used an actor to convey much of the factual information. In all three of the newspaper reviews that survived the production, there are references to an "interlocutor" who speaks directly to the audience. "In structure, the play hardly offered to augment the art of the theater, using an interlocutor to link facts and figures with the story depicted—not a very effective medium—and employing contrasts which were too extreme to create even effective drama."[7] Another reviewer noted that at the end when the young boys call back to their parents, "the interlocutor steps to the footlights and asks the audience, 'can you hear their voices?' which seems an anti-climax to this reviewer anyway."[8] Whether this was a dramaturgical choice or a time/cost shortcut is not clear, although two years later in a subsequent correspondence Flanagan offers to "rent you the slides" if you wish to mount a revival, "for a small fee."[9] At any rate, the presence of a "character" reading statistics must have heightened the propaganda of the occasion and worked against the theatricality and epic quality that the authors intended.

At the beginning of a decade in which propaganda carried a vastly negative connotation, and in a production that replaced epic staging with lectures, it's not surprising that the Hedgerow *Voices* was not reprised extensively in the season. While it took in a quite respectable gross on opening night ($141.50), in subsequent performances it fell to as low as $31.50. Deeter played it three times that September and another in October, but only at midweek (Tuesday and Wednesday evenings) and it finished with a gross income of $303.25[10]

But the patina of a professional production buoyed interest in the play, and four years before *Waiting for Lefty* officially baptized the "thirties," Flanagan and Clifford's searing depiction of the poor, neglected, and dispossessed spoke eloquently to an emerging theatre and audience. *Voices* depicted, as almost no other play had done, the gulf between the rich and the poor. In a short period of time it was produced at a host of other venues. By Christmas, it was drawing praise in Shanghai where the director of the Shanghai People's Theatre wrote to Flanagan that "the aim of the production was to help the struggle for the development of the complete democratization of the Chinese agricultural social system."[11] An emerging

Workers Theatre embraced what they saw as its agitprop characteristics and swelled the number of productions. Working from her correspondence and archives, Flanagan later tallied and reported on the amazing success of the play that she and Clifford had outlined and written in ten days. "It was done by farmers in North Dakota... by Negro Theatre groups in Cleveland, Ohio and Washington, D.C. and by students of Commonwealth College in the Ozarks. The Vineyard Shore School for Women Workers in Industry produced it, as did the Beaux Arts Theatre in Los Angeles and the Boston Ford Hall Forum."[12] It was produced in Vancouver, Newark, and dozens of American cities. The revolutionary Artef Theatre produced it under the title of *Trikinesh* (*Drought*) and made changes without Flanagan's approval to make Harriet a more enlightened character. Flanagan recalled that copies of the play were ordered from theatres in Greece, Hungary, Finland, Denmark, France, Russia, Spain, and Australia. In fact, the buzz created by *Can You Hear Their Voices?* played a substantial part in legitimatizing Flanagan in the theatrical community four years later when Harry Hopkins appointed her as the administrator of the fledgling Federal Theatre Project.

Deeter was disappointed that Flanagan and Clifford's play did not develop a larger following, but it did have two additional echoes in the Hedgerow story. Flanagan, like many others, was impressed by the way that Deeter had created a viable, functioning theatre in a rural corner outside of metropolitan Philadelphia. Four years later she would convince him to become one of her regional directors on the massive WPA Arts project that Harry Hopkins had entrusted her with.[13] And his experiment with an "interlocutor" would reemerge as one of the central features in their celebrated staging of the Dreiser-Piscator's *American Tragedy*.

Dreiser, who was an international celebrity following the success of his novel, had experimented with playwriting for a number of years and had been acquainted with Deeter from Provincetown days. As artists they shared a love of the natural world and mistrust of the modern urban landscape. Dreiser had edited an edition of Thoreau's works and admired Deeter's attempts to create a theatre that was located in, and respectful of, a rural environment.[14] They were both critical of the capitalist money machine that tempted people to value success in accumulation of wealth and were suspicious of the way in which working-class men and women were exploited by the class system. Dreiser was also close to Sherwood Anderson, though his politics were considerably more radical, and it was through Anderson that Dreiser became reacquainted with Deeter and encouraged him to stage the world premiere of a new adaptation of *An American Tragedy*.

The story of Clyde Griffith's attempt to free himself from a relationship with the working-class Roberta in pursuit of the wealthy Sondra, and Griffith's subsequent execution for murdering Roberta by overturning their rowboat, had already been dramatized successfully on Broadway. A version by Patrick Kearney with Miriam Hopkins and Morgan Farley had run for 216 performances in 1926, and Paramount had filmed a disappointing version in 1931 with Sylvia Sidney and Phillips Holmes, directed by Joseph von Sternberg.[15] Dreiser enjoyed the Kearney adaptation, although the emphasis was clearly on the melodrama of the doomed Griffiths rather than the economic and class pressure that were resonant in the story. When Dreiser was approached by a German theatre to make a new translation, he was enthusiastic about the project.

Lena Goldschmidt, a German critic and translator of Dreiser's works, was given permission to prepare a new scenario of the novel and she, in turn, retained the famed director and Epic Theatre theorist Erwin Piscator to write the script. Piscator was fascinated by the political implications in the story, and he focused in his adaptation on the economic "laws" that had driven Clyde to his final destruction. Dreiser was pleased with the theatrical nature of the play but was reluctant to foreground the economic forces at the expense of all the "naturalistic" impulses that had driven the novel. He wrote to Goldschmidt that the script needed to be modified, since in places it was "counter to some of my economic and sociological principles."[16] Ultimately a compromise was reached and Dreiser was satisfied that the script retained the "tragedy" of his original story while focusing on the economic despair that led Clyde to his crime and execution. Following its premiere and a subsequent production at the Group Theatre—where it was renamed *Case of Clyde Griffiths*—Dreiser wrote:

> It has been said of my novel *An American Tragedy* that in it the idea of economic stratification, the wealthy members of the society superimposed on the poor, and the tragic results of the same to the less fortunate were more implied than argued, and with this I agree, since it is what I intended. None the less I hold that any class conscious person who reads the book will see clearly and effectively the determining social and economic forces surrounding the individuals of all classes, and within which they move to their comfort and destruction.[17]

Production plans in Germany stalled after Dreiser approved the new adaptation. Casting problems, the chill of the emerging Nazi ideology, and eventually Piscator's flight to Russia delayed the premiere. A new German production was performed but was actually based on the Kearney adaptation not the Piscator text. In America, Dreiser was convinced by his lawyers not to pursue a production until the Paramount film had been released. Finally, after several frustrating delays, and the opening night of *Winesburg*, Dreiser offered the script—now translated by his friend, Louise Campbell—to Deeter for an American premiere at Hedgerow.

Deeter realized immediately that the scenic demands of the script would adapt remarkably well to the Hedgerow stage. In its epic and symbolic mise-en-scène the play called for a series of platforms that functioned not only to stage the action but also to symbolize the economic status of the characters. Thus the stage was divided into two main levels: the rich on the top and the poor on the bottom with two side-playing areas where actors could comment on the action. It was an arrangement that Deeter had used in *Can You Hear Their Voices?* where Flanagan and Clifford's script called for a clear delineation between the Arkansas farmers on the left and the lavish Washington capitalists on the right, along with a "platea" or middle area allowing the action to expand from each side. In addition, Piscator had created a new character called "The Speaker" who was both in the play and stood outside of the action, commenting on the characters and events and focusing the audience attention on the social implications of character decisions. The Speaker was not bound by any of the physical dimensions of the setting and could also move among the audience members while commenting on the play. The notion was familiar to Deeter who had already created such a character—The Interlocutor—for his production of *Voices* four years earlier, and he was excited about the opportunity to stage this character in the intimate Hedgerow space.

But he was also suspicious of the characterization of the Speaker and wrote to Dreiser that it was vital that the character remain neutral in his commentary on Clyde's struggle. "To my mind the most important asset is the Speaker. This is new and of great value if the character's impartiality is preserved. Now he goes on the rocks on page 54 when he begins to argue with Clyde."[18] Deeter was conscious of the social slant that was driving the play, but he felt strongly that the Speaker had to maintain the narrative and not color the action too overtly. "On page 76 the Speaker shows 'concern' which is what the audience pays to do. The narrator must conceal concern."[19] Deeter recognized the power in the story and because he hadn't read the novel he was able to concentrate on the dramatic action without the distractions of press notoriety or other dramatized versions. He focused his analysis on the love triangle that drove the action and was particularly critical of Sondra. "Wharton says in the novel Sondra's love is real. At this point I can't tell what she's like; I feel a sort of Volksbühne slant."[20] With his well-known penchant for character honesty, Deeter added that

"If Sondra is not a fake why isn't there less of her love and more to it?" and concluded that "a fine love affair...the commentary lets the play down into an obvious *ism* of some sort."[21]

Dreiser responded that he appreciated Deeter's concerns, and that he agreed with "most of them."[22] But the tension between the passionate love triangle and the urge to place the blame for Clyde's behavior on economic forces was a tension in the production that was never totally resolved. Deeter, whose respect for playwrights was genuine, made his position clear early on but did not try to dictate how the script should be modified. "The effort to make a social drama out of it annoys me, but I think a proper finish might easily occur to you."[23]

He cast four of his strongest players in the central roles (Harry Sheppard as the Speaker, Joe Taulane as Clyde, Ann Clark as Roberta, and Ruth Oliver as Sondra) and began working on the two-tiered stage with a minimum of scenery. Chairs and hand props were brought on to suggest various locales, and much of the action was pantomimed to accompanying offstage sound effects. A car was a few chairs, but the opening and closing of its doors was realistically heard. A desk was bare, but the buzzer that was pantomimed clearly rang. A dinner scene featured waiters carrying imaginary trays and dishes, while four actors in straight backed chairs pretended to eat. In one of the most celebrated sequences, Clyde was transformed from poor to rich in a tailor shop where he was fitted for a tuxedo that insured his passage into the moneyed class.

The Speaker was the hit of the production. Deeter let him roam freely over the stage and audience space commenting on the action and calling attention to the economic disparity between the classes. He encouraged Taulane to react with anger and outrage when appropriate, but also to guide the audience to an understanding of the social and economic implications of the character's choices. Deeter tempered the Speaker's comments on the actor's feelings but stressed how their behavior was a product of class and status. Deeter had an intellectual understanding of an "epic style," but he encouraged Clyde and Roberta and Sondra to explore their genuine emotional responses and make the relationships honest and believable.

John Wentz, who wrote about the original production and then later saw a revival, was perceptive about how Deeter tried to balance the "truth" of the human emotions with the intense social critique. "Midway through the play the Speaker declaims, 'This is the crisis; Fate marches unknown. But we have torn the mask from his face...and have given him a name. We call him the law of Economics, that inexorably and without compassion controls the destiny of mankind.' At the play's end Clyde's mother says of her son: 'He dies as a sacrifice to his rebellious, yearning heart, but he will be forgiven.' But the last word is the Speaker's: He dies as a sacrifice to society, and it will not be forgiven!"[24]

The result was a stunning success. Philadelphia and New York newspapers praised Piscator's adaptation and Hedgerow's production. Robert Garland writing in the *New York World Telegram* called it "one of the most provocative plays of the season, a work to rescue a nodding theater" and went on to praise the theatre. "In Hedgerow there remains most of what's left of theatrical zeal and enthusiasm, of theatrical daring, of joy in theatrical production."[25] Sherwood Anderson was ecstatic and wrote to Dreiser, "Saw the *Tragedy* last night and was bowled over... It's gorgeous, beautiful, direct. It is really much stronger than the things the Theatre Union are doing."[26] Dreiser was full of praise for Deeter's direction and encouraged his friend and translator Louise Campbell to make the journey to the Rose Valley. She too was delighted with what she saw, although she wrote Deeter that she "wished for a more sparkling Sondra."[27]

The success of the Hedgerow production created a storm of interest among agents and producers vying to bring *An American Tragedy* to New York. The Theatre Union, which was trying to stretch its appeal beyond working-class audiences and bring the revolution to the middle class, sent representatives to Hedgerow to assess the political correctness of the adaptation. The Shuberts expressed a strong interest in bringing both the script and Deeter to New York to stage a new production. Deeter was flattered by the attention and amused by the commercial squabbling over the play. In July he wrote to Dreiser, "It's a see-saw with four or five Shuberts on one end and four or five Left Theatres on the other... Theatre Union wants to know if it was prepared for a bourgeois or working-class audience... Then young Milton Shubert informed me that Lee is very busy but is interested and I told him that the play and I will be here for three years or so."[28]

Dreiser wanted the Shuberts to produce the play, and he wanted Deeter to direct so he repeated an earlier caution. "They think you are difficult and rehearse too long,".[29] But Deeter's concern was not about going to New York, in fact, it was about scheduling the upcoming season. *An American Tragedy* was the official opening production for 1935, and Deeter was already preparing eight new productions to be introduced over the next few months. He revived *Tragedy* several times that season and it continued to do very good business. Over the next two years the play was a favorite in the repertory and eventually totaled 110 performances. It grossed an average of $104.14 each time it played and eventually earned $11,455.66.

In his study of Hedgerow statistics, John Wentz concluded that the play generated the seventh largest income in the history of the theatre.[30]

Meanwhile Milton Shubert continued his efforts to bring *American Tragedy* to Broadway. He had earlier tried to interest the Group Theatre in doing the American premiere, but Harold Clurman had demurred because he felt that the script was too stylized and lacked emotional appeal. Others, however, were fascinated by the politics of the play and Joe Bromberg had traveled to the Rose Valley to see Deeter's production. When Odet's *Paradise Lost* struggled at the box office, Milton Shubert convinced Lee Strasberg to take another look at *An American Tragedy*, and after discussion with Stella Adler and other company members, Strasberg agreed to direct. To avoid confusion among potential audience members they renamed the play *Case of Clyde Griffiths*, distinguishing it from the earlier Kearney adaptation. Morris Carnovsky was cast in the critical role of the Speaker.

Jasper Deeter's production was the blueprint for the Group Theatre's version, but they made some critical departures from what had been produced at Hedgerow. Strasberg, in an attempt to capture the essence of the "epic acting style," encouraged the company to employ "narrative emotions" as if they were remembering something that had already happened rather than immediate emotional responses. This had the effect of making the action more deliberative and hence, in theory, making the action more susceptible to audience analysis.[31] The Speaker, however, was allowed to play in a more "method" oriented fashion and his staging was modified in several ways. Rather than roaming the house as Taulane had at Hedgerow, Carnovsky was principally stationed in front of the stage at the audience level where he acted as a conduit between the players and the viewers. However, he became intimately involved in the stage action as the play progressed, and in the critical trial scene he climbed onto the set and became Clyde's defense attorney.

Finally, at the suggestion of Mordecai Gorelik, Clyde's story took on the guise of a Christlike earthly journey. Strasberg worked to give the production the aura of a "Passion Play" with Clyde being sacrificed by a corrupt society. His trial became a martyrdom in which a "golden overhead spotlight deified Clyde as he was led to the electric chair."[32]

Beset with such baggage and seeking earnestly to communicate a social message via an Americanized version of "epic acting," it is not surprising that the production faltered under the weight of so much theory. The company was generally praised for their work but as Brooks Atkinson pointed out, "Between the story the play tells and the teaching shouted by the Speaker there is a gap through which the validity of the drama escapes."[33]

For Atkinson and many others the social "laboring" of the evening just did not erase the fact that Clyde Griffiths was basically a "contemptible coward." The play ran for 19 performances.

But at Hedgerow there was a renewed effort to enlist Deeter in the left-wing activism that was increasingly vocal in the American theatre. Virginia Farmer, who had been one of the earliest Hedgerovians before embracing the Group Theatre, wrote a widely read piece on Hedgerow for *New Theatre* in which she praised Deeter's accomplishments but complained that the repertory had "little consistency in social point of view." She went on to argue, "There is a growing desire in the Hedgerow Theatre for plays that speak decisively and to the point on social, economic and political issues of today, and I hope that this attitude will soon dictate the theater's choice of plays and the productions it gives them."[34]

What Farmer, Kline, and others failed to understand was that Deeter was neither a revolutionary socialist nor an ideologue. He certainly was committed to a socialist view of the world and in some discussions would refer to his "Bolshevik side," but if he had a mentor in any traditional sense it was not Marx or Lenin. It was always George Bernard Shaw and often, the courageous and resolute Scott Nearing. In most of his interviews and articles, Deeter always downplayed his grasp of history or his command of theory of any kind. He characterized himself as a "doer," as someone whose thinking and ideas could be determined by his work in the theatre. But, of course, he cared deeply about ideas especially those that had to do with nature, pacifism, class inequity, and racial injustice. All concepts that he shared with Nearing, who was ten years his senior and one of America's most distinguished radicals.

Scott Nearing lived for one hundred years and his lifelong devotion to human rights, equal opportunity, and popular government endeared him to radicals, conservationists, and defenders of civil rights. Deeter first became aware of Nearing at Chautauqua where Deeter was taking drama classes and earning his tuition by learning to cook. Nearing taught classes in social theory and history for six weeks every summer from 1912 to 1917, where he would warn the predominantly middle-class audiences about the futility of chasing money as a way of evaluating success; "that is a game in which the sky is the limit."[35] Nearing was developing his ideas about socialism while renting a cabin each summer in Arden, Delaware, another single tax community that had been founded by David Price with many of the same impulses that characterized the artist colony in Rose Valley. Nearing, who was pioneering contemporary notions of homesteading and getting "back to the land," lived at Arden for several summers between 1906 and

1915. His neighbors included Upton Sinclair, who rented Nearing's cabin during the winter months, and tutored him in socialism. Arden was also an experiment testing how a human community can live in harmony with their environment. "For Nearing life in Arden meant taking produce to the Saturday town market, playing roles in the town theater productions and participating in collective building activities."[36] Nearing's homesteading impulses would grow in the following years climaxing in an experiment in Vermont where he and his wife focused in living simply and where he developed a philosophy about how to live without seeking "profit" even under the harshest conditions. Deeter felt a kinship with Nearing's rejection of urban landscapes and acceptance of a life based on the satisfaction of hard work and invited him to visit Hedgerow and talk to the company about notions of community and environment. Later Ruth Esherick would confide that as a youngster she remembered Deeter reading to the company from essays and books that Nearing had published.[37]

In the Hedgerow files at the Gotlieb archives, there are wonderful letters asking Nearing to come and talk to the students and actors at the Hedgerow School. "We use your ideas all the time," a Hedgerow representative writes to Nearing in 1948 hoping to convince him to come again even though they know he has time conflicts, and they don't have very much money in their budget. Nearing responds, reflecting his affection for Hedgerow, "I never talk for money and would gladly fit into your budget on terms that are advantageous to you."[38]

The two men shared many interests, and Deeter admired Nearing's courage in standing up to the federal government when he was arrested and tried for espionage during the Red Scare in 1919. An outspoken critic of plutocracy—which he saw as the real threat to American democracy—Nearing never wavered in his critique of the capitalist agenda that encouraged wealth and power, and after experimenting with many forms of socialism, Nearing was finally driven into the Communist Party. But there too he had difficulty, with the authoritarian structure of the party and the rampant bureaucracy that drove the agenda of American communism. Deeter believed, like Nearing, that "socialism is a process" but he did not wish to expend his energies in party squabbles or theoretical notions of government. What Deeter relished about Nearing's teachings was his uncompromised commitment to preserving the environment, fighting for civil rights, and pacifism, all issues that Deeter could enact on the stage in the Rose Valley. Nearing paid his own tribute to the theatre that rejected the capitalist pursuit of accumulating wealth. He wrote to his son Scott in 1931 that "the pursuit of profits is so narrow a phase of human activity that it does not permit of much elaboration. Then, the thinness of life left very little to express even where decoration was attempted. Dreiser's *American Tragedy* tells the story. So do the books of Sherwood Anderson."[39]

Nearing was an absolutist in his demands for civil rights for Negroes. As early as 1908, he had recognized the need for education for Negroes in his textbook *Economics* (1908). At first a supporter of Booker T. Washington, he later moved to embrace the more confrontational politics of W. E. B. Du Bois after traveling in the south and seeing the conditions first hand. He contributed to the *New Masses* and *Messenger*, the black journal edited by A. Philip Randolph and Chandler Owen, and eventually wrote his own study of racism in *Black America* (1929). Like the American Communist Party, Nearing struggled with the web of class and race that entrapped the American Negro, and he came to believe that the working class can never be successful in dethroning the oligarchy if it was divided along racial lines. In *Free Born* (1932), his novel of a black laborer coming to radical consciousness by reading the works of Marx, Sinclair, Jack London, and others, Nearing paints a radical but futile picture as Jim is convicted for his beliefs in a trial that resembles Nearing's own in 1919.[40] Jasper Deeter's campaign to foreground the "Negro question" on his stage at Hedgerow in the 1930s was no doubt partially inspired by his admiration for Nearing's commitment to the cause.

But, perhaps, the single biggest influence of Nearing's writings and teachings for Deeter and for Hedgerow was his fierce commitment to pacifism in the face of both oligarchical war machine and the Leninist dictates of the Communist Party. To denounce violence was to deny the "history" of communism as laid out by the revolutionaries who saw it as necessary to complete the transition to a truly classless society. But Nearing was always uncomfortable with grand theories of history and believed that no one could predict the outcome of socialist thinking. His stance led to his expulsion from the party and a new reorientation to the individual; to self-worth and satisfaction. At his Vermont farm he and Helen struggled with the relationship between individuality and community, and Scott eventually came to believe that "socialism," however it was parsed, must stand at some point for individual development and freedom. He came to see that Marxism was fundamentally opposed to free will and incompatible with pacifism. Violence was anathema and it took great courage to reject it fully.

An American Tragedy was a great success at Hedgerow, and in staging it, Deeter found imaginative ways to foreground its class prejudices and its anticapitalist critique.[41] But he was never comfortable with the bellicose preaching and the one-dimensional symbolism that overtook it in New York. For Deeter, the theatre was always grounded in the truth of human behavior, and he could find that truth in farce as well as agitprop harangues. But like Nearing, he was suspicious of the left-wing fervor that vowed to suppress human and civil rights in the name of building a better world. Like Nearing, he too was opposed to any creeds that embraced violence. Those in New York who urged Deeter to take up the revolution—especially in wake of *An American Tragedy*—misunderstood the real cornerstone of his beliefs. They also misunderstood his genuine commitment to repertory and its appetite for many kinds of plays. Dreiser and Anderson were celebrities, but Deeter embraced equally the writers who were not stars and one, in particular, who shared his distrust of Broadway.

5. *The Cherokee Night*: Riggs and the Power of Place

Deeter's disdain for the Broadway theatre was critical in the formation of Hedgerow, and over the years he perfected a public presentation to encourage donations, promote specific productions, or increase public awareness. In October 1939, before an audience of the Council of Jewish Women in Philadelphia, he outlined what he viewed as the critical differences between Broadway and Hedgerow, and in the process revealed a great deal about what he valued as a theatre artist. In a section titled "Production Methods," he contrasted the work in the Rose Valley with the typical New York production.

Broadway	Hedgerow
Expensive	Cheap
Fast	Slow
Type	Acting
Real	Style
Pace	Rhythm
Demonstrative	Suggestive
Recognition	Discovery[1]

While it does indulge in some easy generalizations, and does not have the weight, say of Bertolt Brecht's recipe for an Epic theatre or Peter Weiss's for a documentary one, it does outline a coherent aesthetic and foregrounds a rehearsal process that is about discovery rather than results. Rehearsals at Hedgerow were, by many accounts, long and challenging. Unencumbered by union restrictions and aided by a company of mostly resident performers, it was not unusual for a call to begin after the evening performance and continue for another two or three hours. This schedule led to some excellent ensemble work but such performances were often perceived by

74   A Sustainable Theatre

Figure 5.1   Company photo, 1934. Ruth Esherick is in the window seat behind Jasper Deeter. From the collection of Mark Sfirri.

audiences and critics as overly long. In fact, a recurring theme in Hedgerow reviews is the length of the evening's entertainment.

The long evenings in the theatre, however, were not the result of a stubborn refusal to cut the playwright's text or intended to test audience endurance. They were the result of a belief that authenticity could best be achieved by discovering truths of behavior, with a focus on the rhythm of characters and their relationship to the environment, rather than the "pace" of revelation. Deeter repeatedly told actors that slow rehearsals did not mean long performances, and that pace could be adjusted once the "truth" was distilled. He once told Peter Carnahan, "If we could do just three plays and do them slow enough, we could learn everything there is to know about acting."[2]

Deeter loathed the formulaic approach to commercial theatre that often dictated how long each act should be in order to fulfill a predetermined notion of what "worked." And he disliked intensely the power of producers to dictate to writers and directors what should be cut in order to make the evening successful. The "type" acting that characterized the Broadway theatre was a futile attempt to be "real," he believed, and not compatible with the "style" at Hedgerow that gave the genuine appearance of the "real." Hedgerow actors *acted,* which—in Deeter's judgment—was vastly different than "typed" actors endlessly replicating themselves.

This attention to authenticity and Deeter's respect for the writer's word endeared him to playwrights and helps to account for the vast number of new plays in the repertoire. In addition, Deeter had an acute sense of "place" and was sensitive to how playwrights invoked environments to suggest and color human behavior. Long before critical theorists began to conceptualize the "platial" as a legitimate "character" in drama, Deeter's understanding of the relationship between the natural world and Hedgerow, and his stubborn belief that art could grow out of a sensitivity to the environment that "housed" it, had made him aware of how powerfully "place" and "a sense of the past" could help to mold authenticity on the stage.[3] It was one of the reasons that made *Inheritors* so important in the Hedgerow community. The events in Glaspell's drama were accomplished over a long period of time, but they were dominated by the hill and the land—the place—that housed both the Blackhawk Nation and Morton College.

The combination of these two factors—a distrust of Broadway practice and sensitivity to the power of environment—was alluring to Lynn Riggs, who became one of the most frequently produced authors in the Rose Valley. Hedgerow staged six of Riggs's plays between 1928 and 1936—including three world premieres—and kept three of them in the popular repertoire throughout the next decade. In many ways Riggs's work encapsulates what was distinctive and unique about Hedgerow; an author embraced because of his vision, despite the fact that he was not "popular," and that he often outraged both his audiences and critical press. Riggs's plays appealed to Deeter—the iconoclast—because they often pushed the boundaries of what could be depicted on the stage. The banal (and the comic) was frequently in concert with incest, rape, prostitution, and violence. And the language, earthy and poetic, while frequently objectionable to middle-class reviewers, captured the diction of the Oklahoma territory that Riggs mined in his dramaturgy. This connection to the land was compelling and reading Riggs's revised introduction to *Green Grow the Lilacs* seems eerily familiar, as if Deeter was being channeled.

> For this reason it seemed wise to throw away the conventions of ordinary theatricality—a complex plot, swift action, et cetera—and try to exhibit luminously, in the simplest of stories, a wide area of mood and feeling. This only could be done, it seemed to me, by exploring the characters as deeply as possible, simple as though they appeared to be, hoping to stumble on, if lucky, the always subtle, always strange compulsions under which they labor and relate themselves to the earth and to other people.[4]

Deeter delighted in the work of this shy Oklahoma poet and playwright who aspired to have his plays done on Broadway, but who repeatedly returned to the Rose Valley and a company that prized his iconoclastic vision and theatrical imagination. Deeter loved the outrageous farce of *Roadside* with its larger-than-life characters and its depiction of the lawless Western territories. He found character truth in the dark and hopeless *Rancour* and the equally bleak domestic landscape of *A Lantern to See By*. But it was the visionary imagination of *The Cherokee Night* that most intrigued Deeter and which he chose to commemorate with a special production in their "Tenth Anniversary" season. The play, which puzzled and confused patrons and critics in 1932, is now recognized as Riggs's most powerful and important work and is added testimony to Deeter's instincts in embracing not only Lynn Riggs but also his long-neglected threnody of the Cherokee diaspora.

Prior to the cultural renaissance of the Native American movement in the late twentieth century, Rollin Lynn Riggs was a little known "southwest playwright" best known for providing the book for one of America's iconic musicals. The transformation of *Green Grow the Lilacs* into *Oklahoma!* is a legendary tale in the American theatre, but the original was rarely read or produced and languished along with dozens of plays, poems, and film scripts in a cultural memory that dismissed Riggs as a talented but "regional writer."

A quickening Native American consciousness, however, began noting and then celebrating Riggs's one-eighth Cherokee heritage, and the fact that a bulk of his plays drew on the Oklahoma territory where the Cherokee nation had been banished. While they did not all deal in "Indian" themes, they all drew on the "place" where blacks, whites, and Native Americans contested for land, power, and identity. Some were deeply personal, transcribing the unhappy childhood of the abused young author, others were folk farces rich with local dialect and song, and one majestically captured the place of Claremore, Oklahoma, the loss of Indian lands, and the threatened extinction of the seven tribes.

Far from the obscurity that characterized his reputation after his death from stomach cancer in 1954, Riggs had a productive career in the American theatre. Following a nervous breakdown during his senior year at the University of Oklahoma, (and a possible diagnosis of tuberculosis), Riggs fled to Santa Fe, New Mexico, in 1923 to recover his health. There he became involved in the burgeoning literary community assembled around Provincetown fugitives Mabel Dodge and Ida Rauh and the poet Witter Bynner. Riggs, who was a closeted gay man, was impressed by the talented and controversial Bynner, who lived openly with his homosexual lover and who took an interest in Riggs's writing.[5] Bynner encouraged Riggs to follow his literary ambitions, recommended several of his poems for publication, and maintained a correspondence with the young writer after he had moved to New York. Bynner, who had a substantial reputation in the scuffle over image making in modernist poetry, also wrote a strong recommendation for Riggs to the Guggenheim Foundation in 1927, which allowed Riggs to travel to Paris.

But it was Ida Rauh Eastman who encouraged his interest in drama and playwriting and prompted him to write his first script, *Knives from Syria*, which she directed with the local Santa Fe players in 1926. With her support and connections to the New York theatre, Riggs secured a production with the experimental American Laboratory Theatre of his full-length play *Big Lake* in 1927. That company, which was founded by alumni of the Moscow Art Theatre, included critic Francis Fergusson who played a bit part and Stella Adler who played the lead.[6] *Big Lake* is a haunting and poetic play set in the "Indian Territory" of Oklahoma in 1906. And even in this early work the sense of the characters negotiating a relationship with the earth is distinct. Each of its two acts is named after the geography that frames the action and the movement of the play: The Woods and The Lake. In Act I two young and innocent teenagers journey through the "woods" en route to a high school picnic. Their suppressed physical attraction for one another is palpable, but their behavior is rigidly restrained by both custom and etiquette. In the rich country dialect that is a striking feature of all the Riggs plays, Betty tries to articulate the danger that she feels in the darkened woods while Lloyd picks a wild flower to put in her hair. (I have quoted at length here in order to provide a sense of Riggs's early fascination with "place," a quality that Deeter found compelling.)

BETTY: No, no. Whur'd you git it at?
LLOYD: (*puzzled*) Why, here.
BETTY: (*strangely*) Under the leaves. It growed up through the dead leaves. I don't like it—
LLOYD: Why, Betty!
BETTY: I cain't stand them kind of flowers.
LLOYD: 'S jist a flower. Growin' in the woods.
BETTY: In the dark woods. Lloyd—
LLOYD: (*puzzled*) Whut is it?
BETTY: Lloyd, lets go away frum here—
LLOYD: Whur'd you want to go to?

BETTY: Out of here, out of these woods! (*Pleading for him to understand*) Oh, you think I ain't right. I cain't expect you to know how I feel. They's sump'n—I don't know what it is—Please! It's like the woods wuz waitin'—
LLOYD: Like a animal.
BETTY: To git us. To git us! I'm afeard. They's things growin' here—and fightin'. They's things crawlin' on the ground, under the ground—in the trees—everwhur! I'm afraid![7]

Lloyd takes her to an old cabin to get warm, but his description of the building only increases her anxiety.

LLOYD: It's the funniest kind o' cabin you ever see. It's a log cabin. I been in it a long time ago with Paw. It's a nice log cabin. And they'll have a fa'r.
BETTY: (*reluctantly*) Well, I'll go—if you think—
LLOYD: Frum the outside it looks jist like any log cabin. But when you open the door, and look in—what do you see? Steps! Three steps a-goin' down to the dirt floor. It's part under the ground—
BETTY: Oh! Like it growed up out o' the ground—?
LLOYD: Yes, jist like that! Like it growed out o' the ground!
BETTY: (*with conviction*) It growed out o' the ground. It growed out a' the same ground the big woods growed out of! (*She shudders*)[8]

In Act II the menace of the woods is contrasted with the promise of the lake; the site that will perhaps allow Lloyd and Betty to escape from the terror that they encountered in the log cabin.

LLOYD: (*kneeling*) Out there—look at it—look at the lake! (*Breathlessly*) Sun techin' it. Little waves startin' in the wind, breakin' here on the banks in ripples. Trees—willers leanin' down like they uz prayin' at the edges. I wish I could be a lake. I wish I could be that that big, that deep! I wish I could be ketchin' the sun like it—an' sparklin' an' singin'—an' never afeard o' nuthin'—just a-settin' thar quiet in the sunshine—a-lookin' up at the sky, a-lookin' up at the sun—
BETTY: (*looking up at him*) You make it nice—
LLOYD: No, 'tain't me—
BETTY: You make it nicer'n it is—
LLOYD: No. It looks that a-way t'me.
BETTY: It's that a-way t' me too—

LLOYD: (*relieved*) Betty—
BETTY: When you say it. You make things nicer'n they air—
LLOYD: No, I make 'em the *way* they air.
BETTY: An' the lake?—
LLOYD: It's a deep pond—
BETTY: It's quiet.
LLOYD: It moves when the wind moves. It holds the sun. It's a cup with gold in it-[9]

Unfortunately, the lake does not provide salvation for the young innocents, and they are both shot dead in a bizarre case of mistaken identity that fulfills the dread that Betty anticipated at the beginning of their journey.

The production received mixed reviews but impressed Barrett Clark who would later become Riggs's literary advisor and arrange for the publication of many of his plays. Clark wrote, "*Big Lake* is that rarest of things, a poetic drama that is at once poetry and drama. To one of his later plays Mr. Riggs has given the title *Sump'n Like Wings*, and I can think of no words that so accurately describe what I felt when, over a year ago, I read the manuscript of *Big Lake*. There is a winged lightness in the words that the poet puts into the mouths of his young people, an ecstasy born of the sheer joy of being alive."[10] Riggs also became friends with Kenneth Macgowan at Provincetown, who encouraged his writing and introduced him to other New York artists and authors. In the next five years Riggs wrote a dozen plays, was invited to the prestigious Yahoo writer's colony in Saratoga Springs, and won a Guggenheim trip to Paris; but he struggled to land a successful Broadway production.

Riggs wrote approximately 25 plays, in addition to *Lilacs* and *Oklahoma*, but only three of them were produced in New York; most importantly *Russet Mantle* (1936), which ran for 117 performances and then had an extended road tour. Samuel French published 15 of them and kept Riggs active in the little theatre and college circuit. He made a substantial amount of money in Hollywood and was a sought-after screenwriter and celebrity "date" for Hollywood starlets including Bette Davis, Jean Muir, and Joan Fontaine. He also participated in the "committee" of writers who crafted screenplays for *Garden of Allah* (1936), *Delay in the Sun* (1935), *Wicked Woman* (1934), and *Stingaree* (1933). But he was most satisfied with his script for *The Plainsman* (1935) with Gary Cooper and Jean Arthur, which was distinctive for its sympathetic treatment of Native Americans.

Riggs's difficulty with Broadway—and a quality that endeared him to Jasper Deeter—was his refusal to compromise his vision of a play with the current producing notions of what would "work." It frustrated him immensely and on one occasion led to the cancelation of a Shubert-backed production before it opened. *The Domino Parlor* (1928) chronicles the attempts of a female blues singer in Blackmore, Oklahoma, to rekindle her romance with a former lover whom she has not seen in a dozen years and who has survived by robbing banks. The romance is thwarted by a jealous rival who is finally murdered by the frustrated and cynical singer. The violence though, which is often a hallmark of Riggs's plays, was offensive to Sam Shubert who told the writer that "the heroine could not kill a man, and that the hero had to be a bootlegger rather than an odious bank bandit."[11] Riggs refused to rewrite to Shubert's specifications, and the production was canceled after a brief tryout in Newark. Riggs would later write, "The playwright is always right. If a play seems to have the merit to make production a fact, the author should have the final word on the interpretation. He alone—and not the director or the producer or the actor—knows the exact shade of the meaning he intends."[12] This integrity thwarted him on Broadway, but Jasper Deeter found it admirable.

Deeter read *Rancour* at the suggestion of several of his former Provincetown colleagues and was impressed with the characters and the sexual impulses that seemed to drive the action. *Rancour* is a stark account of an unhappy marriage. In a bleak farmhouse Dorie Bickel struggles to motivate her husband, Ned, to provide for his family and keep the farm from falling apart. In desperation she begins an egg-and-butter business so that she can send their son Julius to college. But both he and his father are laconic and without ambition, and they constantly frustrate and betray Dorie's dreams. While Riggs seems sympathetic with Dorie's unhappiness, he is also careful to detail her shortcomings and failings: her intolerance of Ned's love of hunting, her Missouri "social" background, and her disdain for the coarseness of the frontier. Like many of Riggs's plays, sexuality is a central issue and the behavior that it generates is often destructive or shocking by conventional mores. In *Rancour*, both the philandering husband and the son have affairs with a local neighbor and her daughter. The pressure on Dorie to succeed in spite of personal and business betrayals is intense, as is the loss of manhood that Ned experiences when he is finally rejected by both neighbor and his wife. In a climax that was compared to Greek fate by some critics, Ned kills himself, and Dorie struggles against the landscape that seems constantly to thwart her.

Deeter rehearsed the play in the spring of 1928 and opened it for the public in June. In the rehearsals, he focused on the rhythms of the dialect and the character impulses that forged the sexual relationships. In spite of the potential for audience alienation, the production was reviewed favorably by several Hedgerow critics, most of whom commented on the honesty of the writing and the playing. "The situation Mr. Riggs establishes proceeds toward the final curtain implacably, authentically and with almost no flaws in taste... In the final altercation between Dorie and Ned, Dorie Bickel speaks her inner conflict with expressionistic vehemence and lucidity; and at this point, the naturalistic method evolves into something more stylized but quite acceptable... *Rancour* does not lack guts and has considerable formal beauty."[13] The play, one of the least known of Riggs's works, became a successful addition to the Hedgerow repertory and was revived a number of times. Sixteen years after its debut performance, Deeter wrote to Riggs that *Rancour* is back and "vital, fresh and very timely."[14]

What is most important, however, in the history of Hedgerow is that the production built a bond between Deeter and Riggs that would lead to not only five more Riggs plays but which also typified a way of working that was prized by both men and which was symptomatic of Deeter's commitment to other known and unknown writers and many untested scripts. According to Thomas Erhard, Riggs's total royalty income from Hedgerow over a 15-year period was only $426.[15] But what drew him back to the Rose Valley ("my favorite theatre") was the opportunity to work with a company he admired and a director whom he trusted. Writing about *Rancour* in 1929, he told Deeter, "As for the final line, I wouldn't fight for it. I'll trust your feelings."[16]

The correspondence between them is constantly illustrative of the faith that Riggs placed in Deeter. "The more that I direct, the more insistently I realize what a great director you are." And "I'm delighted that you are doing *Roadside*. I trust you implicitly."[17]

Roadside, Riggs's farcical tall tale of a braggart Texas cowboy and his romance of an equally spirited and sharp-tongued farmer's wife was a great favorite at Hedgerow and was revived successfully into the 1960s. Janet Kelsey remembers it as one of her finest productions and recalls how audiences responded to the broad farce of the characters and the situations. Reviewers, who sometimes objected to Riggs's salty language, were frequently charmed by its "lusty" dialogue. "One minute a character is cussing with swinging eloquence and the next he is rhapsodizing over nature in terms that are no less poetic because they are crudely alive."[18] *Roadside* was an audience delight in the Rose Valley and even had a brief Broadway run in 1930 with Ralph Bellamy in the featured role.[19] But of all the Riggs plays, Deeter was proudest of the "failed" *The Cherokee Night* that had its world premiere at Hedgerow and which Deeter invited Riggs to direct because he wanted to capitalize on the fact that this play was at the heart of the author's connection to the Indian territories and to Riggs's own Cherokee heritage.

In her impressive 2009 study, *Native American Drama: A Critical Perspective*, Christy Stanlake celebrates Lynn Riggs as the first professional playwright of the Native American theatre and finds in his masterpiece, *The Cherokee Night*, "a play that not only confronts directly the harsh prejudices against and within Oklahoma-Native communities at the turn of the twentieth century, but also functions as a ceremonial return to a Cherokee ethos of sacred place and community."[20] In his important study of Native American literature and culture, Jace Weaver concludes, "How Natives relate themselves to the earth and to each other also lies at the heart of *The Cherokee Night*."[21]

In his introduction to a new edition of Lynn Riggs's plays in 2003, Weaver writes that "with its underlying themes of preserving one's culture instead of running from it and of intercultural respect and understanding, this play becomes more contemporary with the passage of time."[22] Of course, the recent rush to restore Riggs's play to dramatic respectability after years of neglect is not shared by all contemporary critics. Julie Little Thunder writes in 2002 that "*Cherokee Night* distorts native cultures and perpetuates racist stereotypes, demonstrating how authors of minority ancestry, with no real connection to their culture, may inadvertently reinforce the views of the dominant society."[23] But even with this reservation, contemporary critics and scholars continue to reclaim Riggs's "masterpiece," as a critical text in the history of Native American drama.[24]

The Cherokee Night in seven scenes traces the downfall of the Cherokee nation as it is assimilated into the white culture of the State of Oklahoma. Set against the backdrop of the Claremore Mound, a hill that marks the infamous site where Cherokee warriors slaughtered Osage women and children while their men were away hunting, the play dramatizes the forces that fragmented and destroyed the culture and heritage of a once proud people. The mound is a contested place in Cherokee lore serving as a backdrop for the violence they perpetuated against the Osage as well as a sacred burial ground for the fallen victims and the warriors. Each scene dramatizes critical moments or impulses in the fragmentation of the Cherokee nation: the loss of territorial lands through bribery and propaganda for statehood; the denial of identity by assimilating into the white culture; the loss of language, schools, and religion; the participation in the slave trade of African Americans after the Civil War; and the betrayal of family and friendship for money, weapons, and alcohol.

Structurally, it is the *place* of the Claremore Mound that unifies the action of the play because the scenes are not presented in chronological order. The play begins in 1915 with a party on the mound attended by young mixed blood Cherokees who are ignorant of the sacred ground as well as their individual connections to the past. In subsequent flashback scenes, Riggs details the loss of Cherokee identity among these youngsters by dramatizing the events of assimilation that have led to this cultural erasure. The Claremore Mound hovers over each scene—sometimes in the distance and sometimes dramatically near—as though its presence operates as a character in the narrative. In one remarkable *interior* scene Riggs stipulates that Sarah, who is denouncing her sister's greed and vanity by denying her heritage, becomes an apparition of the mound. *"The lights begin to go down strangely. A fantastic glow from the stove creeps into the room, blotting out its realistic outline, its encompassing walls, throwing* SARAH'S *shadow, huge and dark, on the wall."*[25]

The last scene in the play takes place in 1895 and introduces the audience to a full-blooded Cherokee chief, Gray-Wolf who tries to help his grandson understand the ways of the past, but at 55, Gray-Wolf is no match for the white law that now rules over all aspects of Cherokee life and is articulated by the vigilante, Tinsley. "(*Briskly, turning, facing nearly front*) Gray-Wolf. Let this be a lesson and a warnin'. Teach your grandson. Tell everybody what it means to oppose the law. You Indians must think you own things out here. This is God's country out here—and God's a white man. Don't forget that."[26]

Riggs attempts to endow Gray-Wolf with the dignity of a full-blooded chief and both the stage directions and his demeanor reflect this. But the viewer is left not with the integrity of Gray-Wolf but with the realization that this scene precedes the opening moments of the play, set in 1915, where it is clear that assimilation has destroyed the Indian culture and replaced it with loss of memory. The final moment returns us to the hill. "The lights fade slowly. The fire flickers. Claremore Mound glitters in the night. A few stars are in the sky."[27]

Jasper Deeter was enormously moved by *The Cherokee Night*. The ideas in the play resonated strongly, recalling his adventure directing Jig Cook's *Spring* years earlier and his own impatience with racial discrimination. In addition, the play thrummed with the same energy and spirituality that had led him to cherish *Inheritors* and make it such an important icon on the Hedgerow landscape. Riggs's Claremore Mound recalled vividly for Deeter the hill that is the central location in Glaspell's play and the connections that it embodied for Native Americans. The surreal moment in Riggs's play where we encounter the ghostly Cherokee warriors were even reminiscent of Silas's drunken vision of meeting the Indian chief Blackhawk.

> SILAS: ...I climbed the hill. Blackhawk was there.
> GRANDMOTHER: Why, he was *dead*.
> SILAS: He was there—on his own hill, with me and the stars. And I said to him—
> GRANDMOTHER: Silas!
> SILAS: Says I to him. "Yes—that's true: it's more yours than mine, you had it first and loved it best. But it's neither yours nor mine,—though both yours and mine. Not my hill, not your hill, but—hill of vision," said I to him. "Here shall come visions of a better world than was ever seen by you or me, old Indian chief." Oh I was drunk, plum drunk.[28]

Although Deeter invited Riggs to direct the production, the program credits and production records suggest that Riggs served more in a dramaturgical capacity and that Deeter actually staged the play. They worked together to establish a sound score—principally drumbeats—that captured emotional moments and provided transitions between the scenes in much the same manner that Deeter utilized in *Winesburg*. They also used the prominent cyclorama to project and establish the presence of the Claremore Mound hovering over each of the individual scenes. The mountain was a constant reminder of the destruction of the Cherokee nation and a looming presence that tied the characters to the violence and loss of their homeland. And it invoked a poetic vision that prepared for the surrealistic moments that Deeter admired in Riggs's writing.

They were concerned, however, about audiences following the arc of the story because the play did not proceed in a linear, chronological fashion but rather dramatized significant events and moments between 1895 and 1931. So Riggs prepared a program note that helped to frame the intent of the production.

> The time sense, or rather the lack of chronological sequences, is not to be thought of as a stunt. The intent of the play, stated in scene one in somewhat supernatural terms, is meant to carry the play forward in space in exactly the same way as the mind—dealing with a subject—draws out of past or future or present, impartially, the verbal or visual images which will serve best to illustrate and illuminate a meaning.[29]

Unfortunately, Deeter's vision of the power of the events and the sacredness of the American landscape was not shared by theatre critics or much of his audience. In spite of a superb cast and Riggs's authorative counseling, the gala opening was greeted with extremely negative, and often savage, reviews. "It is to drama what sawing a woman in two is to surgery."[30] Some of the objections were familiar. "Mr. Riggs should be told that bold expletives are effective in the theater when used in moderation, but when they are used in excess they are downright offensive."[31] Or, "Mr. Riggs's partiality to strong language which was noticeable in both *Roadside* and *Lantern to See By* is here carried to quite unsavory extremes. There is no reason, artistic or otherwise, for the constant use of strong expletives."[32]

While the language did offend critical sensibilities, it was the fractured chronology and confusing character relationships that raised the clearest complaints. Arthur Waters, writing in the *Philadelphia Inquirer*, called it "a rambling, incoherent, over written play which skips rashly backward and forward over a period of 36 years."[33] And the *Bulletin* described it as "a relentlessly wearisome series of incoherent sketches."[34] The direction and the acting were praised in all accounts, but most accounts agreed that "the exact purport of the play remains a mystery to this observer."[35]

An exception, and a fascinating one, was Brooks Atkinson who seemed to have an acute understanding of the meaning in the play although heartily disagreeing with Riggs's dramaturgical program notes. "Let this column state categorically that Mr. Riggs's principle is one of the worst by which a play can be written. It gives a muddled mind the authority of an artist."[36] But Atkinson heartily admired the intent and the meaning of the play. "Although it is a perplexing drama, which holds the conventional theater forms in fine contempt, it has an exaltation of spirit that is honest, solid and moving."[37] He points out that the time leaps are sometimes baffling and often the characters only "fugitive shadows," but he was deeply impressed by the ambition of the play and the skill of the company. "For the anguished mood of *The Cherokee Night* is a purging one; the acting of Jasper Deeter's troupe has also an enkindling sincerity. And before the play is well started you begin to realize that this story of a lost tribe is no isolated episode. It is the story of a world that has lost its heritage. The Cherokee tragedy is the universal complaint."[38]

In spite of the negative press, Riggs was delighted with Deeter's production, and he made arrangements to produce the play at the University of Iowa in August. There he incorporated ideas that they had learned at Hedgerow—including the elaborate sound score—and directed the entire production himself. In 1936, it was revived by the Federal Theatre

Project for a brief run in New York but was largely forgotten until Riggs was "rediscovered" by scholars and artists of the current Native American renaissance.

One mystery does remain, however, from the Hedgerow world premiere. Stanlake points out how critical the number seven is in Cherokee lore and in the dramaturgy of Riggs's play. There were seven clans in the Cherokee nation and the play takes place in seven scenes. There are seven characters in the play and "the number seven alludes to the play's ceremonial nature."[39] And yet it appears that a critical scene was cut in the Hedgerow production. That scene—"Where the Nigger Was Found"—does not appear in the program and there is no mention of it in the surviving notes and correspondence. It is a pivotal scene occurring halfway through—number 4—and its subject is Negro racism, drawing thematically on the fact that Cherokees did enslave black men after the Civil War. Three young boys look for the blood of a slain Negro in a clearing under the Claremore Mound, and in the process enact a frenzied ritual spouting racist oaths and mimicking clichéd "Indian" war dances. At the end of the scene a giant black man emerges from the leaves and poses dramatically in contrast to a slim and attractive Cherokee warrior on the mountain. The racist language is painful, and some critics believe that the profanity, along with the homoerotic ending, discouraged subsequent productions of the play.[40] It's not clear why the scene was cut at Hedgerow. Deeter certainly could have cast a large black man and I don't believe that homoeroticism, however subtle, would have been a problem at Hedgerow. But it does remain a puzzle in the production history of *The Cherokee Night*.

Lynn Riggs's relationship with Jasper Deeter and the Hedgerow community was never about making Riggs a great deal of money nor did it dampen his ambition to be accepted someday by the Broadway establishment. But it is symptomatic of Hedgerow's mission, and Deeter's determination, to make a living by making honest theatre. The Riggs plays—comic and tragic—banal and poetic—are rooted in a dramatic vision that revealed truths about human beings and explored how that humanity was inescapably locked in a sense of "place" in the natural world. And Deeter produced them within the structure of his repertory calendar, joyous to discover a writer who was sympathetic to his goals and vision.

6. *Too True to Be Good*: Consequences of Integrity

Susan Glaspell wrote the anthem for Hedgerow, but it was Bernard Shaw who was their patron saint and most produced playwright. Beginning with *Candida* in their initial season, Deeter worked his way through the Shaw canon with brilliant productions of *St. Joan* (1934) and *The Doctor's Dilemma* (1935), annual summer festivals celebrating Shaw's July birthday, and eventually an epic American premiere of the complete *Man and Superman* in 1939. His fascination with Glaspell's *Inheritors*, with its appeal for "caring people doing," is directly reflected in his admiration of Shaw. "There is a very important sense in all of his writings of what we might do if we learned how to do things together."[1]

For Deeter, Shaw was also great fun and good box office. He relished the delightful humor in *Androcles and the Lion* and the pricking of pomposity in *Arms and the Man*. He reveled in the bluntness and fading ardor of Shotover in *Heartbreak House* and embraced the antiwar fervor of numerous characters, including the articulate "Sergeant" in *Too True to Be Good*. Shaw was the ultimate iconoclast, the master of the smashed idol, and Jasper Deeter was one of his most ardent devotees. For Deeter, as well as Shaw, the goal was always trying to find the truth. David Ralphe, one of Deeter's protégées and a successful director at Hedgerow and later the Simi Valley, recalled, "Jap saying angrily, at times wistfully, but always with determination that would brook no disagreement; 'the search is for truth and beauty.' A reference to Shaw would not be far behind."[2]

Hedgerow had a special relationship with Shaw, and he allowed them to produce his plays for a reduced royalty, which occasionally led to spats with the Theatre Guild who believed that they controlled exclusive Shaw rights in the United States. The squabbling is sometimes humorous when read against the background of the royalty checks that Hedgerow, diligently and precisely, sent on to Shaw's secretary, Blanche Patch, and the Shaw bank account. Two weeks after they had played *Misalliance* for eight

88 A Sustainable Theatre

Figure 6.1 Jasper outside Hedgerow. From the collection of Mark Sfirri.

people in 1933 and sent Shaw 0.20 cents, the same production earned them $345 (132 people at $2.00 and 27 at $3.00) and at 7.5 percent they mailed a check for $25.88.[3] In 1946, Shaw tried to regularize the method of payment and expressed the appreciation that he felt for their work. "Make your payments to me by cheques on your bankers as if I lived in Moylan, which is quite simple, or in dollar notes. Pay by the year if you like, or whenever it is most convenient for you. The fraction that will be left to me when your Inland Revenue authorities and the British Exchequer have taken their rake-off will be negligible and need not burden your conscience while it is in arrear."[4]

Deeter expressed great affection for Shaw and would not be drawn into a public quarrel when the playwright, visiting Hollywood in 1933, reduced Ann Harding to tears in a widely reported verbal spat. On the set of *When Ladies Meet,* Harding told Shaw that she had played in *Captain Brassbound's Conversion* at Hedgerow and would return shortly for a reprise. He replied that it must have been a "pirated production" and the conversation accelerated into loud voices, threats of legal action, and tears of outrage. Shaw walked off the set and Harding fled to her dressing room leaving Myrna Loy and the crew speechless and astonished at Shaw's rudeness to a gifted actress whom they all admired. The episode was reported widely in the newspapers, and Harding claimed the moral high ground: "an uncalled-for bit of rudeness to an organization which has sincerely admired him for years."[5] Deeter, who was aware of Shaw's reputation for confrontations and sometimes boorish behavior, told the press, "We have a special contract for the production of everything George Bernard Shaw ever wrote, with the exception of his latest play *Too True to Be Good*. But even if we had no such contract, we would certainly steal his plays, so highly do we think of them. I am too busy to be greatly concerned over it. I can say, however, that Mr. Shaw is a great artist and anything he says is pretty important."[6]

Too True to Be Good is one of Shaw's most peculiar plays and even after Deeter had found a way to stage it, he was not confident that it would play. "I think I understand the third act, but I don't guarantee I can make it clear to other people," he told Lawrence Davies.[7] The play was introduced into the Hedgerow repertory as part of the fourth annual Shaw festival on July 26, 1937, and was billed as the one hundred and twenty-third production. That summer the festival ran from July 19 to August 14 and featured ten different productions in addition to *Too True*. Playing every day but Sunday in true repertory, the ambition was enormous. During the first week they opened on successive nights *Arms and the Man, Candida, You Never Can Tell, The Devil's Disciple, Getting Married,* and *Misalliance*. The second week opened with *Too True* that played Monday and Tuesday and then alternated with other titles for an additional four performances.[8]

The play begins with a talking microbe who is invisible to other characters and ends with a long sermon by a reformed minister and thief who preaches from no creed and who is second guessed in the stage directions by the author. The action moves on a kind of dreamscape from the sickroom of a spoiled aristocrat to an unnamed "Arabian" desert outpost manned by an English regiment. Unlike *Major Barbara* and other Shaw plays where poverty is the worst sin and the underclass the victims of a cruel capitalism, *Too True* posits that the upper classes are the victims of their own excesses, and it is the acceptance of their ideology that is literally making them sick. The characters struggle to understand the source of their unhappiness, while indulging, at the same time, in the material rewards of their class.

Shaw's search for the truth in human condition was matched by the long and testing rehearsals at Hedgerow where Deeter helped his actors craft their performances around making choices that revealed their inner truth. He was famous for rejecting anything that seemed false or "acting" and encouraged actors to free themselves of acting habits so that they could see the text and their characters in a fresh light. Shaw was a special challenge because he often structured his plays so that they appeared to be embracing one set of ideas and then reversed the stakes by making the opposite more attractive. This iconoclasm appealed to Deeter because it forced him and his company to uncover the ideas and the ideology driving the dramatic action. Speaking about *Too True to Be Good*, Deeter described how he had at first been confused and disappointed in the play, but after considerable reflection and study it now made sense to him within the context of Shaw's other works. "It attacks the light-mindedness in God (as in *Saint Joan*) to I believe in you (as in *Candida*) to I believe in me (as in *Heartbreak House*). In *Too True* there is a question mark: what is there to believe in?"[9]

In the final act the characters come to a significant revelation about their lifestyle and behavior. Major Tallboys abandons his military command to take up a career in painting, and "The Countess" renounces the obligations of motherhood to embark on a quest for communal feminine companionship. The Sergeant rejects the ideology of killing those who are "different" and runs off to marry the working-class Sweetie who, posing as a profligate aristocrat, has experienced only spiritual emptiness. Finally, the minister/thief discovers that he literally believes in nothing but continues to preach as a stage fog slowly envelops him: "I must preach and preach and preach no matter how late the hour and how short the day, no matter whether I have nothing to say or whether in some Pentecostal flame of revelation the Spirit will descend on me and inspire me with a message the sound whereof shall go out unto all lands and realize for us at last the Kingdom and the Power and the Glory for ever and ever. Amen."[10]

The play ends, but in a typical Shavian ploy, the author continues speaking behind the back of the departed actor.

> *The audience disperses (or the reader puts down the book) impressed in the English manner with the Pentecostal flame and the echo from the Lord's Prayer. But fine words butter no parsnips. A few of the choicer spirits will know that the Pentecostal flame is always alright at the service of those strong enough to hear its terrible intensity. They will not forget that it is accompanied by a mighty rushing wind, and that any rascal who happens to be a windbag can get a prodigious volume of talk out of it without ever going near enough to be shriveled up. The author, though himself a professional talk maker, does not believe that the world can be saved by talk alone. He has given the rascal the last word; but his own favorite is the woman of action.*[11]

The long closing sermon/monologue perplexed Deeter as it had others, but it eventually led him to an understanding of the play and to additional admiration of Shaw's work. In rehearsal, Deeter worked to make the monologue as appealing and sympathetic as possible with a view that "we should fear a man who tries to please people with the beauty of thought."[12] The long sermon with its final appeal to God and goodness is too true to be good for anything, especially on a dramatic landscape that highlights the "selfishness and pride of men and women and in nations of men and women."[13] Shaw has the final word in the stage direction, but how do you stage that?

Deeter's prompt script indicates that the curtain call followed immediately after the final "Amen," so there was no attempt to stage the author's closing remarks. But the blocking notes for the end of the sermon provide an idea of how the production was framed for the audience "After 'falling, falling' from here on Aubrey has ad lib moves until seven lines from curtain. At 'I am ignorant' up onto center ramp for crucifix position and light plot."[14] Aubrey, the lapsed cleric and master thief, is stripped of illusions like the other characters in the play, and while his futile preaching might suggest a hope for faith, he is actually crucified in a world of brutal men and failed political systems. Perhaps, there is a chance that women might provide some hope, but it's an afterthought in a blasted aftermath, and Deeter despaired at the bleakness of Shaw's vision.

Henry Murdock, reviewing the production for the *Philadelphia Evening Ledger,* called it "superlative" and added that "of the many Shaw achievements in Hedgerow's record, last night's takes first place." He then tries to articulate what he saw and perhaps what it meant.

> Shaw was 76 years old when he wrote it and, if we have interpreted the play correctly, a frightened man who was encountering a new reality in the form of the World War and the wrecked generation it left in its train... With a courage little short of magnificent this giber at the status quo, this apostle of free thinking, this iconoclast confesses a fear of the naked world that is stripped of illusion. All his characters arrive at a state of Shavian common sense before the play is over, yet he looks at them with something akin to horror. Their world is not the world he wanted to make with his glib phrasing, and hidden beneath his sharp words of wit is a strange and moving plea for a return to the most elemental emotions—faith.[15]

For Deeter, however, faith was evaporating. *Too True to Be Good,* with its nearly existential view of the human condition, fascinated him, but he was uncomfortable looking into the abyss and wrote to Shaw on the eve of another world war, "*Too True* tells the whole story but what now?" He could not understand how Shaw, with his unabashed faith in a kind of creative evolution and an avowed commitment to the power of the life force, would not find a way to say "yes" to human beings. "Do you have anything new and is it like *Heartbreak House* now? We want to know what you think and can we know and help?"[16]

As the shadow of a second great world war loomed, Deeter had reached out to Shaw angling to obtain production rights for *Geneva* and seeking advice and guidance from a man for whom he held tremendous respect. "Thank you for your note about *Geneva*. You have suggested *Too True*," Deeter wrote to Miss Patch, "which was our most successful play in 1937 and will run this year...Let us do *Geneva*. My insistence can be interpreted as my fear that our free speech will be a thing of the past in 1940...I should hate when our repertory would be the brighter comedy of Mr. Milne and the fake satires of the American Kaufmans, who enhance our stupidities by only pretending to make fun of them."[17]

They did not produce *Geneva* but did revive *Too True*. War was anathema to Deeter. Like Robert Sherwood and other theatre artists who had come to maturity in the aftermath of the mud and mustard gas of trench combat, war was humankind's descent into bestiality and was to be resisted at all costs. God's version of solitaire was how Sherwood had characterized it in *Idiot's Delight*, and Hedgerow's repertory was abundant with antiwar sentiments. They were most obvious in the strong support for conscientious objectors that were central to the argument of *Inheritors* and in the powerful antiwar *Unknown Warrior* by Paul Raynal that Deeter produced on Armistice Day in 1933 as their official one hundredth production. In Shaw, Deeter preached his own sermons with productions of *Heartbreak House, Arms and the Man,* and *Too True.* Part of Deeter's attraction to *Too True to Be Good* was its clear-eyed view of how war functions as part of the human condition and how the bureaucracy and incompetence of the military dooms it to perpetual incompetence. War, in Shaw's estimation, was a central hypocrisy in the ideology of English Church and State, and he missed no opportunity to skewer its proverbs and maxims. Aubrey, the failed preacher and thief in *Too True*, explains his fall from grace to his bewildered father. "As a flying ace I won a very poorly designed silver medal for committing atrocities which were irreconcilable with the profession of a Christian clergyman. When I was wounded and lost my nerve for flying, I became an army chaplain. I then found myself obliged to tell mortally wounded men that they were dying in a state of grace and were going straight to heaven when as a matter of fact they were dying in mortal sin and going elsewhere."[18] Shaw constructs in *Too True* a satirical fantasy of

English army encampments overseen by the tyrannical Major Tallboys and functioning only through the pragmatic actions of working-class private Meek, who keeps rejecting promotion and advancement because rank only insulates officers from the reality of command.[19] But the brunt of Shaw's indignation, and Deeter's sympathy, is carried by the Sergeant for whom the Great War taught a horrendous truth.

> You see, miss, the great principle of soldiering, I take it, is that the world is kept going by the people who want the right thing killing the people who want the wrong thing. When the soldier is doing that he is doing the work of God, which my mother brought me up to do. But that's a very different thing from killing a man because he's a German and he killing you because you're an Englishman. We were not killing the right people in 1915. We weren't even killing the wrong people. It was innocent men killing one another.
>
> THE PATIENT: Just for the fun of it.
>
> THE SERGEANT: No, miss; it was no fun. For the misery of it.[20]

It was the hope of communicating some of that misery that prodded Jasper Deeter to commit Hedgerow to a stand for conscientious objecting as a second war loomed. Realizing that a draft would also rob him of the core of young actors critical to his repertory, Deeter was determined to oppose conscription of his company by whatever means he could devise. It was a fateful decision and one that would have grave consequences for the theatre and the community.

In spite of its growing record of excellence, and the publicity generated by the Shaw festivals, Hedgerow remained a reclusive and largely unheralded venue. But Deeter's desire to preserve the company by defying the draft made newspaper headlines across the country and thrust the theatre into national prominence. In the wake of the Pearl Harbor patriotism that swept the country and accelerated the conscription of its young men, Deeter made a courageous stand against war and violence. Vilified by many and under vehement pressure to relent, he undertook a campaign for conscience that reached from the Rose Valley to the White House.

It began with a letter to President Roosevelt in July of 1940 in which Deeter tried to make a case for the deferment from any future conscription of the half dozen company members who would be eligible for the draft. His rationale was that they were performing an important cultural task for the country and were they to be drafted Hedgerow would be severely crippled. Two months later—and still more than a year prior to the attack at Pearl Harbor—Roosevelt signed the Selective Training and Service Act, with the first registration scheduled one month later on October 16, 1940. At Hedgerow, Deeter and company manager, Mahlon Naill, began preparing letters to submit to the local draft board should their actors be called. Working in a theatre did not qualify one to be exempt from the draft, but there was a provision that could exclude young men who were performing a "national service." Deeter seized upon this provision, and over the next four years continually argued that producing plays in their nonsubsidized, nonprofitmaking theatre was not only a national service, but was also a vital cultural resource fundamental to a free and democratic society. He would take an enormous amount of abuse for this line of reasoning, particularly from those who saw it as a self-serving rational to preserve a little bucolic theatre while others were fighting for the survival of a country. Deeter had schooled his company and his audiences in the integrity of war resistance in *Inheritors,* however, and he was not going to back down, especially when it was one of the potential draftees who played the pragmatic Professor Holden in Glaspell's play. Moreover, Deeter's stubborn insistence was buttressed when George Bernard Shaw made the same appeal in England on behalf of the ballet company at Sadler's Wells theatre.

Eventually six young men were called and classified 1-A. Hedgerow immediately undertook an aggressive campaign to have them reclassified. On December 13, 1941, one week after Pearl Harbor, Naill wrote to the Media Draft Bureau requesting a deferment for two of them—David Metcalf and Morgan Smedley—on the basis of their conscience and refusal to participate in warfare. Conscientious objector status was controversial and extremely difficult to obtain. Men who could not document an active and ongoing religious commitment or affiliation were routinely viewed as "slackers," a popular derisive term for those who were cowardly or conniving to escape service to their country. The definition of slacker, however, was problematized when the massive enlistment programs unearthed all kinds of dissenters, including "secular pacifists, non-pacifist Jehovah's Witnesses, Hopi Indians, socialists refusing to enroll in a capitalist war, African Americans protesting Jim Crow in the armed services, and Puerto Rican nationalists incensed over the US occupation of their island."[21]

There were few "actors" who qualified, although in one celebrated case film star Lew Ayres was granted conscientious objector status when he argued that his genuine opposition to war was a result of his leading role in the antiwar classic, *All Quiet on the Western Front.*[22] Ayers was clearly an exception, however, and easily surpassed in public opinion by Gary Cooper whose performance in *Sergeant York* became a model for military defense of the country. Timothy Stewart-Winter quotes one enthusiastic voice from

1942, "I have been raised to be a conscientious objector to war and fighting. I saw a motion picture entitled *Sergeant York*. Afterwards I did some steep thinking. Was my religion worth fighting for, or should I sit back and let my friends and neighbors stick up for it for me? Was my home worth protecting, or should I let some yellow, thieving, killing rebel come in and destroy it?"[23] For the draft board in Media, Pennsylvania, there was no question. Actors in the Hedgerow community were clearly bohemian slackers and all those eligible for the draft were denied exemptions and called to serve.

An examination of "Form 47: Special Form For Conscientious Objector" illustrates how complicated it was to apply for conscientious objector status. Applicants had two choices: to apply for noncombatant service under military direction or to refuse to participate in any service under direction of the military. The first allowed objectors to be drafted into a system that assigned them to ambulance and other duties. The second was frequently regarded as the "slacker" category by local draft boards and required extensive documentation including a narrative of your beliefs and how you came to acquire them. "2. Explain how, when, and from whom or from what source you received the training and acquired the belief which is the basis of your claim made in Series I above."[24] Mahlon Naill, who had been instrumental in helping his fellow actors complete their forms, submitted his own application in June, 1943. It is nine single-spaced typed pages and illustrates both the fervor that was felt by the Hedgerow applicants as well as the connections that they saw between what they did and who they were. "In *Inheritors* Susan Glaspell has shown that it is very difficult to remain within a thing without becoming like that thing," Naill wrote, "I could not see myself joining the Army and still retaining my religious principles, and I have no more wish to undermine the war effort than to help it."[25] Naill lists a number of plays that have continued to enforce his religious beliefs and offers quotations from Shaw's *Back to Methuselah* and borrows one from *Too True to Be Good*. After indicating that he is willing to serve in a CPS (Civilian Public Service) camp or even go to prison, Naill writes, "I realize, however, that fine words butter no parsnips and I am prepared to back up my words with actions."[26]

He also attempts to contradict the prejudice of the local draft board that Hedgerow is some kind of slacker colony where one is brainwashed into bohemian behavior.

> It has been suggested by one of the members of my local draft board that my position as an objector *jelled* at Hedgerow implying that I may have picked up my views there. It is true that the Selective Service machinery forced me to

know and declare my position while I happened to be living and working there, but I sincerely believe that I brought as much of that position to the theater as I picked up there... The C.O. views of my contemporaries were not common property until the situation was laid in our laps. It may look like ostrich behavior, but we were simply too busy building our institution to spend our time that way. As Sherwood Anderson puts it, "Life, not death, is the great adventure."[27]

Undaunted, Deeter wrote to General Lewis B. Hershey, the director of the Selective Service Bureau and appealed to him to grant the conscientious objector exemptions, but Hershey was unmoved by Deeter's attempt to link play production in the Rose Valley with national service in the time of war. In fact, Hershey was not the least bit tolerant of those evading the draft and had already proclaimed that "by one device or another, we can take care of almost every shade of conscientious objecting."[28]

By the fall of 1942, Hedgerow had exhausted its appeals, but Deeter was determined to show that this was not just a quarrel about protecting his turf, but rather a fight to legitimize the position of those who stood up to war and violence as a matter of conscience. In a dramatic flourish he wrote an open letter to the public, clarifying his moral stance and sent copies to dozens of people in the professional theatre, many of whom had worked at Hedgerow or been part of their audience and community. By going over the head of the draft system he hoped to stir public support in sympathy with his belief that the work being done at Hedgerow was the very thing that America should be fighting to support. In part, he urged support because "so far, no officer or branch of the Selective Service System has been fit to include the work of the Hedgerow Theatre within the scope of the national interest."[29]

The upshot was a fistful of letters, both denouncing and supporting the theatre, that increased the clamor and brought the local and national press into the controversy.

Some were very supportive. Eve Avedon wrote to Mahlon Naill, "Hedgerow does for National Unity, Democracy, and the very things this Second World War is being fought for! Hedgerow wages its own war, a cultural one, against poverty, racial discrimination, Nazism, and all the other evils that have caused this world turmoil."[30] Sean O'Casey sent a stirring response from Ireland in support of theatre in a time of war, exhorting Jasper to keep up the fight, and concluding, "Long live the Abbey, the Moscow Art Theatre and Hedgerow."[31]

But others were not so kind. Virginia Farmer, who had been an original Hedgerow member before moving on to the Group Theatre, wrote, "The moment for individual preference, individual decision and judgment is not now."[32] And Paul Green told Jasper that in spite of all the words, he probably should "get on with it...Your COs are right in *attitude* but *wrong* as citizens of a practical world."[33] Some chose to pass: "I'm not the right man to interfere," [34] wrote Irwin Piscator. But one of the most interesting (and provocative) responses came from former company member Maria Coxe, who was totally opposed to the notion of exempting actors from the struggle. "It is not life or death for Hedgerow, it is life or death for the right to have theater, art and freedom to create freedom to live." Coxe then tried to school Deeter by invoking his beloved *Inheritors*, "If you make Hindus Jews, and set *Inheritors* in Heidelberg University you will find a modern parallel—fighting aggression and persecution."[35]

Deeter was vilified by many and several subscribers asked that their names be removed from the theatre's list of supporters, but his tactics insured that the Hedgerow controversy received wide and prominent headlines. On October 7, 1942, the *Philadelphia Record* published a feature story titled HEDGEROW ACTOR AWAITS SERVICE OF WARRANT FOR DRAFT DODGING; OTHER 1-A's CARRY ON THEATER'S WORK OF "NATIONAL IMPORTANCE." With six accompanying photographs, the *Record* reviewed the vital work that each of the 1-A's were doing. "George Ebeling (1-A) was taking telephoned reservations for *The Picnic*, an account of the amorous difficulties of a domineering mother."[36] And Morgan Smedley (1-A) "chairman of the property department and the front-of-the-house department" was talking about "scenery being prepared for the show."[37] The article concludes with disparaging quote from a local and prominent Rose Valley resident and an observation from Congressman Michael J. Bradley of Philadelphia's third district. "For unmitigated gall and nerve, it would be hard to match the statements issued by Jasper Deeter in his efforts to secure exemption from military service by the members of his theatrical troupe."[38] In the same issue an accompanying editorial castigates Deeter, "Look here, Jasper Deeter, you are making an ass of yourself."[39] Two weeks later, *Time* magazine published a feature article on the Hedgerow controversy and noted that "Philadelphia papers last week loosed on Hedgerow a flood of sarcasm and censure for getting too big for its Army boots."[40]

Then in a surprising move, the Roosevelt administration ordered General Hershey to reverse the decision by the Media draft board and grant conscientious objector status to three of the Hedgerow petitioners. The local board was furious but had to comply. But it was a Pyrrhic victory. The three actors were not allowed to continue with the company but were instead assigned to CPS camps where they would be compelled to do volunteer work for the duration of the war.

The work was hard—similar to what Civilian Conservation Corps (CCC) volunteers had done in the previous decade—planting trees, building fire breaks, clearing brush. But in their "free time" conscientious objector inmates struggled to keep their pacifism alive, and the Hedgerow "alumni" sought to establish the kind of theatre that they learned and revered in the Rose Valley. They were idealistic and courageous, but also homesick and dislocated. In the Hedgerow archives there are dozens of letters from the various locations as the men were moved from camp to camp in the conscientious objector network. Joe Leberman describes the living conditions at Camp Marietta in Ohio, and details that he is forming a play reading group so they can keep the Hedgerow spirit and ideas alive. Later, he is moved to Lyndehurst, Virginia, where he pleads for news from the "gang" and describes how plays like *Inheritors* and *Arms and the Man* help him focus on the mission of using theatre and drama to enlighten and uplift his comrades.[41]

But the most poignant and touching accounts are from Joe Gistirak who started out in Big Flats, New York, but was eventually transferred to Camp Waldport in Oregon. There he joined a group of other artists and actors who were deeply committed to making vital theatre as a response to the madness of violence. The Waldport group was deeply influenced by Jasper Deeter's teachings as well as the repertory at Hedgerow. David Jackson who had worked at Hedgerow had come to Oregon in the summer of 1944 and directed a production of *Aria da Capo* by Edna St. Vincent Millay using techniques of acting that he had learned from working with Deeter. When Gistirak arrived that winter they immediately began planning a production of Ibsen's *Ghosts*, another Deeter favorite. Gistirak was excited about the potential of the production and was able to put together a local cast whom he believed could make the difficult text work. His letters are filled with hope and enthusiasm for the potential of theatre in the Waldport community.

From the limited sources available, it appears that the production was indeed a very successful undertaking. "We rehearsed for a period of about six and a half months five nights per week for about four hours straight," he wrote. "This is practically unheard of in the system. Leisure time is so rare and highly valued that it is almost impossible to get people to make any commitment at all. However, I believe the determining factor in this case was the stature of the play. It is quite a tribute to Father Ibsen that he has kept five people whose primary interest is not acting interested for nearly seven months."[42]

But the passion to resist the war and the idealism that drove so many young people into the conscientious objector ranks often diminished as the months and years dragged on. Some walked away from the camps and disappeared. Others were arrested after going absent without leave (AWOL) and sentenced to federal prison. Even Gistirak, in spite of his idealism and belief in the redemptive power of the arts, became discouraged and disillusioned with the mission. "There is only ennui," he wrote, "all idealism lost, this is simply a lower kind of prison without bars and concrete."[43]

In the Rose Valley, the impact of the war was decisive. Gas rationing prevented audiences from making the familiar drive from Philadelphia and nearby communities. The box office income declined dramatically as some patrons refused to support what they perceived as Deeter's unpatriotic support of conscientious objectors. By 1943, the season was curtailed and productions offered only two nights a week. Resident members took part-time jobs to keep the company going. The annual Shaw festival was canceled. With a reduced male population, Miriam Phillips put together a popular review called *Girls in Uniform*, but Deeter was able to add only four new productions to the repertory, and none at all in 1945. And in perhaps one of the most disheartening moments, Glaspell refused to authorize any productions of *Inheritors* that she felt could now be misinterpreted in this different war. She wrote:

> I deeply felt when I wrote it, and I believe that there is much in the play that is not confined to a particular time. But perhaps people who do not think carefully—and there are unfortunately, a good many of them—could relate things said of that time to the present day, which might make it seem that I was not in sympathy with what my country is now doing. The contrary is true. I believe we have to fight and win this war. I think our country is in greater danger than ever before in our history—that all we hold dear, all worth living for is threatened... But as *Inheritors* is written, being written for another time, I think it might do more harm than good, and so I am asking you to withdraw it.[44]

Deeter was terribly disappointed and repeatedly urged her throughout the war years to relent. At one point he asks her if she will grant him permission to do a single-voiced reading for a "Friends" benefit in Philadelphia. Her response is brief and final. "The answer is no. I tried to make myself clear before."[45]

Deeter, however, remained unflagging in his opposition to state-supported wars and sanctioned violence. Like Shaw and Scott Nearing, he believed that individual rights and freedoms were often endangered by the "mass thought" of ignorant politicians and uninformed citizenry.

And with Wharton Esherick he found strength in Thoreau's caution from *Walden* that "say what you have to say, not what you ought. Any truth is better than make believe."[46] Ruth Esherick, who referred to Jasper as her "second father," recalls how this passion would carry over into the postwar years, "He would invite people to the Plumstead bar to watch the McCarthy hearings, because even though we lived in a rural community he always wanted us to be aware of what was going on in the outside world."[47]

Hedgerow survived the war as it had the Great Depression, the loss of many talented youngsters, and the call to abandon the countryside and join the revolution. Everything they believed in and stood for was tested, and Deeter defied those who questioned his sincerity and his resolve. While he found no solace in *Too True to Be Good*, its characterization of the hypocrisy of war and military service was as central to his convictions as his beloved *Heartbreak House*. His strength came from many sources including a well-worn Thoreau quote from his friend Wharton Esherick: "I learned this, at least, by my experiment: that if one advances confidently in the direction of his dreams, and endeavors to live the life which he has imagined, he will meet with a success unexpected in common hours."[48]

7. *Uncle Vanya*: A Way of Acting

For two years they had been unable to mount a new production, but with the war behind them and the company swollen with returning members, Deeter added Chekhov to the 1946 season. *Uncle Vanya* had always intrigued him because of its rich characters and its deft and deceptive story line, and he was anxious to explore the behaviors that motivated and propelled these charming and failed people. In addition, the small cast, limited interiors, and minimal technical demands allowed him to open a new production without an expensive outlay.

Hedgerow had had successes with Chekhov, especially *The Seagull* that premiered in 1932 and was frequently revived. Deeter enjoyed working on the play, especially reminding his cast and classes that Chekhov called it a "comedy." After performing a highly intense and emotional scene, Louis Lippa recalls a long silence after which Deeter remarked, "You do know that Chekhov calls this a comedy." Lippa agreed but pointed out that the play ends with a suicide. "Yes," said Deeter, "He's been trying to get his mother's attention from the outset; what better way to finally get it?"[1] Hedgerow played *Ivanov* in 1926 and introduced *Three Sisters* in 1934. *The Cherry Orchard*, interestingly, was not added to the repertory until after the success of *Uncle Vanya*. *The Cherry Orchard* premiered in 1949 and then subsequently played to good receipts in 1950 and 1952.

Vanya benefited from a superb cast and from detailed and imaginative direction. Both George Ebeling and David Metcalf who played Vanya and Astrov received strong notices as did Audrey Ward as Yelena. And Catherine Reiser was outstanding as the lovesick Sonya. Reiser was a favorite of Hedgerow audiences and of Deeter. She was a splendid St. Joan, and Deeter later remembered her Sonya as one of the best that he had directed. She also was spunky and outspoken and according to one observer, "able to stand up to Deeter in any conversation."[2]

The critics were very complimentary about the new production. One reviewer remarked, "Our strongest impression after seeing Wednesday

Figure 7.1 Jasper Deeter and Rose Schulman taken in the early 1950s. Courtesy of the Hedgerow Theatre.

night's performance is that the play was both directed and acted with affection as well as intelligence. Rarely does one meet in theater such complete individualization of personalities as is found in this production."[3] Moreover, the *Bulletin* reviewer commented, "The talented Rose Valley troupe have gone all out in this, their fourth Chekhov opus, and the result of their efforts—in terms of staging, direction and acting—will delight the serious student of the drama."[4]

Amidst the praise, however, there was a familiar codicil, one that was frequently visited upon Hedgerow productions. "One would never want to see *Uncle Vanya* played fast, but a stepping up of the tempo in certain scenes would help the present production. However, we hasten to note that Wednesday's lags were those of deliberation, not of lack of preparation."[5]

That deliberation is reflective of the way that Deeter worked on *Uncle Vanya*, and an examination of the process yields a great deal about the Hedgerow production as well as insights into Deeter's core beliefs about acting and directing actors. David Ralphe, who worked closely with Deeter, recalls, "I never attended a class with Jap that he didn't have a scene on the floor from *Uncle Vanya* and occasionally *The Seagull*. Every female student he had experienced either Sonya or Irena in the scene following Dr. Astrov's exit."[6] Deeter used this scene and others from the play when he taught acting, and several hours of those rehearsal sessions were tape recorded by Peter Carnahan, the director of the Harrisburg Community Theatre, over two summers in 1966 and 1967. An examination of those tapes, as well as notes from the Hedgerow archives, yields some valuable insights into Deeter as director, teacher, and acting coach, and illuminates why so many actors were forever grateful to him for their training.

Acting is difficult to write about because language cannot capture the immediacy of an emotional moment, and descriptions of a process do not always convey the linkage of thought and impulse that lead to a successful choice. Deeter believed that actors could be taught and could grow in their talent and their craft. But he insisted that besides talent they had to have three important qualities: aptitude, willingness to learn, and humility. This "three legged stool" was the basis for all the work that he undertook and was a measure of whether he believed an actor could find the truths of a character. And, of course, aptitude could not be taught. Penny Reed, who studied with Jasper and who is the current artistic director of Hedgerow, recalls a particularly difficult moment when he said to another young woman, "I'm not taking your money anymore."[7]

Deeter's touchstone of being truthful was rooted in the belief that you had to study carefully the character you were playing as well as the reality of the imagined dramatic situation. He believed that you could "become" the character and, therefore, think and behave as that person. But unlike many of the Strasberg-influenced actors who would popularize the American Method in postwar America, Deeter did not believe that the actor literally became the character. "If you lose yourself in the role," he often remarked, "you are simply lost." Like Stanislavski, Deeter understood the difference between real truth and scenic truth. No matter how immersed in the details of the play, the actor is still a player on the stage capable of watching the "ballet" or finding the light. Penny Reed recalls Jasper saying that "you have to have at least 4% of your conscious mind in charge."[8]

The key to unlocking the character that you are portraying is *empathy* and Deeter taught and coached about the power of empathy that could function like a wave washing over and allowing you to understand the person you are playing.[9] Thus, the presence of the actor plus the empathic response to the character was the basic groundwork for establishing a truthful performance.

Within that framework individual choice was then determined by a precise chain of impulses that started in the mind and which were manifest in movement and language. There was a mantra among the actors at

Hedgerow that encapsulated what Deeter taught and which many of them still trust and recite today.

MIND
BODY
EYES
FACE
TALK

In technical terms, Deeter believed that thought was expressed in the central nervous system and then in a rapid process carried out through the body, crystallized in the eyes and face, and made manifest in the language of the play. Of course, this was an instantaneous process, but the awareness of it encouraged actors to focus and *listen*. Deeter was adamant about listening, because the mind had to have a cue to initiate the process that would result in the next truthful moment.

He was also adamant about the power of the actors creating the reality of the play by working together and not by featuring themselves. Deeter was patient and supportive of his actors, but he was aware of the numerous ways that actors could draw attention to self at the expense of the moment or the ensemble. Sherwood Anderson relates a wonderful story about a young woman who had had a great success and received enormous audience approval. The next day, as the company was shelling peas for the evening meal, the room was tense and quiet. Finally, she spoke:

> "Well, I did it again?" "Yes," says Deeter, "you know you did... You did not want to do it. You did not want to spoil the work of all the other actors on the stage. I understand. Again you were too determined. You were afraid you would not get it done and so you got it all up in your head. You could not let go. The other players on the stage were thrown off. As I have told you many times and as you know full well, playing is always a group matter. When you become like that, all mind, determined, conscious of technique, the others cannot exist in the play. The play and others get lost. Only you remain."[10]

Deeter repeatedly talked about the actor suggesting, rather than showing, how important it was to reach a condition of relaxation and "easy self-control." He stressed that an actor can only reach a "life-like quality" if he/she works freely within limitations. He disliked the term "blocking" because it too strongly suggests a rigid approach to staging plays and inhibits the actor's spontaneity. He did "stage" plays carefully but often spoke in notions of "ballet" rather than blocking. Certainly the actor had to get from point A to point B to make the scene work, but the actor needed the freedom to make the move—a dance or a circle—rather than a "block."

Speed was always the enemy of the actor because it forces you into making decisions before you have absorbed all the information. True to his Crafts heritage, Deeter was fond of reminding everyone that "nothing good was ever made fast," and an actor frequently was reminded that "the more haste, the less speed." He believed that "performing is a social art but learning the techniques is an individual craft."[11] Part of that craft was answering the "W" questions (Who, What, Where, When, and Why) before worrying about the How. The "how" was the "artistic part" and could not be mastered until the other questions were answered. In Deeter's analysis, bad or glib or Broadway actors could score points by showing the "how," but the truth was often missing.

In spite of his insistence on a working methodology, however, Deeter did not believe that all actors created and/or responded in the same way. He hated the term "method" because he felt there was no such thing that could accommodate the variety of actors. Each one was an individual in Deeter's mind and part of the actor's work was to understand his or herself. An actor's "presence" was very important to Deeter, and that always involved courage and endurance and faith and a commitment not to settle for an effect. David Ralph remembers how contemptuous Deeter could be of those who played for "results," rather than letting the moment grow from the presence of the actor in the moment.[12]

Deeter's emphasis on living the part and becoming the character, especially in the theatre of the early 1930s, raises obvious questions about the influence of Stanislavski and the pioneering work of the Group Theatre, which is ordinarily credited with popularizing the Russian "System" in the American theatre. Deeter had mixed feelings about the Group because some of them—Carnovski, Virginia Farmer—had worked at Hedgerow in the early days, and Deeter believed that they had learned a great deal there without perhaps acknowledging their debt. He also believed that their prodigious pamphleteering, columns, and manifestos betrayed an intellectuality that he distrusted. In 1931, he wrote to the critic George Jean Nathan in response to *The House of Connelly,* "The more intellectual their approach the greater their need for a supporting buncombe built out of their appreciation for Stanislavski and their hate of me."[13] For Deeter, the real work of the theatre wasn't in manifestos and consciousness-raising meetings but in the rehearsal room. "I know nothing of Mr. Strasberg," he wrote to Nathan, and ever suspicious of too much talk and theorizing, he concluded, "Here you see we don't know much. We only work. 168 seats can be made to comfortably house and feed 24 persons 7 months of the year and 18 persons 12 months of the year...in the work of being a theater."[14]

Later on, the Group seemed to have earned some respect in Deeter's eyes, perhaps because they had essentially performed his version of the Dreiser-Piscator's *American Tragedy* under the title of *The Case of Clyde Griffiths* after its spectacular success at Hedgerow.[15] He couldn't help reminding them of his success in the Rose Valley, however, he wrote to Carnovsky in 1939 suggesting that perhaps they should explore ways of working together. "Hedgerow has perhaps the strongest history in matters of group solidarity in the American Theater for the last 8 years of its 16 years of life. Maybe we could swap some people from time to time. You and Luther could come into the rep for awhile...?"[16] There is no surviving response to the invitation among the Hedgerow papers and since the Group was nearing the end of its decade-long run, it's unlikely that the experiment was ever carried out.

But it is intriguing that the history of realistic acting and performance is still dominated by the Group Theatre and its alumni at the Actors Studio, the Neighborhood Playhouse, and other assorted studios and companies. Certainly the Group should be honored for their advocacy of Stanislavski and for their notion that rehearsal can also be actor training, but the idea that acting should be more lifelike and believable was widespread in the American theatre prior to World War II and was not confined to any one person or program. Montgomery Clift, for example, often referred to as one of the finest "Method" performers, was always clear that he learned his craft by watching Alfred Lunt and then trying to copy him.[17] And Jasper Deeter had worked out a rather extensive approach to realistic acting that not only produced excellent results, but dozens of students who swore by his approach, peopled his theatre, and often returned for refresher courses.

Actors frequently remarked about Deeter's eyes and how he could see—or see through—what you were doing, and Sherwood Anderson was witness to this power of observation in the first rehearsals that he spent observing *Winesburg*. Anderson was also enthralled by the way that Deeter would patiently and tirelessly compel his actors to perform. In a description of rehearsing, which he later published in a collection of essays called *No Swank*, Anderson provides a record of Deeter at work.

> Once, one night, I heard you—your voice not tired—it a little rasping, exasperated—(this at four in the morning) beginning again, slowly, patiently—
> "This is what the man, who wrote this part, was trying to get said."

"God knows... he may be a damn fool. I don't know... "

"We, all of us wouldn't have tried to do his play unless we thought it was worth doing."

"Listen! The damnfool play writer may be trying to say something."

"We have all agreed that we want to do his play... "

"I wouldn't have any of you think that, as an actor, I take my hat off to any play writer—"

"But."[18]

Later, actors would compare him to a laser who would illuminate what was false. Penny Reed described him as a "declutterer" who could help you eliminate everything that wasn't essential.

Deeter enjoyed decluttering Chekhov and frequently referred to him as "Dr Chekhov" in rehearsals and classes. He believed, along with many others, that the key to playing Chekhov—especially the comic Chekhov—was to remember that the author was observing his characters and not using them as mouthpieces for his social and or political agendas. And he was also not shy about exposing their anxieties and idiosyncrasies. Deeter describes to an actor playing the pompous Professor Serebryakov in Act II of *Uncle Vanya*, how ludicrous it is for the Professor to invoke Turgenev in describing his gout and angina pectoris as if "all the great writers have the same affliction this year."[19] And to a bumbling, love-struck, and tipsy Vanya he announces, "The old bum is gone and she doesn't know you will throw puppy love at her," and then he demonstrates how Vanya pursues Yelena "like a big old dog. He toddles because he can't walk very well when she's around."[20]

Deeter believed that one of the keys to playing *Uncle Vanya* effectively was to recognize that the characters try to think, but—unlike Shaw—they really don't do it very well. Comedy is always about contrast in Deeter's work. The characters are naïve and not good thinkers, thus the contrast is always between their "feelings and the unintelligent expression of opinion."[21] But they are absolutely fascinating to explore because the transitions of feeling are sometimes so abrupt and unexpected. In working with Yelena and Sonya he notes that "there are so many changes in such a short time, that's why I love to work with this man."[22]

The basis for most of Deeter's work with actors in *Uncle Vanya* is a rigorous analysis of "behaviors" and an exploration of relationships. He talks with a young woman playing Yelena about how absolutely trapped she is in her marriage and stresses that there is no way out. Divorce is impossible, and without money to run off to Paris and start over, her choices are limited. But he also cautions that Yelena is not "frustrated." She's "caged." She's caught and caged and in Deeter's words, "I've got to get out of here or go nuts!"[23] In a lovely scene where Dr. Astrov is angling for a drink and the besotted Sonya is trying to stop him, Deeter stops them and points out that the line about Astrov not drinking is simply a lie. That he uses it to change the subject because he is tired of being lectured by her and wants to go home or out to his carriage for the drink.

Deeter is also adamant that these behaviors must always be rooted in the body and must appear to arise spontaneously. Spontaneity is a critical term in Deeter's vocabulary and he invokes it constantly. It originates as energy in what he terms the *sponte* down there "below the belly button" and is released into the body where it finds physical expression and finally in talk that is "energy finding release in words." Coaching an actor (Ray) in Vanya's self-pitying soliloquy in Act II, Deeter reminds him that "Vanya doesn't know what he's going to say but Ray does. We must behave spontaneously. I do know what comes next but what do I do with it?"[24] Akin to William Gillette's "illusion of the first time," spontaneity is critical for the actor, especially in understanding the power and importance of breath. Deeter talks about breath as one of the defining forces in how talk is shaped and released. He urges actors to pursue a kind of athleticism of breathing so that you have as much breath available at the end of a long aria as at the beginning. This is crucial because the character—as opposed to the actor—doesn't know how long the next line or speech is going to be, and if you run out of breath the talk will become strangled and false.

Spontaneity is also determined by what Deeter terms "caring" and it is vital in his approach to acting. "Our talk is never fully expressive unless we care...Caring gives us energy. It's an animal thing that originates way down here in the sex buttons."[25] Caring is a genuine commitment to an idea, a person, an event, and so on. It is what actors must possess and pursue to understand the true commitment of the actor and the integrity of the profession.[26]

In working through *Uncle Vanya*, especially in the scene between Yelena and Sonya in Act II where they determine to be friends, Deeter reminds them of the importance of breathing and an expressive body, but he also returns to his fascination with the Chekhov people who "live on their emotions." It's a fascinating leitmotif in his work because most acting theories and practices following the Stanislavski influx—and the various Method adaptations—eschewed playing emotions in favor of the active verbs that would invoke them. But Deeter's approach recognized the presence and power of "emotions," and he encouraged actors to access and play them. The critical point, however, was that once selected, emotions always had to be "more or less." "They are always true when they are more or less," he was fond of saying.[27] Meaning that the grading of emotions was what the actor should strive for rather than the comfort of embracing one easy thing. He encourages Sonya to take no guff from the Professor and use her anger, and he tells "Ray" that it's okay to be self-pitying in playing Vanya. "All plays other than Chekhov avoid self-pity. The theory is that self-pity will alienate an audience. This guy can be self-pitying because of who he is."[28] It's interesting that Deeter's sense of grades or degrees of emotions might be seen as compatible with the Method dictum of making stronger "choices" in parsing active verbs of action. But in talking about "behaviors," one of the central pillars in his work, Deeter clearly believes that emotions can take over a character. "When feelings take over we may think we are thinking but we are not."[29]

Deeter was also very fluent in music and believed that Chekhov worked much like a composer in constructing scenes and acts. He liked actors to think of the soliloquies in the play as arias. Of course, this use of music and musical terms was not limited to work with Chekhov. Deeter had a love for music that had been initiated by his mother and which had been fostered over a lifetime in silent films, radio concerts, and Broadway musicals. Nearly everyone who worked with Deeter talks about how he often used the piano—which he played very well—to illustrate a point in a scene or to try and solve a problem that he couldn't articulate. A piano was a featured fixture in the "big room" at the Hedgerow house where frequent rehearsals and classes were conducted, and Penny Reed remembers Jasper playing to help her understand a difficult moment in a scene that she was rehearsing. There was also a piano in his family home in Summerdale, and on the Carnahan tapes he uses it to illustrate an important point in *Uncle Vanya*. His directions to actors are often filled with musical terminology, and it's not uncommon to hear him referencing the pace or rhythm of scenes in terms of *vivace* or *andante*. At one point, in directing his favorite scene between Sonya and Irena in Act II, he talks about the tension that has been built up and needs to be released in order to make the scene work. He describes the composition of the scene as one in which the tensions have accelerated and now at the end—in spite of the crushing fact that Yelena is not allowed her music—a certain calm is restored. Then he illustrates the composition of the scene by playing them a short piece from a Sibelius symphony to convey the accumulation of *stretta* and the struggle to get back to "calm."[30]

Deeter's work with *Uncle Vanya* is illustrative of the joy that he found in exploring and staging Chekhov. (At one point he describes a wonderful piece of comic hokum when he had an offstage picture crashing down after Vanya's wild gunshot in Act III.) It is also illustrative of the patient and insightful ways that he worked with actors. Deeter was insistent about actors "absorbing" a part. Not memorization with speed, but a slow understanding of the character with care and patience. There are several moments in rehearsing *Vanya* where he stops and give a note, and the actor will acknowledge the correction and then go on. Sometimes, however, Deeter will stop again immediately and say that you can't make that correction with just the brain. How does the actor absorb the correction? How will it become manifest in the body?

Hedgerow rehearsals were long because Deeter built his plays with this kind of care. Asked once how much time he would need for a certain production, he told the inquirer to ask him again after about five weeks. Then he'd have a better idea of how much time was needed to bring it to life. He was trusted by actors and was trustful of them. He encouraged them to discover and often remarked that his principal job was to be useful. "I don't need to be right," he'd often say, "I need to be useful." If what he suggested was not "useful," then the actor could throw it out and try something else. Of course, he did reserve the right of "interpreting the play" and guided everyone to that interpretation. He could flare and his anger with interruption or inept work could be daunting. But it was, by almost all accounts, the result of an artist who cared genuinely and deeply about his life's work.

In listening to the 18 hours of the Carnahan tapes there are two additional points that shed some further light on Deeter's art and his work in the theatre. One is his awareness of sculpture, of an actor sitting in space, for example, defined in light and hence communicating. That awareness goes to his understanding of theatre as a medium drawing on all of the arts and underscores his sensitivity to his friend Wharton Esherick and how deeply the ideas of the Arts and Crafts philosophy impacted the Hedgerow aesthetic.[31]

The second, and perhaps most revealing, is his ongoing conviction that the central nervous system, which he continually invokes as the engine that drives the actor, is totally sensitive to the environment in which it functions. He tells his *Vanya* class about a recent experience he had shooting a television cameo appearance in a dreary set with a dilapidated couch that Deeter was sure was full of bedbugs. The tension that grew out of that thought (mind) was so disturbing that his (body) began to react in a way that impaired the breath and thus strangled the quality of the energy and voice. Fortunately, the film was spoiled in the lab and they were able to reshoot in a different locale. But the example underscores a fundamental belief that goes to the core of all the work at Hedgerow. That the art of acting is essentially linked to the environment and for that work to be genuine there has to be a sensitivity, appreciation, and understanding of the way that the body is shaped by the given circumstances of the place of the scene.

If there was indeed a Hedgerow aesthetic, however, it was not Deeter alone who maintained it. His presence was without question dominant, but the actors who studied with him always insist that Rose Schulman was also a dynamic and galvanizing force in the theatre, and her own career as actor, director, and teacher bears witness to that claim. Rose, whose plaintive cry for her own place began this study, came to Hedgerow as a 22-year-old actress and died there at the age of 79. She was tough and feisty, loved poker and horse racing, and was in many ways a perfect foil for Deeter in both temperament and skill. Janet Kelsey, herself a longtime and influential Hedgerovian, remembers auditioning for both of them in 1962.

> It was Lady Macbeth's letter scene. I was a farm girl, had on pants and Wellingtons. Jasper told me to use that, to stride confidently in the scene as if through a field of wheat. Rose, who always called a spade a spade, told me to dress like a lady for God's sake![32]

Rose came to Hedgerow as a young actor but she found a home and a teacher whom she grew to admire and imitate. Born in Philadelphia in 1910, she fell in love with the theatre as a teenager, and after high school she took classes at the drama league of the Young People's Society where Deeter saw her in a production of *Uncle Vanya*. In New York, she joined the Yiddish Art Theatre and took classes in elocution with Emilie Kraider Norris and in behavior with Gustav Peck of Columbia.[33] In 1932, she joined the part-time company at Hedgerow, played the Old Nurse in *The Three Sisters*, and impressed Deeter with her commitment to, and love for, the theatre. In 1934, she became a full-time member of the company. After several roles playing "tough broads," Deeter encouraged her to direct, and she made her debut in 1935 with a production of *Engaged* by W. S. Gilbert. After that she worked as both performer and director, but her belief in the Deeter "approach" to acting enabled her to become a gifted teacher, and her talent and temperament became part of a growing Hedgerow mythology.

Deeter was fond of Rose not only because she was insightful and smart, but also because she was very direct in her critiques and opinions. "She has the great genius of extreme patience and the capacity for straight talk of the kind which turns mountains of conceit into molehills of ability."[34] Of course, not all the companies over the years embraced Deeter's synopsis enthusiastically. Many found Rose too aggressive, opinionated, and blunt. In a letter to Deeter during the Draft Board crisis in 1942, Maria Coxe, Hedgerow alumna, commenting on the national importance of actors stated, "I think it might do Schulman good to go to work in a war plant, but her little career of dictatorship at Hedgerow has ill prepared her to take orders."[35]

But there is no doubt that Rose could coach actors and teach with skill and insight. Her approach to acting was similar to Deeter's, but Louis Lippa described a critical difference that differentiated their work and also made them very complementary as a team. Deeter's greatest strength, according to Lippa, was his intellectual analysis of texts "in the best sense of the word." That is, he worked from a playwright's point of view and really concentrated on the "W" categories. He was really interested in *what* we act. Rose, on the other hand, was more focused on the *how*. And the brunt of her focus seemed to be on what the actor is *doing*.[36]

They were in total agreement, however, about the nature and importance of acting as an artistic impulse and as a way of life. In her program for Arthur Miller's *The Price* in 1970, Rose talks about "The Art of Acting" and outlines her approach to training an actor that is remarkably similar to Deeter's.

> A skill is on its way, when you know why you are doing what you are doing, when and where you are doing what you are doing. And now you are ready to BECOME or BEHAVE and include the last of the processes of the skill:—the way, the how, the manner of.
>
> Our enemies in learning these are speed; proceeding to the how first before the groundwork is laid; the imposition of behaviors upon the exterior self.
>
> Our friends are good common sense, an affectionate consideration for material objects, realizing that blood, sweat and tears were used at the source of their creation; a respect for time in its most realistic sense and a respect for space; also in its most realistic sense, and above all an affectionate consideration for mankind.[37]

Joyce Mycka-Stettler, who studied with Rose in 1979 and credits her with her own success as actor and teacher, is adamant about the quality of her teaching. She stood for "no crap" according to Mycka-Stettler and pushed performers to make strong choices "from the guts."[38] Like Deeter, Rose insisted that her students understand the energy flow that originated in the guts and swelled into the rest of the body. "She would interrupt you if she didn't like what she saw," remembers Mycka-Stettler, "but her coaching was always insightful and helpful." She'd say things like "don't hurry," "watch your breath," "be ordinary," and "give the audience time to catch up."

"From the guts" was a kind of mantra for Rose, and Penny Reed remembers her coaching in graphic detail. Having difficulty finding her gut reaction one day, Rose reminded Penny that "use your gut, your pelvis; speak from the gut. It's where you have babies. It's amazing that the only time you've ever used your gut was for having babies!"[39] But Penny always learned from Rose and credits her today with a tremendous gift—that of "teaching me to teach myself."[40]

Richard Wright, who took classes with Deeter after he had retired from directing and also worked with Rose, remembers her with great fondness: "She possessed infinite perception and sensitivity. She had a keen eye for human behavior and a near perfect instinct for human communication. Rose put great emphasis on the use of the body, using every part of your being to express character. She was strong on energy in the expression of one's emotions. Her attitude was tough, and so she appeared tyrannical, ruthless and unmerciful. But beneath the layers there was empathy and heart."[41]

As early as 1927, Deeter was concerned that the achievement of the Hedgerow company would be lost in the accord of *his* accomplishments, and, therefore, intent of the "Virginia Plan" was to democratize the workload as well as the artistic contributions of many others who dedicated themselves to the work. But Deeter was always at war with himself about distributing artistic credit and maintaining the artistic vision that shaped the work over 30 remarkable years. With Rose Schulman he found a unique collaborator. She understood and totally supported Deeter's approach to acting and together they created a school and acting curriculum in the days after the demise of the repertory company that was widely admired. While there were shades of difference about how they approached the *teaching* of acting, their vocabulary, and sense of what was "truthful" was strikingly similar. And as they aged, they became increasingly dependent on each other's opinions and ideas. For Rose, Hedgerow was home and family, and at one point she penned a brief note leaving all that she had to Deeter.[42] He, in turn, enjoyed her company at his summer retreat in

Summerdale, and in the Carnahan tapes she can be heard reading in the place of a tardy student as Deeter guides actors through his favorite scenes in *Uncle Vanya*.

The depth of their friendship can best be illustrated in an exchange of letters in October 1952. Deeter was on a leave of absence and Rose wrote him about her "Tale of Woes" at Hedgerow. She was not feeling well, rehearsals for *Arms and the Man* were not productive, and she was frustrated with the amount of work confronting her. "Of course, underlying it all, is that quality in me that I have never leveled out. I can't stand being disappointed. On one end of the pole this is extremely valuable because it sets a high objective; on the other end it's a mess. And I don't even know if there is value in the leveling of this subject. It seems to me that high hope is still worth the occasional let down."[43] Deeter responded immediately. "We must never level ourselves out!" he thundered, "We may, at times, pretend to do so up to the very utmost of our ability, but close to the easily achieved ability to deceive ourselves."[44] He then goes on for nearly four single-spaced typed pages reminding her about the importance of having a vision—a "grail"—to focus her vision and the pursuit of beauty. He recalls reading Mallory's *Le Morte d'Arthur* as a youngster and how that still lingers in his imagination. "Our Holy Grail is indistinctly envisioned; and this must be so because we do not, sometimes, know that we have found it. Apollo knows." Jasper talked a great deal over his lifetime, in his directing and teaching, about the power and pursuit of *beauty*. And it is always tempting to be cynical about pragmatic people invoking the power of vague and highly charged concepts to stir their soldiers to battle. But beauty was real to Deeter, and it inspired his artistry. Actors talk about how he could inspire in the classroom and the rehearsal room. Here in this letter to his old friend we find a sample.

> The wildernesses, the mountains and the valleys and the pitfalls and the enemies which confront us on our adventures require the faith of Galahad, the sweetness of Gawain, the love of Launcelot, the emboldened strength of Tristram and the comforting Self-Assurance that we are pursuing beauty. How can anyone have in himself these four kinds of chivalry and still find nourishment for his self-assuring Self without becoming, at times, embroiled, entangled and unwisely engaged? When men have answered this question, Beauty will be the Handmaiden of Mankind and she will bring to artists what they desire in little things, and she will guide them unfailingly in their quest for the Larger Beauties and the Better Life. Be assured! That is my frequent blessing and to share it with both hands is the most important lesson of my life.

8. *The Hedgerow Story*: Celebrity and Disappointment

Hedgerow, which was in the national spotlight briefly at the beginning of World War II, was there again for a moment at the end. The State Department, anxious to capitalize on the excellent documentary films that had been produced by the Office of War Information (OWI), created a civilian counterpart in 1946 called the "Division of International Motion Pictures" (IMP). The goal of the IMP was to "initiate, plan and develop motion picture projects to promote the objectives of the United States information and cultural program in other countries."[1] They believed that foreign audiences experienced America primarily through Hollywood movies, and they wanted to provide a broader and more nuanced view. Topics were drawn from cultural events and rural snapshots that, in the words of IMP director, Herbert T. Edwards, reflected "the vast panorama of American life that this nation seeks to have understood abroad."[2]

The IMP, which began with a modest budget, undertook one hundred films on various aspects of America, and in 1948, they were rewarded with a generous allocation of more than $2 million. Unlike the OWI, which contained a complete production team, the IMP hired outside producers for new projects or adapted "reels" that had already been shot for domestic programs. State travel logs, for example, which had been made by Esso and Standard Oil, were easily appropriated, as well as educational films like *Starting Line* that had been shot by the Southern Educational Film Service and dealt with the problems of premature birth.[3] But the enthusiasm in the division was for original films that they commissioned to independent producers. These ranged widely in subject matter and presentation. *The Bridgeport Plan* focused on a community's efforts to help returning veterans find employment; *Trailer 201* examined the highway infrastructure in the United States; and *The Holtville Story* depicted life in a rural Alabama town.[4]

Anxious to present positive views of American culture, the IMP decided to feature a repertory company, since that was the kind of theatre, they believed, European audiences would find most familiar. After some preliminary research, however, they discovered that the choices were extremely limited. The only professional company operating in true repertory fashion—and now approaching their twenty-fifth anniversary—was the Hedgerow Theatre in the Rose Valley near Philadelphia. Edwards, the director of IMP, was a Pennsylvania native with a degree from the University of Pennsylvania, and believed that the company was an excellent choice. He approved the project and requested that a production team be assembled to explore the success of the theatre. Hedgerow, which had inspired outrage and venom over its opposition to Selective Service, was now poised to represent "theater in America."

George Beckwith, who had spent some time studying with Deeter before the war, was chosen to produce *The Hedgerow Story*. He had worked for the OWI during the war and had learned the basics of shooting and editing documentary films. He continued with the new project after the armistice and had already shot a successful short feature called *City Pastoral*. Instead of focusing on skyscrapers and tourist attractions, Beckwith set out to record New Yorkers at play, going to the Zoo, or relaxing in Central Park. The film was a hit with the administrators at IMP and earned the following accolade from his supervisor: "The merit of this film does not lie in its contents, but in its leisurely pace, its unpretentious, human approach, and a refreshing absence of any sales talk."[5]

For the Hedgerow project, Beckwith contracted with Willard Pictures in New York, who provided a promising young director named Lee Burgess described as "an able young woman, who has already directed several documentary films, including one on women voters in New York and another about rural nurses."[6] Beckwith wrote the script that included narration about the founding of Hedgerow, glimpses of daily life of the resident company, and scenes from some of their signature plays including *Inheritors, The Emperor Jones, Uncle Vanya, American Tragedy, Twelfth Night,* and *The Physician in Spite of Himself.*

Deeter had hoped to fit the shooting into their weekly schedule without too much interruption, but he underestimated the time and effort that it required to convert their stagecraft into an acceptable film. Blankets had to be hung in the auditorium to shape the sound, and some seats had to be removed to build dolly tracks for the cameras. The Green Room was appropriated as the sound studio, and after each take Burgess had to rush there to see if there was a match with the film. Norman Bunin, a reporter for the *Wilmington Sunday Morning Star,* attended an afternoon shooting and left this intriguing report.

> I watched a "take" of a scene from *Inheritors.* Hedgerow's tiny stage was filled with lights and microphones, almost obscuring the simple set. The players, Jasper Deeter and Ruth Esherick, stood patiently under the hot lights while the equipment was being adjusted. There were no stand-ins.
>
> The cameramen and soundmen, all young ex-G.I., leaped playfully and competently about their duties. Miss Burgess, casually attired in blue jeans, supervised all the operations and consulted with Rose Schulman, the director of *Inheritors.* The script girl, whose job is one of the most difficult, carefully checked all properties and costumes to make sure that they were exactly the same as they had been for the previous take. Even the kernels of corn strewn on the floor had to be in exactly the right position.
>
> After what seemed an interminable time spent moving cameras, mikes and furniture, everything was ready for a rehearsal. The take lasted only about a minute, but it had to be rehearsed over and over again. First the lights were wrong, then the sound. Finally it was ready to be "shot."
>
> The cameras rolled and the actors went through their paces. Miss Burgess yelled "Cut." We all went into the Green Room to listen to the sound track. It wasn't quite right. So the whole process started again. All for a sequence that lasts just a few seconds on the screen.[7]

The process was frustrating and exhausting, especially since they were struggling to maintain the weekly repertory while also filming sequences to illustrate daily life in the community. For one exterior scene showing the company performing various pre-breakfast routines, Beckwith postponed the shooting for three days until he got the required quality of sunshine. In another extended sequence, which was designed to film a Hedgerow audience, Deeter invited people on the mailing list to come for a special event; but the weather was foul, and they all had to be invited back on the following Sunday to reprise their parts. Bunin reported, "That afternoon the Hedgerow kitchen provided 500 sandwiches for the hungry audience."[8]

Finally, Deeter canceled a full week of performances so that they could concentrate on filming the live theatre scenes. He was reluctant to disappoint his patrons but anxious to capitalize on the good publicity of Hedgerow being chosen to represent theatre practice in the United States.

Unfortunately, the film was never released and, like some other IMP productions, was shelved after an official screening at the State Department.

Anecdotal chatter suggests that a film featuring a communal group that had already opposed Selective Service was not welcome in a country on the verge of a communist scare and a torrent of un-American frenzy. And this is probably accurate. Reviewing the charge of the IMP reveals a very comprehensive agenda including "to give advice to and cooperate with other officials of the Department and with other Federal agencies."[9] The roles of the House Committee on Un-American Activities (HUAC) and other congressional committees have been widely documented during this period, but the State Department and the United States Passport Office also played an active part in determining how American culture would be viewed and exported.[10] Helen Shipley's notorious Passport Office was one of the "other officials" who may have certified IMP films, and as the Cold War intensified, there is no question that the State Department would refuse to endorse films that had "communist" overtones.

Eventually, Hedgerow obtained a copy of the film and Deeter and others continued to anticipate its release. But interest in the project waned as the months dragged on and McCarthyism extended its cultural blight on American entertainment. Copies of the film were misplaced or lost, although a few survived in the personal collections of actors who valued its "snapshot" of a Hedgerow that was an American legend.[11]

Viewing the film today, it's unclear what happened in the editing process, but of all the stage footage only a brief scene from *Inheritors* survives. Deeter is seen as Silas in Act I, along with Ruth Esherick in a white wig as his mother. The entire film is 17 minutes long and includes glimpses of the company at breakfast and dinner, preparing for the evening curtain, moving scenery onto the stage through the open traps, doing costume and prop research in Philadelphia, and working at various chores at the farmhouse. Other than the brief snippet of *Inheritors,* the film has a voice-over narration and a lively soundtrack that includes patriotic songs like *Yankee Doodle* and *Battle Hymn of the Republic.* There are no credits.

What is fascinating about the film, however, is its emphasis on the *company*. Other than the scene from *Inheritors*, Deeter is depicted as just a member of the group. We see him opening the morning mail along with a number of others or walking down the hill for the evening's production, but nowhere is he identified as the leader or the force behind the project. Similarly, we glimpse other members of the company going about the business of making a life in the theatre. Dolores Tanner, who would later direct the theatre for a time in the 1970s, is filmed observing people in a public square in Philadelphia in order to make her acting more "realistic." A young woman in casual working clothes sits on the empty stage helping to focus light levels, and others try on costumes or apply makeup in the tiny dressing areas below the stage level.

In perhaps the most delightful sequence, the entire company is seen outside on the lawn of the farmhouse voting on plays for the next season. The narrator informs us that "election day" is one of the highlights of the year when they all come together and cast their ballots for the season selection. The paper ballots are collected in baskets and then taken to a committee on the porch to be counted. Deeter, by the way, is not amongst the counters but simply another face at a nearby picnic table. At a climactic moment the new season is announced, and everyone applauds and appears appropriately delighted or astonished. Many of the men are wearing jackets and slacks and the women sundresses, and the effect is of a glorious picnic. Reflecting on the travails of the "Directions" committee, however, and the annual wrangling on play suggestions from the company, the moment does connote a certain filmic fantasy.

In fact, the emphasis on the group sharing and decision making may have been a principal reason why the film was not distributed. Members are seen dining communally, taking turns with kitchen chores, and in one nicely etched moment sorting the company laundry. The narrator stresses that the 25 members "live and work together." In a culture where this kind of communal activity automatically raised concerns about "communism," it is not surprising that there were second thoughts at the State Department about endorsing this theatre. And I suspect that concern is what explains the film's efforts to tie Hedgerow to Philadelphia and its vast resources and landmarks of American patriotism. The film not only follows Dolores Tanner into Philadelphia but also devotes two sequences to the theatre's close ties to a bookseller and an antiques dealer. In both scenes, Hedgerow is defined as being aware of and sympathetic to past traditions and American history. In fact the narrator intones that "here the Declaration of Independence was signed," while we watch a landscape composed of Liberty Hall and a statue of Benjamin Franklin. And Hedgerow is praised for its connection to a "city that is rich in its history of the American people." The message here is not subtle. Hedgerow is a cooperative it suggests because repertory demands this kind of close-knit camaraderie, but they are Americans and proud of their past.

The film is also retitled from *The Hedgerow Story* to *A Repertory Company*, perhaps to suggest a more generic brand and thus neuter the supposed radicalism of the Rose Valley. There is one curious sequence, however, which in some respects is quite baffling. It begins with an actor/stagehand fitting a small platform piece into a set on a stage model and then pans to an actor below the actual stage lifting similar set pieces up through the trap. Designed to show how sets were changed and constructed on the small Hedgerow stage, the sequence also allows the viewer to see the famous dome that was a hallmark of the theatre. As each of the several pieces is passed up to the main stage, the actor/stagehands are silhouetted against the dome. All five of the actors—including the middle man straddling in the trap to hand up each piece from below—are costumed. That is, they are wearing jeans and are bare-chested. And the sequence is lit so that we are very conscious of their reflections on the dome. In addition, the camera moves underneath the middle actor essentially foregrounding his crotch as he heaves the pieces over his head to the men above. At the conclusion, all the actors are on the main stage and in highly theatrical lighting they take their leave one at a time. It is a curiously staged vignette in a film that relies on essentially documentary techniques and where many of the carefully staged scenes have been eliminated. The homoerotic overtones are vivid, but one wonders why they would be foregrounded in a cultural climate that despised "queers" almost as much as commies?

The shelving of *A Repertory Company* was a disappointment for the group, but it was a preamble to two other filmic adventures in the Rose Valley. Jasper Deeter and some of the Hedgerow company appeared in the original *The Blob* (1958) that was filmed outside of Philadelphia and which is considered by some a science-fiction "classic." Deeter plays a befuddled old man who can't decide which helmet to wear—civil defense warden or fireman—when alarms wake the townspeople to an impending disaster. The scene is barely 30 seconds long but is a genuine moment in a film whose script and performances are truly awful. And in *4D Man* (1959), another sci-fi thriller filmed in the Delaware Valley, Deeter made a cameo appearance as "Mr. Welles" the owner of a research facility that is destroyed by the secret work of one of his scientists. His wonderfully resonant voice is a highlight of a one-minute scene that does little more than move the plot along.

More significantly, however, the failure of *A Repertory Company* to find an audience was linked in the theatre's history with an equally ambitious venture the following year; one that would test their resources, bring them additional national exposure, and for some, would be equally disappointing. In between takes for *The Hedgerow Story,* and often late at night, members of the company were reading a new book by Eric Bentley called *The Playwright as Thinker.* With its dismissive critique of the commercial theatre and its celebration of artists like Ibsen and Shaw, the book was having a fashionable appeal to theatre artists and academics who were also curious about the plays of the German celebrity, Bertolt Brecht. According to Hedgerow lore, someone wrote a postcard to Bentley, who was then teaching at the University of Minnesota, inviting him to come and see their work. He responded that he had heard good reports about the theatre and hoped to visit there one day. Deeter read the book and decided after a company meeting, and considerable discussion, to invite Bentley to guest-direct a play of his choosing in celebration of their twenty-fifth anniversary season. A correspondence ensued and Bentley accepted Deeter's invitation. With a theatre and all of its resources at his disposal, Bentley decided to use the occasion for the professional premiere of Brecht's *Caucasian Chalk Circle*.

Deeter enjoyed celebrating Hedgerow anniversaries. They gave the company occasions to reflect on what they had accomplished and provided opportunities to prepare and publicize special productions. They had been forced into a truncated season by the war during their twentieth year, and now with the promise of generous publicity from the release of *The Hedgerow Story*, Deeter wanted to create a new work that would be appropriate for a big birthday. Brecht's *Galileo*, with Charles Laughton, was about to open in New York and had generated a lot of publicity. Deeter and the company thought that the professional premiere of *Chalk Circle* would be in keeping with their artistic vision and would create excitement for their anniversary season.

Eric Bentley, who was 32 at the time, was already an enthusiast of Brecht's work and had been trying to encourage productions of his plays in the United States. While teaching at the University of Minnesota, he had prepared his own translation of *Chalk Circle* but was unable to convince the Drama Department to stage it. However, a former graduate student, Henry Goodman, who was teaching at Carleton College in Northfield, Minnesota, thought that his school's progressive agenda would not be threatened by Brecht's "communist" leanings, and together they began to plan a production. With Goodman directing a student cast in Bentley's translation, the play had five performances at Carleton in May 1948. In spite of some amateur and uneven acting, Bentley was delighted to see the script in production and later recalled, "I still remember the performance in the overcrowded little improvised theater, with specially composed music a bit on the sugary side, [and] agreeably naïve, enthusiastic acting by most."[12]

One actor, however, was remarkable in Bentley's appraisal and would be influential in bringing the play to Hedgerow. Alvis Tinnin was the first black man to attend Carleton College.[13] He had been recruited as part of an aggressive administration desire to integrate the student body; a campaign that also brought Japanese, Chinese, and Native Americans students to Northfield, Minnesota. Tinnin had served in the Philippines during World War II, and following his discharge had auditioned for several Broadway musicals. His rich tenor voice and imposing physical presence won him several small roles in Harold Rome's *Call Me Mister,* which ran for two years on Broadway. An undated press release at Hedgerow reminds Philadelphians that they will remember him for his tenor solo in that show's "Going Home Train" about "home-bound veterans on a crowded day coach."[14] Tinnin had left New York, however, after being recruited to Carleton, passing up his brief show business career in favor of a college education. He was older than his undergraduate cast mates, and Goodman had cast him as the pragmatic and rascally Azdak, who eventually decides the fate of the contested child in the climactic scene. Bentley's recollections of Tinnin's performance were still vivid many years later, "a distinctly professional black actor who alone, among the cast, found easy access to the Brechtian irony."[15]

Both Bentley and Deeter were enthusiastic about their collaboration. Bentley was excited about directing at a "professional" theatre and about the opportunity to introduce the Brecht script at a venue that had a rich legacy of presenting new and often controversial work. Deeter was delighted to work with Bentley whose respect for Shaw was widely acknowledged and who, like Deeter, considered *Heartbreak House* a modern masterpiece. Deeter, who was always suspicious of academics, found *The Playwright as Thinker* engaging, especially in its indictment of the commercial theatre, or the commodity theatre as Bentley was fond of saying. "The hope of the theater—I shall maintain—lies outside the commercial theater altogether."[16] Although he was no great fan of O'Neill, Bentley's admiration of Ibsen and Shaw fascinated Deeter, especially in passages such as the following: "Shaw has brought dance back into the drama, not directly, to be sure, but in the lively rhythm of his lines and in the rhythmic and musical, rather than 'well-made' structure of his scenes."[17] Deeter, anxious to make the collaboration successful, promised to turn out the entire company to fill as many of the one hundred *Chalk Circle* roles as possible. He played the piano, recited the prologue, and acted two peasant roles when the production opened.

Bentley wanted to bring two actors with him because he felt that both Tinnin and Minnie Brill, a Minneapolis actress and theatre student at the University of Minnesota, were critical to his vision of the play. Brill had organized a civic repertory group in Minneapolis, taught acting at the university, and had an impressive resume including Katherine in *Taming of the Shrew* and Emilia in *Othello*. In addition, Bentley suggested that he bring Henry Goodman to serve as his assistant director. Deeter was sympathetic with Bentley's request because he wanted him to have his choice in casting and because he was intrigued about introducing Tinnin to the Hedgerow community. But he was also adamant about the strengths of his own actors and reluctant to "showcase" the play at the expense of their current repertory. Eventually, they reached a compromise whereby George Ebeling from the Hedgerow company would play the "Story teller" and then alternate with Tinnin as Azdak. Similarly, Renee Gorin from Hedgerow would alternate with Brill in the role of Grusha. Eight performances were scheduled into the current repertory, and Tinnin was slated for Azdak at a preview on August 18 and then again on the 21, then 26, and finally on September 4.

The setting for the production was fairly simple and rather stark. The title of the play was spelled out across the top of the proscenium, and a large projection screen/cloth was centered against the upstage wall. Wharton Esherick made stereopticon sketches of four scenes that appeared to represent the town square, a river valley, the mountains, and a cabin by the road.[18] Production photos show an unadorned setting with a two-step rise in the back and two vertical beams that could rotate to serve as a gallows for the hanged judge or to provide a curtain in the last scene. Stage right is a placard stand to designate the place of the action, and there is also a curtain downstage that can be drawn to conceal the upstage area. Neither Bentley nor records at Hedgerow reveal very many detail about the production, but Bentley has recorded some brief remarks that suggest that its spare quality was intentional although, perhaps, not what he really wanted. Reacting to a Harold Clurman remark that Brecht must have been unconcerned about the setting and the traditional trappings of theatre, Bentley wrote, "It is true that our stage was too empty, too formal, and too abstract for Brecht; we were saving money; it would be a mistake to imagine that Brecht's ideas can be carried out inexpensively."[19]

Still the Hedgerow audiences responded very positively to the anniversary present and the company stretched their talents playing a variety of roles. Miriam Phillips, perhaps the company's most gifted actor, played four different parts including Grusha's sister-in-law, and Rose Schulman played her mother and a chorus member in the prologue. Bentley worked with them on the "distancing" required to accomplish the "Epic" style, but it seemed to vary considerably among the players. As assistant, Henry Goodman was most active in trying to explain the differences between fully embracing the emotions and allowing the audience to observe them. Looking back, Goodman remembered that "the audience was allowed to consider the reasons for the pathetic situation without sacrificing the pathos. The lovers

124   *A Sustainable Theatre*

Figure 8.1   Production photo, *Caucasian Chalk Circle*, 1948. Courtesy of the Hedgerow Theatre.

were deliberately kept apart by an imaginary stream. There were no movie embraces, no choking up, no straining of facial muscles. The detached Story Teller, with delicacy and restraint, but with firmness, spoke what the lovers 'thought but did not say.'"[20] In spite of its Spartan quality, Bentley believed the production to be successful and wrote, "The Hedgerow production was probably the most Brechtian of American Brecht efforts up to that time."[21] And it did attract critical attention outside of the Hedgerow/Philadelphia communities. *Variety* sent a reviewer who was appropriately impressed with the magnitude of the evening. "By all odds one of the most ambitious productions seen at Hedgerow in a long time and one of the most interesting plays seen in the Rose Valley playhouse in the last decade."[22] "Waters" enjoyed the production although it was clearly "artistic," and in spite of some places where it dragged, "it is distinctly interesting and has something on the ball." He was particularly impressed by Tinnin, "a giant of a man resembling Paul Robeson," who was "magnificent" as Azdak, and found Minnie Brill "a highly satisfactory heroine." In addition, he praised Deeter's performances and George Ebeling's "Story Teller." As for Bentley, Waters reported that he had "done a noteworthy job in his staging of this sprawling, panoramic, unpublished play by Bertolt Brecht."

Harold Clurman reviewed the production for *The New Republic* and spent most of his column discussing Brecht and the text of the play. He believed that Brecht has never "been adequately presented" in America in spite of Laughton's *Galileo* and "the remarkable intelligence evident in the present production."[23] But that intelligence did not seem to be reflected in the performances that Clurman largely ignored and suggested that "Brecht is not easy to render on the stage by actors and directors schooled in an entirely different mode."

This ambivalence about *Caucasian Chalk Circle* is reflected in much of the press and in the documentation that survives the "anniversary" play. *The Philadelphia Evening Bulletin* devoted most of an opening night review to describing the events leading up to the collaboration and the episodes of the play. Minnie Brill is praised for her Grusha as are Tinnin and Eabling, but the critic concludes that "the second act suffers by comparison with the first."[24] And in spite of the enthusiasm at the outset, Bentley is largely silent about the work in several subsequent books and articles. In a 1965 essay that serves as a revised introduction to *Parables for the Theatre,* he reviews the stage history of *Caucasian Chalk Circle* and discusses several textual variances and the context of its famous "Prologue." The Hedgerow production is given almost no mention aside from a brief sentence where he states that he was invited to direct it there in 1948.[25]

Perhaps, the collaboration had not been as successful as everyone hoped? It certainly did not generate the same kind of enthusiasm that was typical of many Hedgerow offerings, and participants are oddly silent about the production. Obtaining eyewitness observation more than 70 years after the event is daunting, but eventually Wharton Esherick's younger daughter, Ruth, was able to provide a few insights into the rehearsal process. Ruth, who grew up at Hedgerow and played many roles—including her appearance in *The Hedgerow Story*—served as production manager for *Chalk Circle.* After reflection, she recalled some of the tensions that characterized the days and evenings leading up to opening night.

She remembers Bentley as "difficult to get along with, making ever more difficult demands."[26] As production manager it was her obligation to "procure or produce whatever he wanted for the show." As time passed, this apparently became more difficult, since budgets at Hedgerow were always small. In addition, it soon became clear to the company that while Bentley was a university professor and scholar, he "had no theatrical experience." For a company who prized "the work in the room," this may have led to tensions on many fronts. It's impossible to understand how the grafting of the "Epic" style onto the quest for "truth," which characterized much of the work at Hedgerow, was received, but it may have been fertile ground for uneasiness, especially if Bentley's assistant Goodman was charged with reconciling the stylistic tensions. Deeter, a genial host and probably valiant peacemaker, may have struggled to ease the production forward to opening.

Finally, Ruth recalls that "Wharton's images were too far out for Bentley and he didn't use them." This may have also been fertile ground for conflict. Wharton Esherick is recognized today as a major American wood sculptor who recently had a superb show at the University of Pennsylvania. Of course, in 1948 he was not a significant voice on the national scene, but he was revered at Hedgerow and was part of the artistic vision that made the theatre prominent. In addition, he was Ruth's father. For Bentley to reject Wharton's designs for the anniversary production—which was totally his right—must have been unsettling for many in the company.

It's difficult to appreciate the visual aspects of the production from the surviving photos, but Bentley did comment on the slides that they used in an article that he wrote for a German book shortly after *Chalk Circle* had been added to the Hedgerow repertory. Slides were constantly projected onto the backdrop "mostly black and white, very simple and strong: a couple of mountain peaks, some roofs and towers and so on. The final scene, the dance, is emphasized by a color reproduction of Bruegel's famous work 'Outdoor Dance.'"[27] He also noted about the photo of the hanged judge's scene? that "one must imagine the projection of a small window through which the Russian city can be seen."[28] Also, in a photo of the opening scene of the first act he cautions that the darkness of the picture neither represents the production nor "modern directors who stage plays in semi-darkness. That would certainly contradict the spirit of the play and is uncalled for."[29]

Whatever the conflicts, Bentley was gracious to reporters before he departed for Europe. Speaking of Hedgerow he told the *Evening Bulletin*, "It has impressed me that there is something which ought to exist in the theater but doesn't—a group that works together as a team. Standards are on a company level and the general standard of the company is excellent."[30] And in Europe he wrote that "they at least have full houses, and the audiences seem to be entertained. We have experienced none of the enmity or indifference with which the professional production in New York was received."[31]

It seems probable that Bentley was disappointed with the technical and scenic support that he received at Hedgerow. In keeping with their repertory orientation, they maintained a huge stock of flats, set pieces, and furniture, many of which were carpentered to sit against the angles of the permanent cyclorama. They were cautious about building or buying new pieces because the budgets were limited, and each expense had the potential to reduce box office income. Even after 25 years they were still committed to the old sustainable notions of living on what you make. It's very likely that a production manager would be tested daily to find ways to please a formidable guest director whose suggestions for more things was constant, and it's also likely that those tensions were exacerbated by the company's increasing concern about the director's lack of experience.

Whatever tensions accompanied the professional premiere of *Caucasian Chalk Circle,* however, did not sour Bentley on casting Rose Schulman (an old whore) and George Ebeling (Third God) in his production of *The Goodwoman of Setzuan* four years later at the Phoenix Theatre in New York. Deeter continued to promote their twenty-fifth anniversary season with splendid productions of *American Tragedy, The Seagull,* and *Uncle Vanya.* Alvis Tinnin left Hedgerow after his four performances and returned to Carleton for his senior year. Following that he got an advanced degree in French at Yale and had a successful academic career. *The Caucasian Chalk Circle,* disappointing on many fronts, was performed briefly in 1949 but was never revived.

But the prospects for continuing the celebration into their thirtieth year seemed remarkably bright. The company was strong, many had now been there over the course of their professional lives; they still did not pay salaries but had modest living expenses plus medical care for the resident company.[32] Of course, their "sustainability" had withered somewhat during the turbulent war years. They were no longer able to keep the gardens thriving and the livestock had been phased out. The corporate models, which were regularizing their operations, were also seen by some as removing the passion that had sustained them, replacing Deeter's "fire" with majority votes. And their repertory, still leaning on O'Neill, Glaspell, Shaw, and the "moderns," was feeling a bit tired to postwar sensibilities. The decade of the 1950s posed extraordinary challenges, which Deeter at first embraced joyfully, but which slid away with alarming swiftness.

9. Aftermath

Rose Schulman prepared a statement announcing their demise. Dated February 16, 1956, it is brief and blunt. "As of March we are shut."[1] They were $15,000 in debt.

Money had always been an abscess in the smooth outer shell of Hedgerow's idealism. Deeter was earnest and articulate about their desire to work for the value of the labor and the art of the enterprise, but he, too, had to pay the monthly bills and support the modest needs of the company. They had struggled bitterly at times, especially in the early years when both housing and food was meager, and they had depended on the garden and the sheep and hens to supplement their diet. After they purchased the farmhouse, the outer buildings, some of which were formerly chicken coops, were "remodeled" to provide additional sleeping quarters.

But in spite of the financial pressures, Deeter refused to inflate ticket prices because he wanted the work to be affordable and accessible. Instead, he tried to market their work in other ways. In 1934, for example, he arranged a tour throughout the Midwest that generated some enthusiastic reviews and additional income. The tour, which featured *Inheritors* and O'Neill's *Beyond the Horizon*, along with *The Romantic Age* and *Mary, Mary Quite Contrary*, covered 15 states, 8000 miles, and involved a dozen performers traveling in two cars and a bus. Deeter divided the resident company so that they could keep the theatre open; the tour generated enough income that undertook a more extensive version in 1935. Buoyed by the hope that they could substantially increase their earnings, they closed the theatre, doubled the repertory of plays, and carried their own "aluminum stages, portable light boards, collapsible furniture and more than 350 costumes."[2] Following the route of the previous year across the Midwest, into Oklahoma and Texas, they returned through the south playing across Tennessee, Georgia, and Florida. It was an exhausting journey, lasting nearly six months, and the expenses of traveling ate into Deeter's imagined profits. Again the reviews and the publicity were positive, but the prospect

Figure 9.1   Hedgerow exterior, 2002. Courtesy of the Hedgerow Theatre.

of closing their theatre each year for an extended period soured Deeter on subsequent touring.[3]

He decided instead to expand the annual summer Shaw festivals, which began as a weeklong repertory celebrating Shaw's birthday in 1934, increased to two weeks in 1935, and then grew into month-long celebrations. The festivals became a signature event for Hedgerow, attracting larger audiences each year, and Deeter added performances from their permanent repertoire in order to insure rehearsal time for new Shaw titles. The seventh festival, for example, in 1940, lasted from July 22 to August 10 and included nightly performances of six Shaw plays interspersed with Hedgerow favorites like *The Emperor Jones* and *Henry IV* as well as a July 4 matinee of *Inheritors*.[4]

Of all the summer Shaws, possibly the most discussed was the 1939 production of the uncut *Man and Superman*. Deeter was fond of the play, especially the *Don Juan in Hell* interlude that was intended to be performed as integral to the production but was ordinarily omitted because of the enormous running time. The Hedgerow production—another American premiere—debuted on July 26, 1939, at 7:30 p.m. and ran until nearly 1:00 a.m. There was an intermission following Act III during which refreshments were served in the Green Room. In spite of the marathon, the play received remarkably positive reviews and Deeter played it more than 30 times during the following two seasons.[5]

He was pleased with the success of the Shaw festivals, but as time passed he realized that the effort in preparing them detracted from the principal goal of expanding the permanent repertory. "I am tired of festivals," he told Lawrence Davies in 1939, "they upset the whole year's planning. They mean that instead of being able to produce nine new plays a year we can do only three."[6] But the festivals did help the box office, and Deeter maintained them for another two seasons before the wartime rationing and the loss of men to the draft forced him to give them up.

Hedgerow survived the war, but the loss of income forced Deeter into one more attempt to capitalize on their reputation and support their faltering box office by playing outside the Rose Valley. He believed that they could control touring expenses and earn needed income by performing during the winter in New York City. He hoped that a return of *The Emperor Jones* to a downtown theatre with the opportunity to reprise his Smithers role would attract interest and provide a platform for other Hedgerow offerings. With Arthur Rich in the title role, they opened a four-week engagement at the Cherry Lane Theatre in New York in January 1945.

It's unclear why Deeter believed that he would prosper in a city that he had bashed for so many years in both interviews and letters to the editor of the *New York Times* and other papers. He was not only disdainful of the commercial theatre but arrogant about his accomplishments at Hedgerow.

> I have seen none of this season's New York productions. By virtue of this fact I occupy an unusually clear position from which I see plainly everything which is wrong about your drama, its creatures and its critics. Why not give gracious ease to yourselves and to each other by letting your empty heavy enterprise fall to earth of its own dead weight? Show business can afford beauty only when it is popular. Critics can afford to call show business beauty only when it can be made popular... Hedgerow can afford to manufacture beauty all the time... an institution which is entirely independent of the overhead, the lying, the cheating and the profitable sensationalism which so rightly hardened your beloved artery.[7]

The Cherry Lane engagement, predictably, was only partially successful because a harsh winter and painfully mixed reviews curtailed attendance. Indeed, some of the reviews reminded him of the difference between the friendly environs of the Rose Valley and the brutality of the "commercial" leviathan. Lewis Nichols was not particularly impressed by Arthur Rich whom he found "workmanlike" and added, "As an offering upon coming home, Mr. Deeter is entitled to his *Emperor Jones*. Unfortunately, it is necessary to shoot the silver bullet at this point; the Hedgerow production is not the best that the play has been seen hereabout during recent years."[8] Others were less kind. Arthur Pollock found "no life or vitality" in *The Emperor Jones* and went on to observe that "it seems nothing but a silly little exhibition of an old fashioned futile dilettantism."[9] And Willeta Waldorf, reviewing their second offering, *Tomorrow's Yesterday* by Jack Kinnard, pronounced it an "appalling piece of drivel."[10] The New York engagement was disappointing and confirmed for Deeter that their success and livelihood was linked to the Rose Valley. It also empowered him a decade later to oppose the lobbying of company members and the newly formed Hedgerow Corporation who wanted to open a winter season in Philadelphia.

Deeter had made it a maxim that the work at Hedgerow was for the value of the product and not a quest for financial enrichment. But he was also realistic about securing basic needs and paying their bills and royalties. There was always chatter in and about Hedgerow that Deeter was too idealistic and determinedly stubborn to ask for money. John Wentz, in his dissertation study, observed that "the theater has never asked money from its former players."[11] In reality, however, Deeter was deeply concerned about their finances and keeping the company together, and he often appealed to others for help. In addition to his application to the Rockefeller Foundation (cited in chapter 2), he pursued alumni to remember the training that they had received at Hedgerow and encouraged them to donate. This was especially true of Ann Harding, with whom he carried on a correspondence for many years, and who was a frequent recipient of his pleas for financial relief. After her initial Hollywood success, she responded to his inquiry with the following: "No money at this time. For now it's all going into furniture and retaining walls for the mansion."[12] And 25 years later, as the theatre was approaching its final days, she wrote that she "can't help. Jannsen cleaned me out."[13]

Following the Virginia Plan in 1935, Deeter had tried to turn the organized financing of the theatre over to committees, but the bulk of the burden still remained with him. Eventually, Rose Schulman helped him with the planning, and along with Ferd Noffer, guided the theatre into the partnership reorganization in 1942. But as audiences dwindled after the conscientious objectors flare-up and rationing restrictions on gasoline and rubber, Deeter once more sought outside help. This time he decided to appeal to the highest authorities and explore how funds might be secured from the federal government to support Hedgerow's mission. In 1944, at the height of both the European and Pacific campaigns, he wrote to

Vice President Henry Wallace stating his desire to make a contribution by maintaining "a true Democratic theater" and asked, "Where might we apply for funds?"[14] A month later Wallace said "No" to any government funding.[15]

Money was always nagging, but Deeter would not abandon the repertory idea for longer runs. Repertory had been the inspiration for everything that they had accomplished. It was the signature for his theatre and his career. When the box office improved again after the war, he decided to reach out to another institution that he believed shared his vision about a quality of life in the Arts. Deeter had been intrigued about Frank Lloyd Wright's experimental school, Taliesin, since he had first read about it in the 1930s. He had occasional discussions with both Wharton Esherick and Scott Nearing about Wright's philosophy of learning by doing and of bringing all the arts together in educating a new generation of young artists/architects. He was sympathetic with Wright's belief that the young students at Taliesin should make the program work by sharing the labor of the entire enterprise—cooking, cleaning, gardening, caring for the animals. And he believed that Hedgerow embodied ideas that Wright so often articulated about "organic architecture." Deeter, the reclusive and idealist theatre artist, felt a kinship with Wright, and in 1949 reached out to him to explore whether they could find ways of working together on a shared vision. "We feel that your purpose in Art and Life so clearly parallels ours. There is an enormous similarity between Hedgerow and Taliesin. The way of life, the social and political attitudes, the distribution of labor, the striving of finding a way of working for the sake of the job as opposed to the money, all these things we hold in common."[16]

Deeter was also hoping that if Hedgerow flourished in the 1950s, they could not only find ways of supporting each other, but he could also persuade Wright to design a new theatre that would expand and modernize the mill site that had been their home since 1923. Wright responded the next week to Deeter's inquiry with a very brief letter saying that "we would like to help."[17] Unfortunately, nothing came of the venture, because both organizations became absorbed in their own struggles, but Deeter was impressed with the emphasis on teaching in the Taliesin model, and he believed that classes could impact Hedgerow's quest for solvency.

Deeter had given classes in acting as early as 1933—initially at the behest of Libby Holman who sheltered at Hedgerow after the scandal of her husband's death—but the meetings were irregular and devoted mostly to scene work. With the war, however, and the attendant drop in income, teaching was viewed as a critical component of their mission. Rose Schulman remembered, "We were always doing more than we could afford. So that's the reason for starting a school."[18] Jasper had been experimenting with classes at Hedgerow for young people who wanted to learn about acting as well as some evening sessions in Philadelphia, but in 1945, he and Rose "over much alcohol" sat down and planned a three-year full-time school designed specifically to train actors.[19]

The result was a carefully detailed curriculum that took the actor through some basic introductory classes in such topics as "Breathing," "Energy," and "Imagination" to scene work in "self knowledge and self use endeavoring to release and channel energy from the lowest source," and eventually rehearsal for mounted productions.[20] The curriculum had classes with a variety of Hedgerow professionals and could enroll up to 40 students per year with an annual tuition that was $470.00. The Hedgerow School, which codified the Mind-Body-Face-Eyes-Talk for a generation of professional actors, was active in its first phase until 1952 when it, too, was curtailed for taking too much time and energy from the production calendar. It was subsequently revived in 1955 and continued in a variety of configurations after the theatre closed in 1956.[21]

The tension between keeping faith with the original vision of Hedgerow—a rooted theatre doing a provocative repertory in an environment that they nurtured and which nurtured them—and the increasing pursuit of the dollar was stretching the artistic choices of the theatre as well as the fiber of Jasper Deeter. Hedgerow did rebound in the years after the war; in fact, John Wentz reports that 1951 had the highest box office totals in their history—$28,897.81.[22] But in clinging to its past, Hedgerow was seen by some as a museum removed from the postwar boom and the vigorous cultural changes in advertising, marketing, and mass communications. There was increasing pressure inside the company, and among the partners, for having a second home; a theatre in Philadelphia where they could play a fall and winter season, returning to Moylan for the spring and summer. And there was an increasingly vocal concern for the theatre to incorporate; to abandon the partnership model in favor of a corporation.

Jasper Deeter was tired. He had worked passionately and utterly for nearly 30 years and weariness haunted him. He was also sitting too long at Larry's, the local bar that was prominent among Hedgerovians, and alcohol was stripping his energy. In the summer of 1952, he took a leave of absence for a year to assess the future. Among other things, he wanted to write a book about acting, and many people encouraged him to record the insights and observations that characterized his "genius" as actor and director. In July, he resigned from the board of the partnership with the intent of enjoying a long deferred vacation and writing a manuscript about his life work in the theatre.[23]

In his absence, however, pressure to "modernize" the theatre continued to swell. The enthusiasm for a Philadelphia season continued and seemed viable to members of the board if an appropriate venue could be found. The repertory could be modified so that plays could alternate weekly instead of daily, with special productions on the weekends. Deeter was opposed to the move because he believed that the cost of doing business in two locations would not offset the increased income, and he was convinced that their "character" was deeply rooted in the Rose Valley. He had even reprised their production of the complete *Man and Superman* in July 1952 with many from the original cast and scheduled a new Shaw festival for the following summer, which would include a revival of *Too True to Be Good*.

Deeter's leave of absence also stimulated a new discussion among the partners about creating the Hedgerow Corporation. There was concern about protecting the physical properties of the theatre as well as their financial assets, and they wanted Hedgerow to be eligible for the pending 501 (c) 3 legislation that would allow contributions to the theatre to be tax deductible. They were also sensitive to the passage of control and power. According to a company roster published in 1950, at least 10 members had been with the theatre for 15 years when Deeter went on leave and others (Joseph Leberman, David Metcalf, and Miriam Phillips) had been there for over 20. They were sensitive to the heritage and legacy of the theatre as well as to updating and modernizing the repertory. Although they no longer relied on the gardens for their daily meals, they were still a cooperative community and their lives were invested in the success of the theatre, especially the box office income. What was Hedgerow and who would control and speak for it after Jasper Deeter was gone?

When Deeter returned from his leave, he elected not to be a full member of the company but rather a "guest artist," no longer directing and choosing when to perform. He lived in the farmhouse and focused on his teaching. And he was pessimistic about the notion of a corporate theatre. The plan for Philadelphia season went forward, however, and against his reservations and his "gut," Deeter agreed to support the venture. After investigating several options, the board voted to install a theatre space in the foyer of the Academy of Music and to introduce a Hedgerow season from October to March, 1953. The move was complicated, however, by the fact that they would be required to employ two union stage hands as well as maintain a separate box office. The consequences of that would be significant, but the board agreed and accepted the union demands. Louis

Lippa, who was a young apprentice, remembers trying to coach one of the stage hands about pulling the final curtain in *House of Bernada Alba* to preserve the mood of the final moment. "I have fast, medium, slow," he told Lippa, "which one do you want?"[24]

They planned a season of 13 plays with weekly runs to cut down on the expensive nightly changeovers and to acclimate the Philadelphia audiences to their repertory. They played Wednesday through Saturday evenings with weekend matinees, often of a popular title from their repertory. But attendance was not up to expectations, and combined with the remodeling expenses, they netted a loss of $15,000. After a summer season at home, however, and a disappointing box office, they determined to go back. With no remodel overhead and sold-out performances of *The Crucible*, they reduced their losses. They played a popular season including *Twelfth Night*, *The Physician in Spite of Himself* and *The Emperor Jones* but still could not make the venture profitable. After two Philadelphia seasons they were $8,000.00 in the red. Deeter had cautioned them about the overhead expenses and abandoning their signature repertory, but the board was committed to one more year. They mounted a new production of one of their most popular works, Shaw's *Androcles and the Lion* featuring Deeter and Richard Brewer, but were unable to attract an audience. With losses accumulating nightly,they abruptly abandoned the Philadelphia season in February 1956 after a final production of *Androcles*. They had lost an additional $5,000.00.[25] It was fitting that they ended with Shaw, who had been so entwined with their success, but deeply painful that the last curtain call was not in the old mill in Moylan where *Candida* had promised so much 30 years earlier.

The Hedgerow Corporation survived and became a formal and legal entity in 1957, although they had been operating with a board of directors since 1954. The bylaws stipulated that the purpose of the corporation now was "to produce and present to the public all sorts of shows, exhibitions and amusements and to establish and carry on schools where students may obtain a sound education in all phases of the theater."[26] Eight board members were stipulated including Jasper Deeter and other members of the resident company. Membership in the corporation could be secured by board approval and a $10 annual investment, or $500 for a lifetime shareholder. The board was empowered to manage, control, and govern all the "business and property" of the corporation and to appoint an "Executive Committee" to function on its behalf. Regular meetings of the board were stipulated for the third Saturday of each month along with an annual meeting for all the shareholders.

After the official closure in 1956, Rose resurrected the "Theatre School" and she and Jasper continued to teach and expand the offerings. It was now their primary source of income. The board of directors immediately launched a campaign to pay off the debts of the theatre. Over the next several years the board, with advice from Rose and Ralph Roseman, experimented with several different plans and productions. The most successful venture, according to David Ralphe who began there as an apprentice in 1957 and would eventually be appointed managing director in 1968, was "the Ernestine Perry season with Lonny Chapman, Pat Hingle, Albee, Buck Henry, Michael Christopher and others. I remember Jap as being 'around' but not engaged."[27]

The board kept Hedgerow from going completely dark, preserved its assets and claims of continuous operation, but for Deeter the meetings were a chore that he found discouraging and frequently frustrating. He understood the strategy of having to plan their literal survival, but felt that the corporate decision making was antithetical to everything that Hedgerow represented. Louis Lippa recalls asking the board permission to rehearse a new play that he was writing when the theatre was dark and being rejected because they felt that the apprentices already had enough to keep them occupied. He also recalls Deeter scolding the board for not encouraging young people to pursue their own ambitions. Others remember both Deeter's impatience with having to deal with a board of directors and his increasing unease that the work of the theatre had somehow been lost in the quest for material things. "Driving him by the theater one afternoon he pointed at the building, as we drove past, and said 'a building is only as good as the people in it.' ... 'Torch the building and get on with the work.' was another comment that I remember him making after a contentious meeting."[28] Deeter was wary of what had happened to the theatre in the quest for solvency and the desire to make a corporation out of a dream about making theatre as a life's work. The Arts and Crafts ideals that had stimulated him and Esherick and many others in the 1920s seemed to have slipped away. Actors who had been at Hedgerow for more than a dozen years were gone. Was Hedgerow destined to become another theatre factory?

Deeter continued to teach, and his reputation and the reputation of the theatre attracted students to the Rose Valley. He directed an occasional student production, but most of his focus now was on his classes and his afternoon visits to the Plumstead (formerly Larry's). A younger company of actors was coalescing around David Ralphe, who had grown up in the area, and who shared much of Deeter's passion for the art of the theatre and the power of acting. Ralphe was viewed by some as the best hope to restore Hedgerow to its former status, and he and his company negotiated a lease with the board that allowed them to perform in the theatre. In hindsight he recalls, "In five years we established a strong board of directors, produced thirty two productions playing in weekly rotating repertory. We supported twelve fulltime actor/staff and because of our success we were able to begin to provide neglected maintenance to the building of just under $100,000."[29]

In spite of their success, however, David Ralphe was not viewed by the board as the inheritor of the Hedgerow legend. Dolores Tanner, who had been a longtime company member and who had left in 1953, came back to Moylan in 1968 at Rose Schulman's urging, to help "save the theater." Tanner, a vibrant and flamboyant Texan who had taken some time off to finish a college degree, including a thesis on Hedgerow, was anxious to restore Hedgerow's prominence and reputation. Charley Walnut, who directed at Hedgerow throughout the 1970s and 1980s, and who left an unpublished manuscript of his time there, remembers that Tanner "always considered the Rose Valley her spiritual home. She now intended to make herself useful to the theater in the valley in every way she could. Hearty, outgoing, with enormous energy and a ready smile (she called everyone Sweetie or Doll regardless of gender) it was nonetheless wise to keep on the good side of her."[30] Tanner had a strong ally in Rose, Jasper was fond of her, and she had enthusiastic support from the board. Together with David Ralphe—whom Jasper admired—she was determined to build a strong company.

But there were tensions between the two over play selection, generational values, alcohol abuse, and infighting among company members. David Ralphe was young and talented, but Dolores Tanner was revered by many of the old timers who still came to work in the theatre and by Rose Schulman who supported her without reservation. Later, in 2002, the Hedgerow staff published a brief ten-page "History" of the theatre and included among its highlights the following tribute to Tanner who had died in 1982.

> She directed at Hedgerow for thirteen years and left an impressive mark on the theater both in terms of direction and management. She took part in virtually every area of Hedgerow life—cooking, laundry, teaching, directing, designing sets and costumes, supervising Hedgerow's printing department and running lights—she was a truly holistic artist. Dolores was able to balance the practical with the extraordinary, keeping faith in the middle of chaos. Her major accomplishments were holding the theater together, keeping the tradition of doing fine plays from all theaters, and imbuing the company with a passion for excellence through a strong work ethic.[31]

Her work ethic and schedule was indeed prodigious. Between 1973 and 1982, Hedgerow produced 108 plays. Dolores Tanner directed 65 of them. There is far less tribute to Ralphe, who by that time had moved on to successful ventures with Philadelphia's People's Light and Theatre Company and the Simi Valley RepertoryTheatre, but Walnut recalls the impact that he had: "The company was gaining momentum. Outside membership increased, some organizational input was becoming apparent. David Ralphe was at the forefront. His good looks and charisma were certainly a factor. And some of JD's autocratic prowess seemed to have rubbed off on him."[32] He may have had the arrogance of the young, but Deeter supported him and that support protected him in the infighting that developed between the board, which controlled the physical space, and the young company, which was attracting ever larger audiences. It would not be possible, Walnut recalled

> to pinpoint the exact moment when the partners, the real owners of the theater property (which was leased to the Hedgerow Corporation for a token amount) began to feel threatened by the resurgent company, so bustling and full of ideas and organizational skills... David Ralphe and Co. certainly appeared to be on the crest of a wave with the opening of *Boys in the Band*... it was a sell-out, and the actors knew the sweet smell of success. No one could deny that it was well staged and acted... It was good theater! Cast and crew were pretty cocky. What did Dolores and Rose think? Well, they weren't exactly asked.[33]

As the conflicts between Dolores Tanner and David Ralph escalated, Jasper withdrew letting Rose and the board and Dolores make the critical decisions for the theatre. He spent more time at the "Plum" and weekends at his home in Summerdale. He had devoted the last years of his life to teaching, and the work—from eyewitnesses and the Carnahan tapes—continued to be dynamic and focused. He might come downstairs to the big room looking disheveled and even on occasion with "his business hanging out," but he could still "nail you at any false moment."[34] He might appear to be sleeping or not paying attention but would still hear every note. And on the Carnahan tapes you can experience his legendary eruption when he believes that his understanding of a text is being challenged.[35]

Deeter spent his last years living with Richard Brewer, a talented performer and director who also taught at the Hedgerow School and would later team with Rose Schulman and others as the Hedgerow Studio Theatre. Deeter told Peter Carnahan that he had stopped seeing theatre in New York and couldn't comment on contemporary playwrights or productions. He did reminisce, however, about some of his early days in New York and his friendship with Eugene O'Neill.[36]

Jasper Deeter died on May 31, 1972. He fell and broke a hip in the apartment in Media that he shared with Brewer. Kevin Hughes remembers the event vividly because "it happened the day before I was opening as Christy Mahon in *Playboy of the Western World* at Hedgerow. My first time on stage there. Obviously, the news of Jasper's death was overwhelming and rattled many of the company members."[37] His ashes were spread over the garden at his boyhood home outside Harrisburg. Shortly after, the board declined to renew the lease of the David Ralphe Company and looked to Rose and Dolores and other veterans to continue the story and renew the vision that had made them the most prominent repertory company in the country.

How far Jasper Deeter had traveled from the dream that inspired him is incalculable. How much the corporate Hedgerow had disappointed him is unknowable. David Ralphe believes that he had little use for things—corporations, buildings, or people—that didn't move the work forward. "He was one of the most unsentimental men that I ever met."[38] We do know of occasional moments though that render vividly the distance he had journeyed from the joy of making a living library of plays to the corporate squabbling over Hedgerow. One such was Louis Lippa's determined quest to rehearse his new play after he had been turned away by the board.

A few days later, he and a friend cleared out a corner of the lower barn that housed mostly props and some costumes and christened it "Theatre in the Dirt." They began rehearsing. "I had read in the newspaper a small article about a young dancer whose body was found washed up on the shore of an island somewhere in the South Pacific. It was later determined that he had been murdered by a jealous lover. It all sounded tragically romantic. I wrote a few scenes and asked Ruth Esherick to play the part of the dancer's lover. Rose attended a rehearsal."[39] But the new space didn't last long. "Maybe a week or so. Someone complained that the barn wasn't meant to be used as a theater. I don't blame them. It was a silly idea." Before they were closed, however, Deeter wandered in one day and just stared at the little space they had clawed out of the dirt. "Maybe we should just start over," he murmured. He didn't stay long. "I've always thought he was tired of how complicated Hedgerow had become. Perhaps he was just tired physically. I don't know."[40]

Epilogue

The day after Thanksgiving, 1985, Hedgerow closed its production of *Cat on a Hot Tin Roof,* and by midnight the building was empty. Someone returned, however, in the early morning and set fire to the theatre. It burned unnoticed until approximately 7:00 a.m. when a passerby alerted the South Media Fire Department of smoke pouring from the building. By 8:30 a.m. the fire was extinguished; the fieldstone exterior walls survived, but the interior was gutted. Blackened beams collapsed through Deeter's beloved cyclorama and stage floor and settled in the basement of the old mill.

June Prager, the artistic director, told the *Philadelphia Inquirer* that "there are actors now who are walking by and standing like they're at a funeral, crying. Hundreds of people have put their souls into this building."[1] Hedgerow had long since abandoned repertory, but there was a resident company in the old farmhouse up the road who received their room and board and a small weekly stipend. Dolores Tanner was dead, but Rose Schulman was still teaching, and in spite of a changing cast of characters, there was a core of people who tried to keep the spirit and traditions of Hedgerow alive. Anniversaries were still celebrated and people still came to make their permanent homes in the Rose Valley.

No one was ever charged with arson, and the board of directors immediately moved to raise money to rebuild the theatre. It took them nearly five years and over $600,000, and finally in 1990 the theatre reopened and has recently celebrated its ninetieth anniversary.[2] In the interim, they had played at a variety of venues including the "big room" at the farmhouse where Jasper Deeter used to play the piano and which became a studio space while the renovation proceeded. After Rose died in 1989, her leadership passed to others who also admired Deeter and the Hedgerow legends and wanted to carry them forward. Most prominent was Janet Kelsey who had come to Hedgerow in 1962 with her family to study with Jasper and who, with Rose's support, became an imposing presence. Janet's mother-in-law had been a company member in the early years, and Janet was determined to maintain the Hedgerow mystique. She managed the books and eventually emerged as a superb actor and director. In 1992, her daughter Penelope Reed, who also had taken classes with Deeter before her degrees at Carnegie Mellon and Marquette and a distinguished career at Milwaukee Rep and McCarter Theater, was appointed artistic director at Hedgerow and came home to energize the programming and the theatre's reputation.

As for Jasper Deeter, he has paid the price for his insistence upon living and making his art in rural America. In spite of his extraordinary record, he is little more than a footnote in most theatrical accounts, marginalized by many factors but principally because he believed in a kind of theatre that was at odds with most conventional practice in the twentieth century. And he didn't flourish in New York. "Do you mean that guy in *Tobacco Road*?" was a question that I frequently encountered in researching this book.

Deeter was a theatre artist who dreaded the spotlight and wanted mostly to live a life making and remaking plays in his tiny rural theatre. Like Thoreau, who renounced the trappings of civilization in order to understand his relationship with the natural world, Deeter renounced the commercialization of the theatre and spent his adult life making it an art and a way of life in the Rose Valley. His commitment to ideals like "truth" and "beauty" were not just buzz words but the core of a commitment that sustained him for 30 years. He loved acting and came to see it—and teach it—as an expression of the relationship between the central nervous system of the human being and the natural environment that housed him. The Hedgerow mantra of "Mind, Body, Eyes, Face, Talk" was not only about technique to be sure, but it was also the distillation of a belief that embodied an approach to acting that could result in "truth" for the actor and ultimately "beauty" for the experience of theatre. And it was made possible by his insistence, above all else on generosity. Hedgerow survived not because of Deeter alone, but because year after year other artists were willing to share his dream. His generosity inspired them. The sharing of food, space, and labor was central to the Hedgerow experience, but sharing was most prominent in the realm of ideas. Deeter never claimed to be an original thinker, but he channeled things that he cherished, and in those transactions inspired countless others. He was fierce about equality across class, gender, and racial lines, and he was resolute about attacking ideologies that suppressed under the guise of nation, patriotism, or religion. "Pretend and Be Saved" was not phraseology but devotion to a way of life. In David Ralphe's words, "The clearest insight that I ever had of Jap was to think of his heart belonging to Susan Glaspell and his head to Bernard Shaw."[3]

Appendix A: Hedgerow Repertory 1923–1956

There are several lists of the complete Hedgerow repertory with many inconsistencies and omissions. Some include only the major productions; others include one acts and curtain raisers but confuse calendar years with season offerings. Some publications from Hedgerow, for example, list only eight productions in the initial season and omit the one act plays which were also performed. The following seasonal list is compiled from a variety of sources and cross-checked against holdings in the Hedgerow Collection at Boston University's Gotlieb Archive. There may still be some errors, since Hedgerow maintained their own records, which sometimes contradict each other. A handwritten list, maintained over the years by the company, can be found in Box 77 at Gotlieb.

1923: *Androcles and the Lion, Aria da Capo, The Bravest Thing in the World, Brothers, Candida, Clarence, A Constant Lover, The Dragon, The Emperor Jones, Inheritors, The Master Builder, Mr. Pim Passes By, Swan Song, Sweet and Twenty, The Turtle Dove, Where the Cross is Made, The Yellow Jacket.*

1924: *Androcles and the Lion, The Artist, Autumn Fires, Bernice, Candida, Cast up by the Sea, The Dragon, The Dreamers, The Emperor Jones, The Heart of Youth, The Hero, His Honor the Mayor, Inheritors, King Hunger, Make Believe, March Hares, The Master Builder, Misalliance, Mr. Pim Passes By, Paolo and Francesca, The Pillars of Society, Richard II, Trifles.*

1925: *Beyond the Horizon, Candida, Cast up by the Sea, Captain Brassbound's Conversion, Dulcy, The Emperor Jones, Diff'rent, He Who Gets Slapped, The Hero, Inheritors, March Hares, The Master Builder, The Mermaid, Misalliance, Mr. Pim Passes By, The Pillars of Society, Rollo's Wild Oat, The Romantic Age, The Sabine Women, Six Characters in Search of an Author, The Taming of the Shrew, Wolves.*

1926: *Alice in Wonderland, Captain Brassbound's Conversion, Diff'rent, The Dragon, Dulcy, The Emperor Jones, He Who Gets Slapped, Hedda Gabler,*

144 *Appendix A*

The Hero, In a Garden, Inheritors, Ivanov, Lucky Sam McCarver, March Hares, Mary, Mary Quite Contrary, Misalliance, Mr. Pim Passes By, The Romantic Age, Six Characters in Search of an Author, Taming of the Shrew, Ten Nights in a Barroom, The Verge.

1927: *Alice in Wonderland, Arms and the Man, Candida, He Who Gets Slapped, Hedda Gabler, In Abraham's Bosom, Inheritors, Ivanoff, The Lucky One, The Master Builder, Paolo and Francesca, The Romantic Age, Welded, You Never Can Tell.*

1928: *Alice* in *Wonderland, Arms and the Man, Beyond the Horizon, From Morn to Midnight, The Hairy Ape, He Who Gets Slapped, Hedda Gabler, Inheritors, Lucky Sam McCarver, Mary, Mary Quite Contrary, Mirage, Mr. Pim Passes By, The Pillars of Society, The Prisoner, Quittin' Time, Rancour, The Romantic Age, The Star, Uncle's Been Dreaming, Welded, You Never Can Tell.*

1929: *Alice in Wonderland, Arms and the Man, Beyond the Horizon, The Devil's Disciple, A Doll's House, The Dragon, The Emperor Jones, The Hairy Ape, In Abraham's Bosom, Inheritors, Liliom, Martine, Mary, Mary Quite Contrary, The Man Who Died at 12 O'Clock, Mirage, Misalliance, The No'Count Boy, Mr. Pim Passes By, Poker Face, The Prisoner, Rancour, The Romantic Age, The Star, The Stronger, Sweeney, Thunder on the Left, Uncle's Been Dreaming, White Dresses, White Man.*

1930: *Alice in Wonderland, Arms and the Man, Beyond the Horizon, Captain Brassbound's Conversion, Cast up by the Sea, The Devil's Disciple, A Doll's House, Dulcy, The Emperor Jones, The First Man, The Hairy Ape, Inheritors, Like Falling Leaves, Liliom, Limelight, Lucky Sam McCarver, Martine, Mary, Mary Quite Contrary, The Mask and the Face, Mr. Pim Passes By, Othello, The Playboy of the Western World, Poker Face, The Prisoner, Rancour, The Romantic Age, Sweeney, Thunder on the Left, Uncle's Been Dreaming, When We Dead Awaken.*

1931: *Alice in Wonderland, Arms and the Man, Beyond the Horizon, Can You Hear Their Voices?, Candida, Captain Brassbound's Conversion, Cast up by the Sea, Champagne, The Devil's Disciple, A Doll's House, The Emperor Jones, The First Man, The Hairy Ape, Happy Ending, Heartbreak House, Hedda Gabler, Inheritors, A Lantern to See By, Like Falling Leaves, Liliom, Limelight, Lucky Sam McCarver, Mary, Mary Quite Contrary, The Mask and the Face, Merry-Go-Round, Mr. Pim Passes By, Nellie the Beautiful Cloak Model, Othello, The Physician in Spite of Himself, Pinwheel, The Playboy of the Western World, Poker Face, The Queen of Chinatown, Rancour, Roadside,*

The Romantic Age, Solitaire Man, Ten Nights in a Barroom, Thunder on the Left, Whirlpool, The Witch.

1932: *Alison's House, Arms and the Man, Beyond the Horizon, Candida, Cast up by the Sea, The Cherokee Night, The D. A., The Devil's Disciple, The Emperor Jones, Happy Ending, Heartbreak House, The Heavenly Express, Hedda Gabler, Inheritors, A Lantern to See By, Like Falling Leaves, Make Believe, Mary, Mary Quite Contrary, The Mask and the Face, Merry-Go-Round, Misalliance, Mr. Pim Passes By, The Physician in Spite of Himself, Pinwheel, A Place in the World, Roadside, The Romantic Age, The Seagull, The Ship, Solitaire Man, Spring Song, A Sunny Morning, Sweeney, The Taming of the Shrew, Thunder on the Left, The Whiteheaded Boy, Wife to a Famous Man, The Witch, You Never Can Tell.*

1933: *Alison's House, Androcles and the Lion, Arms and the Man, Beyond the Horizon, Cast up by the Sea, The Cherokee Night, The Countess and the Conductor, The Devil's Disciple, The Emperor Jones, Engaged, The Hairy Ape, Heartbreak House, The Heavenly Express, Hickory Dickory, Inheritors, John Gabriel Borkman, A Lantern to See By, Love and Geography, Mary, Mary Quite Contrary, Merry-Go-Round, Misalliance, The Physician in Spite of Himself, The Pillars of Society, Roadside, The Seagull, The Ship, Son of Perdition, Spring Song, A Sunny Morning, Turnstile, Unknown Warrior, Wife to a Famous Man, Years of the Locusts, You Never Can Tell.*

1934: *Alison's House, Androcles and the Lion, Arms and the Man, Beyond the Horizon, Candida, Cast up by the Sea, The Devil's Disciple, The Emperor Jones, Engaged, Happy Ending, Heartbreak House, Hickory Dickory, The Inheritors, Is Life Worth Living?, John Gabriel Borkman, Let the Punishment Fit the Crime, Love and Geography, Martine, Mary, Mary Quite Contrary, Misalliance, Mr. Pim Passes By, The Physician in Spite of Himself, Saint Joan, The Shining Hour, Spring in Autumn, Spring Song, Three Sisters, Thunder on the Left, Twelfth Night, Unknown Warrior, Wife to a Famous Man, Winesburg, Ohio.*

1935: *An American Tragedy, Androcles and the Lion, Arms and the Man, Beauty Slain, Beyond the Horizon, Candida, Cast up by the Sea, The Doctor's Dilemma, The Emperor Jones, The Emperor's New Clothes, Engaged, Heartbreak House, Inheritors, Is Life Worth Living?, Mary, Mary Quite Contrary, The Mask and the Face, Moon of the Caribbees, The Physician in Spite of Himself, Plum Hollow, Rancour, Saint Joan, The Shining Hour, Twelfth Night, Winesburg, Ohio.*

1936: *An American Tragedy, The Anchor's Weighed, Androcles and the Lion, Arms and the Man, Behold Your God, Beyond the Horizon, Candida, Cast up by the Sea, The Devil's Disciple, The Doctor's Dilemma, The Emperor Jones, The Emperor's New Clothes, Getting Married, Heartbreak House, Inheritors, Is Life Worth Living?, Kit Marlowe, Like Falling Leaves, Liliom, The Lonesome West, Love and Geography, Mary, Mary Quite Contrary, The Mask and the Face, Misalliance, One Way to Heaven, The Physician in Spite of Himself, The Plough and the Stars, Plum Hollow, Rancour, Saint Joan, Twelfth Night, Winesburg, Ohio.*

1937: *An American Tragedy, The Anchor's Weighed, Androcles and the Lion, Arms and the Man, Autumn Fires, Beyond the Horizon, Bystander, Candida, Dark Lady of the Sonnets, The Devil's Disciple, The Emperor Jones, Getting Married, Heartbreak House, Inheritors, Liliom, Misalliance, Noah, One Way to Heaven, Penny Wise, The Plough and the Stars, The Round Table, Saint Joan, Too True to Be Good, Twelfth Night, Wife to a Famous Man, You Never Can Tell.*

1938: *Arms and the Man, Beyond the Horizon, Candida, The Emperor Jones, The First Mrs. Fraser, The Frodi, Inheritors, Is Life Worth Living?, Liliom, Noah, Penny Wise, Roadside, Saint Joan, The Simpleton of the Unexpected Isles, Too True to Be Good, Twelfth Night, You Never Can Tell.*

1939: *An American Tragedy, Androcles and the Lion, Arms and the Man, Beloved Leader, Beyond the Horizon, Candida, The Emperor Jones, The Frodi, Ghosts, Heartbreak House, Honey!, In Abraham's Bosom, Inheritors, Is Life Worth Living?, Juno and the Paycock, Macbeth, Man and Superman, The Nuremberg Egg, Penny Wise, The Romantic Age, Saint Joan, The Simpleton of the Unexpected Isles, Too True to Be Good, Twelfth Night.*

1940: *Androcles and the Lion, Anna Christie, Arms and the Man, Beloved Leader, Candida, Chocolate, Diff'rent, The Emperor Jones, The Frodi, Ghosts, Heartbreak House, Henry IV, Part One, Honey!, Inheritors, Macbeth, Major Barbara, Man and Superman, Misalliance, Mr. Pim Passes By, The Old Homestead, Once Upon a Time, The Romantic Age, Twelfth Night, The Whiteheaded Boy.*

1941: *Anna Christie, Back to Methuselah, Bride of the Moon, The Comic Artist, Diff'rent, The Emperor Jones, Family Portrait, Ghosts, Gospel of the Brothers Barnabas, Heartbreak House, Henry IV, Part One, In the Beginning, Inheritors, Macbeth, Major Barbara, Mary, Mary Quite Contrary, Mr. Pim Passes By, The Old Homestead, Once Upon a Time, Saint Joan, Skaal!, Twelfth Night.*

Appendix A 147

1942: *Anna Christie, Arms and the Man, Bride of the Moon, Candida, The Devil's Disciple, The Emperor Jones, Family Portrait, Gospel of the Brothers Barnabas, In the Beginning, Macbeth, Mary, Mary Quite Contrary, Mr. Pim Passes By, The Physician in Spite of Himself, The Picnic, Pudding Full of Plums, Saint Joan, Skaal!, Thunder on the Left, Turpentine Boy.*

1943: *L'Absence, Arms and the Man, Candida, The Emperor Jones, The Physician in Spite of Himself, Thunder on the Left, Tomorrow's Yesterday.*

1944: *The Emperor Jones, Girls in Uniform, Martine, The Physician in Spite of Himself, Quintin Quintana, Rancour, Thunder on the Left, Tomorrow's Yesterday.*

1945: *The Emperor Jones, Girls in Uniform, Gospel of the Brothers Barnabas, Martine, Quintin Quintana, Rancour, The Seagull, Thunder on the Left, Tomorrow's Yesterday.*

1946: *Androcles and the Lion, The Devil's Disciple, The Emperor Jones, Gospel of the Brothers Barnabas, Inheritors, Martine, The Seagull, Twelfth Night, Uncle Vanya.*

1947: *An American Tragedy, Among Ourselves, And He Did Hide Himself, Androcles and the Lion, Cadenza, The Devil's Disciple, The Emperor Jones, The Great Big Doorstep, Inheritors, She Stoops to Conquer, Twelfth Night, Uncle Vanya.*

1948: *An American Tragedy, Among Ourselves, And He Did Hide Himself, Androcles and the Lion, Cadenza, The Caucasian Chalk Circle, The Cherokee Night, The Devil's Disciple, Gospel of the Brothers Barnabas, The Great Big Doorstep, Inheritors, The Mistress of the Inn, Saint Joan, She Stoops to Conquer, Twelfth Night, Uncle Vanya.*

1949: *Androcles and the Lion, The Caucasian Chalk Circle, The Cherry Orchard, Gospel of the Brothers Barnabas, Ladies in Arms, The Mistress of the Inn, The Quick and the Dead, The Romantic Age, Saint Joan, She Stoops to Conquer, Twelfth Night, Uncle Vanya.*

1950: *Androcles and the Lion, The Cherry Orchard, The Imaginary Invalid, Ladies in Arms, The Man Who Corrupted Hadleyburg, Nathan the Wise, The Quick and the Dead, Saint Joan, She Stoops to Conquer, Skipper Next to God, Thunder on the Left, Uncle Vanya.*

1951: *Androcles and the Lion, The Boor, Gospel of the Brothers Barnabas, A Highland Fling, The Imaginary Invalid, In the Summerhouse, Julius Caesar,*

The Man Who Corrupted Hadleyburg, Nathan the Wise, No Exit, A Phoenix Too Frequent, The Seagull, She Stoops to Conquer, Six Characters in Search of an Author, Thunder on the Left, Uncle Vanya, Yes Is for a Very Young Man.

1952: *The Affairs of Anatol, Arms and the Man, The Cherry Orchard, Cycle for Concern, De Adamses, Heartbreak House, A Highland Fling, The Imaginary Invalid, In the Summerhouse, Julius Caesar, Man and Superman, Nathan the Wise, No Exit, A Phoenix Too Frequent, Six Characters in Search of an Author, Yes Is for a Very Young Man.*

1953: *The Affairs of Anatol, Arms and the Man, The Cherry Orchard, The Great Gesture, Heartbreak House, The House of Bernada Alba, Man and Superman, No Exit, A Phoenix Too Frequent, Ring around the Moon, The Rivals, Six Characters in Search of an Author, Too True to Be Good.*

1954: *The Crucible, The Emperor Jones, The Great Big Doorstep, The Great Gesture, The House of Bernarda Alba, Heartbreak House, Man and Superman, Noah, The Physician in Spite of Himself, A Phoenix too Frequent, Queer People, Ring around the Moon, Twelfth Night, Unfinished Portrait.*

1955: *The Cherry Orchard, The Confidential Clerk, The Crucible, A Difficult Widow, Diff'rent, The Emperor Jones, Ghosts, The Man Who Corrupted Hadleyburg, Noah, The Physician in Spite of Himself, Right You Are, Twelfth Night, Unfinished Portrait.*

1956: *Androcles and the Lion.*

Appendix B: Repertory for *Shaw Festival*, July 19–August 14, 1937

The Shaw festivals varied somewhat as Deeter sought to find the best mixture of new and old titles. The following calendar, from one of their most successful seasons, illustrates how productions were introduced and maintained over the month-long celebration of Bernard Shaw.

Mon.	July 19	*Arms and the Man*
Tue.	20	*Candida*
Wed.	21	*You Never Can Tell*
Thu.	22	*The Devil's Disciple*
Fri.	23	*Getting Married*
Sat.	24	*Misalliance*

Mon.	26	*Too True to Be Good* (Opening—123rd production)
Tue.	27	*Too True to Be Good*
Wed.	28	*Androcles and the Lion* with *Dark Lady of the Sonnets*
Thu.	29	*Heartbreak House*
Fri.	30	*Saint Joan*
Sat.	31	*Too True to Be Good*

Mon.	August 2	*Misalliance*
Tue.	3	*Arms and the Man*
Wed.	4	*Candida*
Thu.	5	*Too True to Be Good*
Fri.	6	*The Devil's Disciple*
Sat.	7	*You Never Can Tell*

Mon.	9	*Getting Married*
Tue.	10	*Androcles and the Lion* with *Dark Lady of the Sonnets*
Wed.	11	*Saint Joan*
Thu.	12	*Heartbreak House*
Fri.	13	*Too True to Be Good*
Sat.	14	*Too True to Be Good*

Appendix C: Repertory Calendars

Repertory is a grueling and demanding schedule, and that Hedgerow maintained it for 30 years is remarkable. In 1931, Deeter expanded their April to October calendar to a full year. By 1934, for example, the theatre operated 51 weeks performing 34 of their announced repertory of 108 plays. Eight were new productions and they played a total of 318 performances. Over the years, Deeter made a number of modifications, allowing more time to rehearse new plays or adjusting the nightly changeovers to accommodate popular offerings. In the 1940s, they reverted to their April to October seasons. The following two snapshots are typical of their monthly schedules; first during the expansive years of the 1930s and second, during the 1940s when weather or finances forced them to do shortened weeks or reduced offerings.

Sample Repertory Calendar, June, 1938.

Wed.	June 1	*You Never Can Tell*
Thu.	2	*Candida*
Fri.	3	*The Emperor Jones*
Sat.	4	*The Frodi*

Mon.	6	*Inheritors*
Tue.	7	*Too True to Be Good*
Wed.	8	*Beyond the Horizon*
Thu.	9	*Noah*
Fri.	10	*Liliom*
Sat.	11	*Liliom*

Mon.	13	*Penny Wise*
Tue.	14	*You Never Can Tell*
Wed.	15	*Candida*
Thu.	16	*The Emperor Jones*
Fri.	17	*The Frodi*
Sat.	18	*Inheritors*

Appendix C

Mon.	20	*Too True to Be Good*
Tue.	21	*Beyond the Horizon*
Wed.	22	*Roadside*
Thu.	23	*Liliom*
Fri.	24	*Penny Wise*
Sat.	25	*You Never Can Tell*

Mon.	27	*Candida*
Tue.	28	*The Emperor Jones*
Wed.	29	*The Frodi*
Thu.	30	*Inheritors*

Sample Repertory Calendar, September, 1947.

Mon.	September 1	*The Great Big Doorstep*
Wed.	3	*An American Tragedy*
Thu.	4	*Androcles and the Lion*
Fri.	5	*Among Ourselves*
Sat.	6	*Uncle Vanya*

Wed.	10	*The Emperor Jones* (Sold)*
Thu.	11	*The Emperor Jones*
Fri.	12	*An American Tragedy*
Sat.	13	*The Great Big Doorstep*

Wed.	17	*Androcles and the Lion*
Thu.	18	*The Great Big Doorstep*
Fri.	19	*The Great Big Doorstep*
Sat.	20	*Among Ourselves*

Wed.	24	*Among Ourselves*
Thu.	25	*An American Tragedy*
Fri.	26	*Uncle Vanya*
Sat.	27	*The Seagull*

*Indicates a performance sold entirely to a group or business which would then resell the tickets to their members or patrons.

Notes

INTRODUCTION

1. Rose Schulman to Morgan Smedley, n.d., Hedgerow Theatre Collection, Howard Gotlieb Archive, Boston University, Box 10, Folder 4. Hereafter, Gotlieb.
2. Miriam Phillips to Board of Governors, Jan. 1943, Gotlieb, Box 10, Folder 2.
3. Jasper Deeter to Bernard Shaw, Sep. 3, 1939, Gotlieb, Box 18, Folder 4.
4. Jasper Deeter quoted in Dolores Tanner, "Hedgerow Theatre," Master's Thesis, University of Texas, 1957, Gotlieb, Box 178, Folder 1, Chapter IV, 24.
5. Ann Harding to Jasper Deeter, Nov. 1, 1930, Gotlieb, Box 8, Folder 4.
6. Sherwood Anderson, "To Jasper Deeter: A Letter," *No Swank* (Philadelphia, PA: The Centaur Press, 1934), 128.
7. Lynn Riggs to Jasper Deeter, Aug. 23, 1932, Gotlieb, Box 18, Folder 1.
8. Jasper Deeter to Bernard Shaw, Sep. 3, 1941, Gotlieb, Box 18, Folder 4.
9. William Smallwood Ayers, "A Poor Sort of Heaven; A Good Sort of Earth: The Rose Valley Arts and Crafts Experiment," Master's Thesis, University of Delaware, 1982, 26.
10. Ibid.
11. Ibid., 27.
12. Jasper Deeter to Bernard Shaw, Nov. 14, 1930, Gotlieb, Box 18, Folder 4. Deeter was acutely sensitive to box office, and the unofficial Hedgerow policy was, "We produce what we like and will be happy to re-produce what you like."
13. Deeter wrote and talked a great deal about beauty and often contrasted it with the ugliness of urban America. "What is the quality of life which makes it easier for us to work together when we are doing a play? I think it is a quality of life we hate and I think its name is ugliness. The world and its cities hit our eyes so dirtily—an ugly lack of order. Its sounds strike our ears unmercifully—an ugly lack of harmony." Jasper Deeter quoted in David Fiebert, "The Hedgerow Theatre: A Remarkable Time," Dramaturgy Paper, Villanova University, 1988, 10.
14. Jasper Deeter to "Clea," Mar. 21, 1938, Gotlieb, Box 2, Folder 2.

15. Jack Wade, who designed at Hedgerow in the 1980s, recalls the huge stock of furniture and flats in the Hedgerow barn and attests to the quality of the construction. "The flats were very well made and the furniture pieces were solidly built." Phone interview Barry Witham with Jack Wade, Jun. 25, 2012.
16. Jasper Deeter to company, quoted in Tanner, "Hedgerow Theatre," Chapter III, 16.
17. Paul Green quoted in Phyllis Cole Braunlich, *Haunted By Home* (Norman: University of Oklahoma Press, 1988), 123.
18. Theodore Dreiser to Jasper Deeter, Jul. 20, 1935, Gotlieb, Box 120, Folder 3.
19. Jasper Deeter quoted in Tanner, "Hedgerow Theatre," Chapter IV, 24.
20. It is difficult to fix an exact number because one acts or curtain raisers were sometimes not counted. This figure is taken from a compilation of lists in the Hedgerow archive at Boston University. See Appendix A for the Hedgerow repertory.
21. Tanner, "Hedgerow Theatre," Chapter II, 11.

1 *INHERITORS*: GROWING A THEATRE

1. Deeter was homosexual and tended to be very private about his personal life. He was somewhat reclusive and is a background figure in all the accounts of Provincetown. While he never was "closeted" and had several partners, people then were—and today are—reluctant to discuss his sexuality. I suspect that it was (1) not an issue for most since he was so widely respected and (2) that "naming" him may have given detractors and homophobes a way to diminish the significance of the work at Hedgerow. The only clue to his own thinking came in an interview with Wharton Esherick's daughter, Ruth, who as a youngster considered Jasper her "second father" and who acted with him for many years. She told me that something had upset her as a youngster—she doesn't recall the actual incident—but Jasper comforted her and told her that "there was nothing wrong with being homosexual and it had been around since the time of the Greeks." Barry Witham interview with Ruth Esherick, Feb. 16, 2011, Paoli, PA.
2. Transcript of interview with Jasper Deeter conducted by Richard K. Doud, Media, PA. 1964, Smithsonian Library, 2.
3. Quoted in John Calely Wentz, *The Hedgerow Theatre: An Historical Study*, Doctoral Dissertation, University of Pennsylvania, 1954, 14.
4. Anne Fletcher, *Rediscovering Mordecai Gorelik* (Carbondale: Southern Illinois University Press, 2009), 27.
5. Ibid., 54.
6. Henry Miller, *Remember to Remember* (New York: New Directions, 1986), 117.
7. Deeter later told Peter Carnahan that the plays he saw at Provincetown were so bad that he thought he could "do some good work there." Carnahan Tapes, G-4, 18:00.

8. Deeter claimed to have saved a copy of the play that he subsequently lost. As I write, *Exorcism* has been found again and produced by the Arena Stage in Washington, DC, apparently from a copy preserved by O'Neill's second wife, Agnes Bolton.
9. *The Spring* played 21 performances at the Princess Theatre beginning on September 21, 1921. George Cram Cook was credited as "staging the play." There was no directing credit for Jasper Deeter.
10. There are excellent discussions of the play in both Ben-Zvi and Gainor and an excellent piece about the play and Hedgerow in Jonathan Shandell, "The Inheritors of 'Inheritors' How Susan Glaspell Inspired the Hedgerow Theatre," *Journal of American Theater and Drama* 22, no. 3 (Fall 2010): 5–21.
11. Susan Glaspell, *Inheritors* (London: Ernest Benn Ltd, 1924), 31.
12. Ibid., 60.
13. Ibid., 95.
14. Linda Ben-Zvi, *Susan Glaspell: Her Life and Times* (New York: Oxford University Press, 2005), 233.
15. Scott O'Brien, *Ann Harding: Cinema's Gallant Lady* (Albany, GA: Bear Manor Media, 2010), 39.
16. Doud interview, 11.
17. Jasper Deeter to Susan Glaspell, Dec. 9, 1936, Gotlieb, Box 16, Folder 4.
18. Jasper Deeter to Sherwood Anderson, Dec. 4, 1934, Gotlieb, Correspondence File A.
19. Daniel Cashman, "Grotowski: His Twentieth Anniversary," *Theatre Journal* 31, no. 4 (1979): 465.
20. Miller, *Remember to Remember*, 116.
21. Deeter told Peter Carnahan that he had no intention of founding a theatre when he arrived in Moylan, but "after that first summer I saw that we had a chance to make a theater." Carnahan tapes, G-4, 23:30.
22. Shandell, "Inheritors," 8.
23. Ibid., 9.
24. Hoag Levins, *A Thoreau in the Woods*, www.levins.com/esh5.html, p. 13, accessed Sep. 1, 2010. Esherick was recently the subject of a major exhibition at the University of Pennsylvania, "Wharton Esherick and the Birth of the American Modern," Sep. 7, 2011 to Feb. 13, 2011. His work is also celebrated in Mansfield Bascom's excellent book, *The Journey of a Creative Mind* (New York: Abrams, 2010); and Eugene Halton, *The Great Brain Suck* (Chicago: University of Chicago Press, 2008).
25. Wentz, *Hedgerow Theatre*, 60.
26. Jasper Deeter to Eleanor Price Mather, quoted in Shandell, "Inheritors," 8.
27. Wentz, *Hedgerow Theatre*, 94.
28. Popular lore suggests that the name "Hedgerow" came from Ann Harding who told a local sheriff when the company was threatened with eviction from the Mill theatre that they would continue playing, even if it was in the hedgerows that surrounded the building. There was such an incident and it

probably led to the naming, but the speaker was probably Deeter and the attribution to Harding is largely public relations.
29. Rose Schulman quoted in Tanner, "Hedgerow Theatre," Chapter III, 19.

2 *THE EMPEROR JONES*: A PASSION FOR EQUALITY

1. Eugene O'Neill, *The Emperor Jones* (New York: Random House, 1954), 176–177.
2. Doud interview, 8.
3. Jasper Deeter to Bernard Shaw, Nov. 14, 1930, Gotlieb, Box 18, Folder 4. Deeter made this claim in numerous places and on numerous occasions. I have no reason to doubt it, but it clearly was not a position unique to Deeter at Provincetown. Black actors had been cast there prior to Gilpin, and both O'Neill and James Light—and others—were sympathetic to "colored" casting. For an excellent account of both Light and Deeter in subsequent minority casting see Cheryl Black, "After the Emperor: Interracial Collaborations between Provincetown Alumni and Black Theatre Artists c. 1924–1946," *Journal of American Drama and Theatre* 20, no. 1 (Winter 2008): 5–26. Louis Sheaffer, in *O'Neill: Son and Artist* (Boston, MA: Little, Brown and Co, 1973), 32, records that Ida Rauh was a leading pro-Negro advocate at Provincetown, but he credits Deeter with suggesting and then pursuing Gilpin on behalf of the players. See also Paul Robeson's recollection that it was Deeter who approached him about playing Brutus Jones prior to Gilpin. The racism in the text so offended Robeson that he "almost threw Jasper Deeter out of the house." Sheila Tully Boyle, *Paul Robeson: The Years of Promise and Achievement* (Amherst: University of Massachusetts Press, 2001), 90.
4. Jasper Deeter press release, Gotlieb, Box 2, Folder 2.
5. Review of *The Emperor Jones* by Herman L. Dieck. Quoted in Wentz, *Hedgerow Theatre*, 24.
6. Le Gallienne recounts the last troubled days of Machet in *At 33* (New York: Longmans, Green and Company, 1935), 206–210. The spelling of Machet's name varies among sources. Sometimes his first name is spelled Sidney.
7. See David Krasner for an excellent discussion of the tensions between Gilpin and O'Neill as well as an account of Gilpin's skill as an actor. David Krasner, *A Beautiful Pageant* (New York: Palgrave Macmillan, 2002).
8. Mansfield Bascom, *Wharton Esherick: The Journey of a Creative Mind* (New York: Abrams, 2010), 34.
9. This important article, extolling the virtues of Hedgerow's integrationist stance, was referenced by Cheryl Black in *After the Emperor* and subsequently became the site for a stimulating series of seminars at the American Society for Theatre Research annual meetings.
10. O'Brien, *Ann Harding*, 82.

11. Wentz, *Hedgerow Theatre*, 61.
12. Paul Green to Jasper Deeter, Dec. 31, 1926, Gotlieb, Box 16, Folder G.
13. Paul Green to Jasper Deeter, Jan. 13, 1927, Gotlieb, Box 16, Folder G.
14. Hughes was commissioned by a Russian film company to write and oversee a project exposing the horrors of segregated America. Along with 22 other actors and leftists artists, he sailed for Russia in May 1932, where they were greeted as heroic revolutionaries. By September, however, the project had fallen apart due to shoddy planning and bureaucratic bungling. Most of the company returned to America but Hughes stayed on to travel and Rudd to pursue a career. See Langston Hughes, *I Wonder as I Wander* (New York: Hill and Wang, 1993) for details.
15. *Daily Worker*, Feb. 1, 1939.
16. *Philadelphia Independent*, clippings dated July 1, 1934 and August 19, 1934. Clipping File, Hedgerow Theatre. The *Pittsburgh Courier* published photos of Rudd and Arthur Rich, when Rudd visited Hedgerow, in a story titled "Emperors Laud Each Other," Jul. 7, 1934, A6.
17. Jasper Deeter to Paul Green, Jan. 4, 1930, Gotlieb, Box 16, Folder G. There is little recorded information about Rudd's historic *Othello* or indeed about much of his career prior to Hedgerow. James Hatch and Errol Hill quote a letter from Elinor Winsor to Rudd praising his Othello in their *A History of African American Theatre* (Cambridge University Press, 2003), 229. Jonathan Shandell has pieced together a fascinating narrative in which he places Rudd in Washington, DC, as a young man attending Howard University and appearing briefly with the Krigwa Players. Deeter apparently saw him performing with an amateur group in Philadelphia prior to his debut as the Emperor Jones on May 29, 1929. See Jonathan Shandell, "The First *Emperor* of Pennsylvania: Wayland Rudd at Hedgerow Theatre," unpublished paper presented at the ATHE Convention in Los Angeles, Aug. 13, 2011.
18. I'm not sure what the duties included or whether the title was simply honorable. Biographical information about Rich is scant. I have tried to contact both of his surviving sons, Arthur Jr. and Jordan, but most of my information is gleaned from various clippings and press releases in the Hedgerow Archives and interviews with his niece, Rachel Neal.
19. Interview with Ruth Esherick, Feb. 16, 2010.
20. "Racial Equality: Raising the Jim Crow Issue," *The Literary Digest*, Sep., 1935, 18.
21. Ibid.
22. Frances Williams Interview ("To Hell with Bandannas") conducted by Karen Anne Mason and Richard Candida Smith, Oral History Program, University of California, 1997, 57.
23. Jasper Deeter to Frank Sheils, Jul. 28, 1939, Gotlieb, Correspondence File S. Deeter had invited Langston Hughes to be a resident playwright at Hedgerow in 1931, where he worked on the text of *Mulatto*. Deeter read the first draft and felt that the play was "too sensational" given its murder and mob

violence. Hughes stayed in Moylan for approximately six weeks participating in all the company duties and chores and discussing with Rose McClendon the role of Cora in the play. But he left in October without making significant revisions to *Mulatto*. See Arnold Rampersad, *The Life of Langston Hughes, Volume 1:1902–1941* (New York: Oxford, 1986), 191–192.

24. See http://www.poetryfoundation.org/bio/countee-cullen, accessed Jan. 30, 2011. Shortly after the marriage, Cullen moved to Paris by himself where he continued to write and pursued, by most accounts, a homosexual lifestyle.
25. Countee Cullen to Jasper Deeter, Jun. 13, 1933, Gotlieb, Box 15, Folder 5.
26. Countee Cullen to Jasper Deeter, Jun. 16, 1933, Gotlieb, Box 15, Folder 5.
27. Jasper Deeter to Leah Salisbury, Jun. 1936 [*sic*] Gotlieb, Box 15, Folder 5.
28. Prompt Script for *One Way to Heaven*, Gotlieb, Box 27, Folder 6.
29. Ibid., Act III, Scene 2, 29.
30. Minutes dated Jan. 3, 1937, Gotlieb, Box 11, Folder 7, "Negro Theatre."
31. Review Sep. 27, 1936, Gotlieb, Oversize Scrapbook, Folder 4.
32. Jasper Deeter to Susan Glaspell, Dec. 9, 1936, Gotlieb, Box 16. Folder 4. Deeter believed that Cullen's depiction of upper class Negroes made a substantial contribution to racial discussions and countered some of Van Vechten's clichés.
33. Figures are from Gotlieb, Box 15, Folder 5.
34. David Stevens to Jasper Deeter, Apr. 30, 1940, Gotlieb, Correspondence File S.
35. Deeter was adamant about the need for a theatre by, and about, Negroes, and praised them as having "a natural gift for histrionics and almost an instinct." See "Stage Director Rates Negro Actors as Equal of Whites," *The Pittsburgh Courier*, Aug. 7, 1928, A3.
36. Thomas Richardson to Jasper Deeter, May 10, 1935, Gotlieb, Box 11, Folder 7.
37. Abram Hill to Jasper Deeter, Jan. 25, 1944, Gotlieb, Box 11, Folder 7.
38. Loften Mitchell to Jasper Deeter, Apr. 10, 1939, Gotlieb, Box 11, Folder 7.

3 *WINESBURG, OHIO*: DEMOCRACY BETWEEN THE HEDGEROWS

1. Doud interview, 32
2. Ibid.
3. Wentz, *Hedgerow Theatre*, 65.
4. Kevin Hughes, who grew up in Media and later became general manager of the company, remembers hearing "third hand" references to the "dirty old man" in the 1960s. Witham interview with Hughes, Jan. 9, 2012.
5. Wentz, *Hedgerow Theatre*, 65.
6. John P. Guyer, "A Look Behind Scenes at Hedgerow Theatre," *Harrisburg Patriot*, Oct. 12, 1934. Clipping Files, Hedgerow Theatre.

7. Ibid.
8. Nofer was Lettie Esherick's brother and along with his nieces, Ruth and Mary, played an important part in the growth and success of the theatre. Ferd became an accomplished actor and also had a shrewd financial sense that helped guide Hedgerow through numerous difficult seasons.
9. Guyer, "A Look Behind Scenes at Hedgerow Theatre,"
10. Ibid.
11. Ibid.
12. Sherwood Anderson, *Plays: Winesburg and Others* (New York: Charles Scribners Sons, 1937), xvi.
13. Ibid., xvii.
14. Ibid., xxi.
15. Sherwood Anderson quoted in John Wentz, "Anderson's *Winesburg* and The Hedgerow Theatre," *Modern Drama* (May 1960): 42. For a fuller treatment of Anderson's meetings with Copeau see Ray Lewis White, ed., *Sherwood Anderson's Memoirs* (Chapel Hill: University of North Carolina Press, 1969), 361–364.
16. *Wonder Boy*, a satire on Hollywood film, was directed by Jed Harris and ran for 44 performances in 1931.
17. Barton retained a 20 percent share of the royalties because Anderson recognized the work that he had done. Barton committed suicide three years later.
18. Walter Rideout, *Sherwood Anderson: A Writer in America*, vol. 2 (Madison: University of Wisconsin Press, 2007), 177.
19. Holman, whose bisexual lifestyle was a source of gossip and tabloid stories, felt comfortable at Hedgerow and admired Deeter whom she thought might help her career as an actress. When she gained international fame as a blues singer she did benefits for the theatre. Janet Kelsey remembers fondly a night where she and Josh White had to shovel coal to keep the fires going at Hedgerow.
20. Rideout, *Sherwood Anderson*, 208.
21. Jack Wade phone interview with Barry Witham, Jun. 25, 2012. The proscenium opening at Hedgerow was 17 feet 6 inches wide and the depth of the playing area was barely 10 feet. An apron gained them another 3 feet of depth but the space was deceptively small.
22. The line that provoked the greatest criticism was at the opening of Scene 4 where one of the youngsters asks his pal, "did you ever have a piece?" Wentz reports that Deeter and Anderson consulted, and Anderson agreed to cut it. See Wentz, "Anderson's *Winesburg*," 49.
23. Quoted in Wentz, *Hedgerow Theatre*, 174.
24. Sherwood Anderson to Jasper Deeter, Jul. 9, 1934 in Howard Mumford Jones, ed., *Letters of Sherwood Anderson* (Boston, MA: Little, Brown and Company, 1953), 307.
25. Rideout, *Sherwood Anderson*, 206.
26. Wentz, "Anderson's *Winesburg*," 50.

27. Ibid.
28. In 1958, Christopher Sergel adapted a new version featuring James Whitmore and Dorothy McGuire as the dysfunctional parents and Ben Piazza as George. It closed after 13 performances. The Hedgerow version was published by Scribner's in 1937 along with three Anderson one-act plays and a tribute to Jasper Deeter. It was prepared from the text at Hedgerow and is fascinating to read, especially the vocal and sound scores that overlap and link the scenes and seem utterly contemporary in the way that they complement the action and forecast the next scene.
29. Rideout, *Sherwood Anderson*, 249. Among the many Hedgerow legends is that Deeter never drank until he began imbibing with Anderson. It is certainly not true, but he did enjoy drinking with Anderson and other visitors to the theatre. In the Carnahan tapes, he quotes Anderson on the pleasures of drinking. (D-2, 57:30) Later, of course, Deeter's own drinking did become excessive and was a topic of conversation around the theatre. Anderson, ironically, died from peritonitis in March 1941 from ingesting a toothpick either from a martini or snack. Wharton Esherick carved a wonderful wood sculpture for his grave site that was eventually removed because of weather damage. It stands imposingly today in the home of Ruth Esherick and Mansfield Bascom in Paoli, PA.
30. The Van Gogh show was a highly promoted and anticipated event. Opening in New York in November 1935 to large crowds, it moved to Philadelphia in January 1936 and subsequently to six American cities. There were rumors that his severed ear was part of the exhibition and that it may have added to the attendance rush.
31. In my conversation with Ruth Esherick in February 2011, she remarked that Jasper wanted them to be aware of what was going on in the world and he would often read to them. Two of his favorites were essays by Scott Nearing and selections from Van Gogh's letters.
32. Bill Ulrich to Jasper Deeter, Aug. 28, 1939, Gotlieb, Correspondence File U.
33. Mr. Orlovitz to Jasper Deeter, Aug. 14, 1944, Gotlieb, Correspondence File O.
34. Audrey Ward Metcalf quoted in Wentz, *Hedgerow Theatre*, 86.
35. Ann Harding to Jasper Deeter, Dec. 1, 1936, Gotlieb, Box 8, Folder 4.
36. These Guest Arrangement Contracts stipulated that "to further the interests of the organization by accepting labor and money from a number of persons of whom you are one. In granting you this arrangement we expect you to pay us $40 per month in advance." Hedgerow Theatre Files. Moylan, PA.
37. Carnahan tapes, Reel G-4, 26:00. With Deeter's approval Basehart chose replacements from the company and taught them the "business" of each role. Deeter was never happy with legal contracts that bound people to an agreement rather than a way of life. Visiting Hedgerow in 1952, Henry Murdock wrote of the company in *Theatre Arts*, "They work at Hedgerow on a long-range basis and by an unwritten law, announce each Christmas whether they are staying or leaving at Christmas of the next year. That is their version of the

'run-of-play' contract." Henry Murdock, "Behind the Hedgerows," *Theatre Arts*, 36, no. 8 (Aug. 1952): 77.
38. Minutes of the Hedgerow company, n.d. From the personal library of Kevin Hughes, Seattle, WA, 38.
39. Ibid.
40. Ibid.
41. Ibid., 40.
42. Murdock, "Behind the Hedgerows," 77.
43. Minutes of the Hedgerow company, Dec. 7, 1941. From the personal library of Kevin Hughes, Seattle, WA.

4   *AN AMERICAN TRAGEDY*: WHOSE SOCIAL CONSCIENCE?

1. Curt Conway, "Open letter to Jasper Deeter," *New Theatre* (Dec. 1934): 18.
2. Herbert Kline, Review of *An American Tragedy*, *New Masses*, May 28, 1935, Gotlieb, Scrapbook, Box 120.
3. Emmet Lavery, "In the Dramatic Mailbag," *New York Times*, May 10, 1931, X2.
4. Hallie Flanagan to Jasper Deeter, n.d., Gotlieb, Box 16, Folder "F."
5. Unsigned review, Gotlieb Scrapbook, Box 120.
6. Review signed D. A. H. Gotlieb, Box 94, Envelope 14.
7. *Hedgerow Stages 2 Somber Dramas*. Gotlieb, Box 120, Scrapbook clipping signed L. G. D. Reviews are also in Box 94, Envelope 14.
8. *Propaganda Play Given at Hedgerow*. Gotlieb, Box 120, Scrapbook clipping signed D.A.H.
9. Hallie Flanagan to Jasper Deeter, n.d., in response to a letter from him dated Feb. 10, 1933. Gotlieb, Box 16, Folder "F."
10. These figures are taken from a correspondence between Deeter and Flanagan fixing the royalties for the production at $30.33. Hedgerow, Box 16. The theatre seated 156 with a top price of $1.65. There appears to have been a delay, however, in paying the royalties and Flanagan reminded Deeter about their agreement in January 1933. He apologizes in a letter dated Feb. 10, 1933 and adds that "somehow our business end slipped up on this and we thought it had been paid."
11. Hallie Flanagan, *Dynamo* (New York: Duell, Sloan and Pearce, 1943), 106.
12. Ibid., 108.
13. Deeter's tenure with the Federal Theatre was brief. He admitted to Doud that he didn't really know what he was getting into, and he became impatient with the paperwork and the naivete that productions would be free from censorship. Doud interview, p. 35.
14. Theodore Dreiser, ed., *Theodore Dreiser Presents the Living Thoughts of Thoreau* (New York: Fawcett, 1958).
15. For an authoritative account of the stage and film history as well as the copywright quarrels among the principals see John C. Wentz, "*An American*

Tragedy as Epic Theatre: The Piscator Dramatization," *Modern Drama* (Feb. 1962): 365–376.
16. Quoted in Wentz, *"An American Tragedy* as Epic Theatre," 371.
17. Theodore Dreiser, "Four Cases of Clyde Griffiths," *New York Times*, Mar. 8, 1936, X1.
18. Jasper Deeter to Theodore Dreiser, n.d., Gotlieb Box 120, Folder 3. This letter is not dated but Dreiser's response is on Aug. 20, 1930.
19. Ibid.
20. Ibid.
21. Ibid.
22. Theodore Dreiser to Jasper Deeter, Aug. 20, 1930, Gotlieb, Box 120, Folder 3.
23. Jasper Deeter to Theodore Dreiser, n.d., Gotlieb 120, Folder 3.
24. Wentz, *"An American Tragedy* as Epic Theatre," 372.
25. Robert Garland, *New York World Telegram*, Jun. 3, 1935. Clipping in Box 120, Folder 3.
26. Howard Mumford Jones and Walter Rideout, eds., *Letters of Sherwood Anderson* (Boston, MA: Little, Brown and Company, 1953), 315.
27. Louise Campbell to Jasper Deeter, Apr. 23, 1935, Gotlieb, Box 120, Folder 3.
28. Jasper Deeter to Theodore Dreiser, Jul. 16, 1935, Gotlieb, Box 120, Folder 3.
29. Theodore Dreiser to Jasper Deeter, Jul. 20, 1935, Gotlieb, Box 120, Folder 3.
30. John Calely Wentz, *The Hedgerow Theatre: An Historical Study*, Doctoral Dissertation, University of Pennsylvania, 1954, 79. Trailing only *Emperor Jones, Twelfth Night, Romantic Age, She Stoops to Conquer, Androcles and the Lion and Saint Joan*.
31. The best record of the production is provided by X. Theodore Barber in "Drama with a Pointer: The Group Theatre's Production of Piscator's *Case of Clyde Griffiths*," *Drama Review* 28, no. 4 (1984): 61–72. Unfortunately there are no sources listed in the article—or a bibliography—so it is difficult to authenticate the information. I have drawn here on what I believe can be substantiated from newspaper reviews and other accounts of the production.
32. Ibid., 69
33. Brooks Atkinson, "The Play," *New York Times*, Mar. 14, 1936, 10.
34. Mary Virginia Farmer, "Memorandum on Hedgerow," *New Theatre* (Oct. 1936): 27.
35. Scott Nearing, *The Making of a Radical* (New York: Harper Colophon Books, 1972), 213.
36. John A. Saltmarsh, *Scott Nearing: An Intellectual Biography* (Philadelphia, PA: Temple University Press, 1991), 56.
37. Barry Witham interview with Ruth Esherick, Feb. 16, 2011.
38. Scott Nearing to Hedgerow Theatre, Sep. 29, 1948, Gotlieb, Box 7, Folder 7.
39. Scott Nearing quoted in Saltmarsh, *Scott Nearing*, 250.
40. Ibid., 234.
41. A revised version of *An American Tragedy* was staged successfully again at Hedgerow in 2010. Based on the Dreiser novel, the new adaptation by Louis

Lippa and Penelope Reed, was coproduced by the University of Pennsylvania and the Wharton Esherick Museum and ran from September 22 to October 10.

5 THE CHEROKEE NIGHT: RIGGS AND THE POWER OF PLACE

1. Jasper Deeter transcript of speech in Gotlieb, Box 2, Folder 1.
2. Peter Carnahan, *Accumulating Lives* (Bloomington, IN: Xlibris Corporation), 105.
3. The foundational text for theories of "place" is Una Chaudhuri, *Staging Place: The Geopathology of Modern Drama* (Ann Arbor: University of Michigan Press, 1995). Christy Stanlake develops a theory of the palatial as a way of illuminating Native American dramaturgy with particular attention to *The Cherokee Night* in Christy Stanlake, *Native American Drama: A Critical Perspective* (Cambridge: Cambridge University Press, 2009).
4. Lynn Riggs, "Introduction to *Green Grow the Lilacs*" in *The Cherokee Night and Other Plays* (Norman: University of Oklahoma Press, 1988), 4.
5. Witter Bynner (1881–1968) was a talented and controversial American poet who achieved some celebrity in 1918 when he and fellow Harvard alumni, Arthur Davison Ficke, were exposed as the authors of a hoax volume of poetry by the "Spectrists" that satirized the "Imagist" poets. Later Bynner was dismissed from Berkeley for serving drinks to undergraduates. In the 1920s, he became part of the arts colony in Santa Fe and was portrayed by his friend D. H. Lawrence as Owen Rhys in *The Plumed Serpent*. For a gossipy and delightful account of the Santa Fe-Taos arts colony see John Pen La Farge, *Turn Left at the Sleeping Dog* (Albuquerque: University of New Mexico Press, 2001).
6. Thomas Erhard, *Lynn Riggs Southwest Playwright* (Austin, TX: Steck-Vaughn, 1970), 8.
7. Lynn Riggs, *Big Lake* (New York: Samuel French, 1927), 7–8.
8. Ibid., 10–11.
9. Ibid., 66–67.
10. Ibid., foreword, vii.
11. Quoted in Phyllis Cole Braunlich, *Haunted by Home* (Norman: University of Oklahoma Press, 1988), 62.
12. Quoted in Ibid., 118.
13. Evelyn Scott, Review of *Rancour*, n.d, Gotlieb Scrapbook Collection.
14. Jasper Deeter to Lynn Riggs, Jun. l, 1944, Gotlieb, Box 18, Folder 1.
15. Erhard, *Lynn Riggs*, 10.
16. Lynn Riggs to Jasper Deeter, Mar. 23, 1929, Gotlieb, Box 18, Folder 1.
17. Lynn Riggs to Jasper Deeter, May 8, 1931, Gotlieb, Box 18, Folder 1.
18. Review in *Philadelphia Evening Ledger*, May 26, 1931, Gotlieb, Box 120, Folder 3.

164   *Notes*

19. The play was revived again in 1950 as *Borned in Texas* with Anthony Quinn but played only eight performances.
20. Stanlake, *Native American Drama*, 44.
21. Jace Weaver, *That the People Might Live* (New York: Oxford University Press, 1997), 100.
22. Ibid., 108.
23. Julie Little Thunder, "Mixed Bloods and Bloodlust in *Cherokee Night*," *Midwest Quarterly* 4, no. 4 (Summer 2002): 355.
24. Stanlake has an extended discussion of the play's intricate dramaturgical patterns and its significance in Native American theatre. See also Jaye Darby, "Broadway (Un) Bound: Lynn Riggs's *The Cherokee Night*," *Baylor Journal of Theatre and Performance* 4, no. 1 (Spring 2007): 7–23.
25. Riggs, *Cherokee Night,* 152.
26. Ibid., 209.
27. Ibid., 211.
28. Susan Glaspell, *Inheritors* (London: Ernest Benn Ltd, 1924), 115.
29. Program for *The Cherokee Night*. Hedgerow Theatre.
30. J. H. Keen, "The Cherokee Night," *Philadelphia Daily News,* Jun. 21, 1932, Gotlieb Box 120, Folder 3.
31. Arthur Waters, "The Cherokee Night," *Philadelphia Enquirer,* Jun. 20,1932, Gotlieb, Box 120, Folder 3.
32. "The Cherokee Night," unsigned review in *Philadelphia Bulletin,* Jun. 20, 1932, Gotlieb, Box 120, Folder 3.
33. Waters, *Inquirer,* Jun. 20, 1932.
34. *Bulletin,* Jun. 20, 1932.
35. Unidentified clipping, Gotlieb, Box 120, Folder 3.
36. Brooks Atkinson, "Riggs Worships Great Spirit," *New York Times,* Jun. 21, 1932.
37. Ibid.
38. Ibid.
39. Stanlake, *Native American Drama*, 45.
40. See Darby, "Broadway (Un) Bound." I have not been able to locate the promptbook for the play but all evidence suggests that only six scenes were played. I spoke to Phyllis Braunlich, Riggs's biographer, and she was unaware of a missing scene in the Hedgerow production. Phone interview Barry Witham with Braunlich, Dec. 14, 2010.

6   *TOO TRUE TO BE GOOD*: CONSEQUENCES OF INTEGRITY

1. Jasper Deeter quoted in Laurence Davies, "Patron Saint GBS," *New York Times,* Jul. 21, 1935, X1.
2. David Ralphe to Barry Witham, email, Mar. 8, 2011.

3. Hedgerow Royalty notes, Gotlieb, Box 18, Folder 4.
4. George Bernard Shaw quoted in Grant Code, "Shaw at Hedgerow," *Bulletin Shaw Society of America* 7 (Jan. 1955): 22.
5. See O'Brien, *Ann Harding*, 323–325, for a fuller report of the incident. O'Brien also reports that Harding later had a very pleasant meeting with Shaw when she was in England for a celebrated production of *Candida* in 1936.
6. "Tells of Shaw Contract," *New York Times*, Mar. 30, 1933, 15.
7. Ibid.
8. Lawrence E. Davies, "Hedgerow Plots a Shaw Festival," *New York Times*, Jul. 18, 1937, X1. See Appendix B for a calendar of productions.
9. Ibid.
10. Bernard Shaw, *Too True to Be Good* (New York: Dodd, Mead and Company, 1934), 134.
11. Ibid., 135.
12. Jasper Deeter, Gotlieb, Box 2, Folder 2.
13. Ibid.
14. *Too True to Be Good*. Prompt Script, Gotlieb, Box 29, Folder 6, Act III, 39.
15. Henry T. Murdock, "Hedgerow Presents Shaw Play," *Philadelphia Evening Ledger*, Jul. 27, 1937.
16. Jasper Deeter to Bernard Shaw, Sep. 3, 1941, Gotlieb, Box 18, Folder 4.
17. Jasper Deeter to Miss Patch, Gotlieb, Jan. 24, 1939, Box 18, Folder 4. *Geneva*, Shaw's satire on political ideologies in Europe, was produced at the Malvern Festival Theatre for four performances in August 1938 and successfully for 237 nights at the Saville and St. James theatres in London. In New York it was a spectacular failure in 1940.
18. Shaw, *Too True to Be Good*, 107.
19. Meek, the delightful realist, was based on Shaw's friend, the celebrated T. E. Lawrence.
20. Shaw, *Too True to Be Good*, 118.
21. Timothy Stewart-Winter, "Not a Soldier, Not a Slacker: Conscientious Objectors and Male Citizenship in the United State during the Second World War," *Gender and History* 19, no. 3 (Nov. 2007): 525.
22. Ibid,. 522.
23. Ibid., 528.
24. Mahlon Naill, "Form 47, For Conscientious Objector." Completed Jun. 5, 1943. Hedgerow Theatre, Moylan, PA. This file, along with other clippings, programs, and pictures, is from several still uncatalogued box in the "back room" at Hedgerow House.
25. Naill, "Form 47, For Conscientious Objector." 5.
26. Ibid., 9
27. Ibid., 6.
28. Lewis B. Hershey quoted in Stewart-Winter, "Not a Soldier, Not a Slacker," 524.
29. Jasper Deeter "open letter" is quoted from clippings in the uncatalogued boxes at Hedgerow House.

166 *Notes*

30. Eve Avedon to Mahlon Naill, Oct. 12, 1942, Gotlieb, Box 21.
31. Sean O'Casey to Jasper Deeter, Oct. 31, 1942, Gotlieb, Box 21.
32. Virginia Farmer to Jasper Deeter, Oct. 23, 1942, Gotlieb Box 21.
33. Paul Green to Jasper Deeter, Sep. 22, 1942, Gotlieb, Box 21.
34. Irwin Piscator to Jasper Deeter, Oct. 2, 1942, Gotlieb, Box 21.
35. Maria Coxe to Jasper Deeter, Oct. 8, 1942, Gotlieb, Box 21.
36. *Philadelphia Record*, Oct. 7, 1942.
37. Ibid.
38. Ibid.
39. Ibid.
40. "The Theater: Arms vs. Art," *Time,* Oct. 19, 1942.
41. Lieberman correspondence, Gotlieb, Box 9, Folder 2.
42. Joe Gistirak to Hedgerow, May 12, 1945, Gotlieb, Box 8, Folder 3. For an excellent summary of the work at Waldport see Andrew Ryder, "To the Heart of It: American Theatre from Hedgerow to the Oregon Coast," *Theatre Annual* 63 (2010): 27–44.
43. Joe Gistirak to Hedgerow, Mar. 13, 1945, Gotlieb, Box 8, Folder 3. Gistirak returned to Hedgerow after the war and resumed his career. Louis Lippa recalls auditioning for him in New York after he left Hedgerow.
44. Susan Glaspell to Jasper Deeter, Dec. 12, 1941, Box 16, Folder 4.
45. Susan Glaspell to Jasper Deeter, Nov. 28, 1943, Box 16, Folder 4.
46. Henry David Thoreau, *Walden or Life in the Woods* (New York: Dodd, Mead and Company, 1946), 365.
47. Ruth Esherick interview with Barry Witham, Feb. 16, 2011.
48. Thoreau, *Walden*, 358.

7 *UNCLE VANYA*: A WAY OF ACTING

1. Phone interview with Louis Lippa, Jun. 22, 2011.
2. Written notes from Richard Wright to Barry Witham, Jan. 1, 2012.
3. W. L. H. Bunker, "*Uncle Vanya,*" *Philadelphia Record*, Oct. 28, 1946. Clipping File, Hedgerow Theatre.
4. H. H. "*Uncle Vanya,*" *Philadelphia Bulletin*, Oct. 24, 1946. Clipping File, Hedgerow Theatre.
5. Bunker, *Uncle Vanya*.
6. David Ralphe to Barry Witham, email, Jan. 19, 2012.
7. Penelope Reed interview with Barry Witham, Feb. 16, 2011.
8. Ibid.
9. Interestingly the notion of empathy was critical to Stanislavski. Sharon Carnicke writes, "Stanislavski reminds the actor that one's empathy (*sochuvstvie*, a derivative of the word "to feel") can be as powerful as one's own emotions in creative work." See Sharon M. Carnicke, *Stanislavski in Focus* (London: Harwood Academic Publishers, 1998), 170.

10. Anderson, *Plays*, xxi.
11. Carnahan tapes, Reel A, 29:00.
12. David Ralphe to Barry Witham, email, Jan. 14, 2011.
13. Deeter to George Jean Nathan, Dec. 30, 1931, Gotlieb Box 6, Folder 2. In the same letter he says that "the New York Group has in it 8 or 9 who have worked here and 4 or 5 who wanted to work here."
14. Ibid.
15. See chapter 5 for a discussion of the production.
16. Jasper Deeter to Morris Carnovsky, Nov. 27, 1939, Gotlieb Box 6, folder 2.
17. See Michelangelo Capua, *Montgomery Clift: A Biography* (Jefferson, NC: McFarland & Co., 2002), 23–24
18. Anderson, "To Jasper Deeter," 128–129.
19. Carnahan tapes, Reel C, part 2, 33:00.
20. Ibid., Reel B, part 2, 15:00.
21. Ibid., Reel A, 51:00.
22. Ibid., Reel D, part 2, 16:12.
23. Ibid., Reel E, part 1, 31:00.
24. Ibid., Reel E, part 1, 11:00.
25. Ibid., Reel D, part 1, 20:37.
26. Ibid., Reel D, part 2, 17:10. In an interesting sidelight Deeter, who is usually very supportive of "actors," describes how sometimes actors can be less genuine as people because they have the ability to quickly inhabit contradictory poses. He was also fond of remarking that if you wanted to act on stage then you couldn't act in life.
27. Ibid., Reel D, part 2, 5:30.
28. Ibid., Reel E, part 1, 3:00.
29. Ibid., Reel D, part 2, 4:28.
30. Ibid., Reel D, part 2, 10:40.
31. Many of Esherick's sculptures were inspired by rehearsals or performances that he watched at Hedgerow. In 1933, he created a life-size wooden figure of his daughter, Mary, as she appeared as Essie in Deeter's production of *The Devil's Disciple*, which was exhibited on opening night. Another stunning piece called *Oblivian* (1934) celebrates his love for Hedgerow actress Miriam Phillips and was inspired by her performance in Lynn Riggs's *Song of Perdition*. An oft repeated Hedgerow story is how Esherick drew a quick sketch for Phillips during a rehearsal in order to help her understand a moment in the play that Deeter was trying to explain.
32. Janet Kelsey interview with Barry Witham, Feb. 16, 2011.
33. Penelope Reed, "A History of the Training of Actors at the Hedgerow Theatre School under the Direction of Jasper Deeter and Rose Schulman," Master's Thesis, Marquette University, 1976, 13.
34. Jasper Deeter quoted in program for *Prelude to France*, 1964. Program Files, Hedgerow Theatre.

35. Maria Coxe to Hedgerow, Oct. 8, 1942, Gotlieb, Box 21, Folder 1.
36. Phone interview with Louis Lippa, Jun. 22, 2011.
37. Hedgerow program for *The Price*. Program Files, Hedgerow Theatre.
38. Joyce Mycka-Stettler interview with Barry Witham, Mar. 24, 2012.
39. Reed, "A History of the Training of Actors," 60.
40. Ibid., 71.
41. Written notes from Richard Wright to Barry Witham, Mar. 10, 2012.
42. Dated Aug. 13, 1962, the note reads, "Everything I own belongs to Jasper Deeter." Signed by Rose Schulman and witnessed by Jane Harmon, Gotlieb, Box 10, Folder 4.
43. Rose Schulman to Jasper Deeter, Oct. 6, 1952. Personal collection of Janet Kelsey.
44. Jasper Deeter to Rose Schulman, Oct. 8, 1952. Personal collection of Janet Kelsey.

8 *THE HEDGEROW STORY*: CELEBRITY AND DISAPPOINTMENT

1. *Register of the Department of State*, Department of State Publication 3202 (Washington, DC: US Government Printing Office, Apr. 1, 1948), 46.
2. Herbert T. Edwards quoted in Robert Katz, "Projecting America through Films," *Hollywood Quarterly* 4, no. 3 (Spring 1950): 300.
3. Katz has a good summary of some of the films that captured the variety of the IMP agenda.
4. See Katz, "Projecting America through Films," 304. *Holtvillle* was withdrawn because it painted an idyllic view of a small southern community but totally ignored the Negro population in "shanty town."
5. Katz, "Projecting America through Films," 301.
6. Norman Bunin, "Global Audiences See Film of Theatre Near Wilmington," *Wilmington Sunday Morning Star*, Jul. 27, 1947, 5.
7. Bunin, "Global Audiences See Film of Theatre Near Wilmington," 5. Aside from a handful of titles, Richard Barsam concludes that the films were not "memorable." See Richard Meram Barsam, *Nonfiction Film: A Critical History* (Bloomington: Indiana University Press, 1973), 278.
8. Ibid.
9. *Register of the Department of State*, 46.
10. See Milly S. Barranger, *Unfriendly Witnesses* (Carbondale: Southern Illinois Press, 2008) for a particularly lucid analysis of the State Department involvement in passport clearances. Shipley was a fervent anticommunist and was the "final authority" on trips abroad. Barranger reminds us that "all petitioners, regardless of gender, had to pass through the gates of her Passport Barony." P. 134.

11. I am indebted to Kevin Hughes and John Harvey for sharing a copy of the film with me.
12. Eric Bentley, *The Brecht Commentaries* (New York: Grove Press, 1981), 166.
13. According to the Carleton College archives, Tinnin was brought to the school when newly installed President Laurence McKinley Gould undertook a policy after World War II to insure that the campus was integrated. Carleton had already established its progressive credentials by admitting Japanese students during the war who were unable to continue their studies on the West Coast because of the Internment Act. And in 1941 Harold Rainwater had been the first Native American to receive a Carleton degree. See www.carleton.edu /alumni/gathering2000/1940.html, accessed Feb. 22, 2012.
14. Undated press release at Hedgerow Theatre. Clipping file: *Chalk Circle*.
15. Bentley, *Brecht Commentaries*, 166.
16. Eric Bentley, *The Playwright as Thinker* (Cleveland, OH: The World Publishing Co., 1963), xx.
17. Ibid.,118
18. Gene Rochberg, ed., *Drawings by Wharton Esherick* (New York: Van Nostrand Reinhold Co., 1978), 58–61.
19. Eric Bentley, *Bentley on Brecht* (New York: Applause Books, 1999), 56.
20. Henry Goodman, "Brecht as Traditional Dramatist," *Educational Theatre Journal* 4, no. 2 (May 1952): 112.
21. Bentley, *Bentley on Brecht*, 166.
22. "Waters." "Caucasian Chalk Circle," *Variety*, Aug. 25, 1948. Clipping File, Hedgerow Theatre.
23. Harold Clurman, "Theatre: A Dramatist," *New Republic*, Sep. 6, 1948, 28.
24. "New Poetic Drama Narrative Has Premiere at Hedgerow," *Philadelphia Evening Bulletin*, Aug. 22, 1948. Clipping File, Hedgerow Theatre.
25. See Eric Bentley, ed., *Parables for the Theatre* (Minneapolis: University of Minnesota Press, 1965), 8.
26. Ruth Esherick Bascom to Barry Witham, email, Feb. 24, 2012.
27. Eric Bentley, "Brecht on the American Stage," in *Theater Der Welt Ein Almanach*, ed. Herbert Ihering (Berlin: Verlag Bruno Henschel und Sohn, 1949), 75.
28. Ibid., 72.
29. Ibid., 71.
30. *Philadelphia Evening Bulletin*. Clipping File, Hedgerow Theatre.
31. Bentley, "Brecht on the American Stage," 75. The New York reference is to *Galileo*, which ran for only six performances in 1947.
32. The amount that each member received for "living expenses" changed over the years depending on box office income. Living expenses included cigarettes, beer, movies, and any special things like Cashmere Bouquet instead of regular soap. Here is how Rose Schulman described it in 1942: "We receive no salaries. Any of the profit we make, which usually isn't very much, goes

into equipment. We receive for ourselves our laundry, our doctor's and dentist and optical bills paid for, and a minimum of four and a half dollars a month." Quoted in Fiebert, "Hedgerow Theatre," 8.

9 AFTERMATH

1. Rose Schulman announcement, Gotlieb, Box 10, Folder 4.
2. "Hedgerow Opens Tour around the Country," *Philadelphia Record*, Oct. 13, 1935, Gotlieb, Box 113, Folder 2.
3. Hereafter they toured occasionally through Pennsylvania with a brief foray into New England.
4. The festivals were discontinued after 1941 due to casting difficulties during the war and revived for one summer in 1953. See Appendix B for a sample Shaw schedule.
5. Deeter reprised the production in the summer of 1952 with many members of the original production.
6. Quoted in Wentz, *Hedgerow Theatre*, 164.
7. Jasper Deeter, "From the Drama Mailbag," *New York Times*, Apr. 12, 1942, X2.
8. Lewis Nichols, "The Visitors," *New York Times*, Jan. 17, 1945, 18.
9. Arthur Pollock, "Theatre," *Brooklyn Eagle*, Jan. 23, 1945, 5.
10. Willeta Wilford, "Column," *New York Evening Post*, Jan. 28, 1945, 25.
11. Wentz, *Hedgerow Theatre*, 185.
12. Ann Harding to Jasper Deeter, Nov. 1, 1930, Gotlieb, Box 8, Folder 4.
13. Ann Harding to Jasper Deeter, Feb. 27, 1955, Gotlieb, Box 8, Folder 4. Reference is to the musical conductor Werner Janssen who was Harding's second husband. They were finally divorced in 1962.
14. Jasper Deeter to Henry Wallace, Apr. 12, 1944, Gotlieb, Box 7, Folder 3.
15. Henry Wallace to Jasper Deeter, May 6, 1944, Gotlieb, Box 7, Folder 3.
16. Michael Kahn (for Hedgerow) to Frank Lloyd Wright, Aug. 19, 1949, Gotlieb, Box 126, Folder 5.
17. Frank Lloyd Wright to Hedgerow, Aug. 27, 1949, Gotlieb. Box 126, Folder 5.
18. Rose Schulman quoted in Reed, "A History of the Training of Actors," 17.
19. Ibid., 18.
20. Ibid., 37.
21. After Deeter's death in 1972, Rose became the head of the school with Dolores Tanner as associate director.
22. Wentz, *Hedgerow Theatre*, 67.
23. Deeter wrote about individual plays as well as theories about acting, directing, and teaching. The book was never finished, but there are many pages in the Gotlieb archive.

24. Phone interview Barry Witham with Louis Lippa, Apr. 29, 2012.
25. The Philadelphia figures quoted here are from a "Thumbnail Chronology" prepared by the theatre and available among the papers in the uncatalogued boxes at Hedgerow House.
26. Bylaws of the Hedgerow Theatre Corporation, Article 2 (a). From the personal library of Kevin Hughes, Seattle, WA.
27. David Ralphe to Barry Witham, email, Apr. 8, 2012.
28. Ibid.
29. Ibid.
30. Charles Walnut, "Green Grow the Hedgerows: The Hedgerow Theatre in Rose Valley," unpublished manuscript. From the personal library of Kevin Hughes, Seattle, WA, 1988, 48.
31. Pamphlet. *The History of Hedgerow Theatre*, Publicity Office, Hedgerow Theatre, 2001, 7.
32. Walnut, "Green Grow," 51.
33. Ibid., 56.
34. Phone interview Barry Witham with Tom McCarthy, Jan. 14, 2011.
35. In the Carnahan tapes, Deeter scolds an actress who is inquiring about her "motivation" when he perceives she is questioning his interpretation of *Uncle Vanya*. Carnahan, D-2, 35:00.
36. Deeter talks about how O'Neill really loathed human conflict and how his face often masked his feelings. He was fond of O'Neill and recalls their work creating a sound plot for *The Hairy Ape* and Deeter's role in *Exorcism*. Deeter also states that it was his sister Jane Deeter Rippin who encouraged O'Neill to show his early plays to the Provincetown Players when he was her neighbor in New London. Carnahan, G-4, 10:00. The Carnahan tapes also include a six minute excerpt of Deeter reading Jamie's monologues from O'Neill's *Long Days Journey into Night*.
37. Kevin Hughes to Barry Witham, email, Apr. 19, 2012
38. David Ralphe to Barry Witham, email, Apr. 8, 2012.
39. Louis Lippa to Barry Witham, email, Apr. 4, 2012.
40. Ibid.

EPILOGUE

1. Ellen O'Brien, "Historic Theatre is Gutted," *Philadelphia Inquirer*, Dec. 1, 1985.
2. During the rebuilding, the company played a season at Widener University where a fire also broke out following a production of Coward's *Nude with Violin* and gutted the building. In spite of the coincidence, it was determined to have started at an electric box and was not arson.
3. David Ralphe to Barry Witham, email, Apr. 8, 2012.

Bibliography

PRIMARY SOURCES

Carnahan tape recordings of Jasper Deeter made by Peter Carnahan in June 1966 and 1967 in Summerdale, PA. Approximately 18 hours. Property of Peter Carnahan. CD conversions by Barry Witham, 2011.
Hedgerow Theatre Collection, Howard Gotlieb Archival Research Center, Boston University Library, 771 Commonwealth Avenue, Boston, MA. 02215.
Interviews by Barry Witham with Ruth Esherick Bascom, Kevin Hughes, Janet Kelsey, Louis Lippa, Tom McCarthy, Joyce Mycka-Stettler, David Ralphe, Penelope Reed, Richard Solomon, Ann-Marie Spata, Jack Wade, and Richard Wright.
Records of Hedgerow Theatre, 64 Rose Valley Road, Moylan-Rose Valley, PA. 19063.

MANUSCRIPTS

Doud, Richard K. "Interview with Jasper Deeter." Smithsonian Library, 1964.
Fiebert, David. "The Hedgerow Theatre: 'A Remarkable Time.'" Prepared for Dramaturgy Class with Jim Schlatter. Villanova University, May 11, 1988 (Courtesy of Janet Kelsey).
Interview with Frances Williams. "To Hell With Bandannas." Conducted by Karen Anne Mason and Richard Candida Smith for Oral History Program. University of California, 1997.
Jackson, Nagle. "Kafka in the Hedgerows." 2007.
Naill, Mahlon. "Form 47: For Conscientious Objector." Hedgerow Theatre, Moylan, PA, June 5, 1943.
Walnut, Charles. "Green Grow the Hedgerows." 1988.
———. "The Hedgerow Idea." 1982.

FILM

A Repertory Theatre, US State Department, 1947.

174 Bibliography

SECONDARY SOURCES

Anderson, Sherwood. *No Swank*. Philadelphia, PA: The Centaur Press, 1934.
———. *Winesburg and Other Plays*. New York: Charles Scribners Sons, 1937.
Ayers, William Smallwood. "A Poor Sort of Heaven; A Good Sort of Earth: The Rose Valley Arts and Crafts Experiment." Master's Thesis, University of Delaware, 1982.
Barber, X. Theodore. "Drama with a Pointer: The Group Theatre's Production of Piscator's *Case of Clyde Griffiths*." *The Drama Review* 28, no. 4 (1984): 61–72.
Barnard, Rita. *The Great Depression and the Culture of Abundance*. Cambridge: Cambridge University Press, 1995.
Barsam, Richard Meram. *Nonfiction Film: A Critical History*. Bloomington: Indiana University Press, 1973.
Bascom, Mansfield. *Wharton Esherick: The Journey of a Creative Mind*. New York: Abrams, 2010.
Bentley, Eric. *Bentley on Brecht*. New York: Applause, 1999.
———. *The Brecht Commentaries*. New York: Grove Press, 1987.
———. *The Brecht Memoire*. Manchester: Carcanet Press, 1989.
———. "Brecht on the American Stage." In *Theater Der Welt Ein Almanach*, ed. Herbert Ihering, 70–75. Berlin: Verlag Bruno Henschel und Sohn, 1949.
———. *Parables for the Theatre*. Minneapolis: University of Minnesota Press, 1965.
———. *The Playwright as Thinker*. Cleveland, OH: The World Publishing Company, 1963.
Ben-Zvi, Linda. *Susan Glaspell: Her Life and Times*. New York: Oxford University Press, 2005.
Bigsby, C. W. E. *A Critical Introduction to Twentieth-Century American Drama, Vol. One, 1900–1940*. Cambridge: Cambridge University Press, 1940.
Black, Cheryl. "After the Emperor: Interracial Collaboration between Provincetown Alumni and Black Theatre Artists, c. 1924–1946." *Journal of American Drama and Theatre* 20, no. 1 (Winter 2008): 5–26.
Black, Gregory D. *Hollywood Censored*. Cambridge: Cambridge University Press. 1994.
Bloomfield, Maxwell. *Peaceful Revolution*. Cambridge, MA: Harvard University Press, 2000.
Bosworth, Patricia. *Montgomery Clift: A Biography*. New York: Harcourt Brace Jovanovich, Inc., 1978.
Boyle, Sheila Tully. *Paul Robeson: The Years of Promise and Achievement*. Amherst: University of Massachusetts Press, 2001.
Braunlich, Phyllis Cole. "*The Cherokee Night* of R Lynn Riggs." *The Midwest Quarterly* 30, no. 1 (Autumn 1988): 45–59.
———. *Haunted By Home*. Norman: University of Oklahoma Press, 1988.
Bryer, Jackson. ed. *The Theatre We Worked For: Letters of Eugene O'Neill to Kenneth Macgowan*. New Haven, CT: Yale University Press, 1982.

Bunin, Norman A. "Global Audience Sees Film of Theatre Near Wilmington." *Wilmington Sunday Morning Star*. July 27, 1947, 5.
Campbell, Louise, ed. *Letters to Louise*. Philadelphia: University of Pennsylvania Press, 1959.
Capua, Michaelangelo. *Montgomery Clift: A Biography*. Jefferson, NC: McFarland & Co., 2002.
Carb, David. "The Hedgerow Players: A Little Theater Bulwark." *The Literary Digest* (September 1934): 43–44.
Carnahan, Peter. *Accumulating Lives*. Bloomington, IN: Xlibris Corporation, 2010.
———. *Opposable Lives*. Bloomington, IN: Xlibris Corporation, 2009.
Carnicke, Sharon M. *Stanislavski in Focus*. London: Harwood Academic Publishers, 1998.
Cashman, Daniel. "Grotowski: His Twentieth Anniversary." *Theatre Journal* 31, no. 4 (1979): 460–466.
Chaudhuri, Una. *Staging Place: The Geopathology of Modern Drama*. Ann Arbor: University of Michigan Press, 1995.
Code, Grant. "Shaw at Hedgerow." *Bulletin of Shaw Society of America* 7 (January 1955): 22–24.
Conn, Peter. *The American 1930s*. Cambridge: Cambridge University Press, 2009.
Conway, Curt. "Open Letter to Jasper Deeter." *New Theatre* 1, no. 11 (December 1934): 18.
Crichton, Kyle. "Directed by Simon Legree." *Colliers* (June 13, 1936): 14, 68.
Cullen, Countee. http://www.poetryfoundation.org/bio/countee-cullen. Accessed January 30, 2011.
Darby, Jaye. "Broadway (Un) Bound: Lynn Riggs's *The Cherokee Night*." *Baylor Journal of Theatre and Performance* 4, no. 1 (Spring 2007): 7–23.
Dawson, Gary Fisher. *Documentary Theatre in the United States*. Westport, CT: Greenwood Press, 1999.
De Grazia, Victoria. *Irresistible Empire*. Cambridge, MA: The Belknap Press of Harvard University Press, 2005.
Dickstein, Morris. *Dancing in the Dark*. New York: W. W. Norton and Company. 2009.
Dreiser, Theodore. ed. *Theodore Dreiser Presents the Living Thoughts of Thoreau*. New York: Fawcett, 1958.
Durham, Weldon B. *American Theatre Companies, 1888–1930*. Westport, CT: Greenwood Press, 1987.
Eldridge, David. *American Culture in the 1930s*. Edinburgh: Edinburgh University Press, 2008.
Erhard, Thomas. *Lynn Riggs: Southwest Playwright*. Austin, TX: Steck-Vaughn Company, 1970.
Everding, Robert G. "Planting Mulberry: A History of Shaw Festivals." *Shaw* 18 (1998): 67–91.

Farmer, Mary Virginia. "Memorandum on Hedgerow." *New Theatre* (October 1936): 13–14, 27.
Fletcher, Anne. *Rediscovering Mordecai Gorelik*. Carbondale: Southern Illinois University Press, 2009.
Gainor, J. Ellen. *Susan Glaspell in Context: Theatre, Culture, and Politics, 1915–1948*. Ann Arbor: University of Michigan Press, 2003.
Glaspell, Susan. "Inheritors." In *Plays of Susan Glaspell*, ed. C. W. E. Bigsby, 104–157. Cambridge: Cambridge University Press, 1987.
———. *Inheritors*. London: Ernst Benn Ltd., 1924.
Hatch, James and Errol Hill. *A History of African American Theatre*. Cambridge University Press, 2003.
Halton, Eugene. *The Great Brain Suck*. Chicago: University of Chicago Press, 2008.
Harris, Harry. "Theatre in a Mill." *Theatre Arts* (October 1941): 766–770.
Harris, Laurilyn J. "Hedgerow Theatre." In *American Theatre Companies, 1888–1930*, ed. Weldon Durham, 212–220. Westport, CT: Greenwood Press, 1987.
Herrmann, Eileen J., and Dowling, Robert M. eds. *Eugene O'Neill and His Early Contemporaries*. Jefferson, NC: McFarland and Company, 2011.
Hughes, Langston. *I Wonder as I Wander*. New York: Hill and Wang, 1993.
Jones, Howard Mumford. ed. *Letters of Sherwood Anderson*. Boston, MA: Little, Brown and Company, 1953.
Katz, Robert. "Projecting America through Films." *Hollywood Quarterly* 4, no. 3 (Spring 1950): 298–308.
Kline, Herbert. ed. *New Theatre and Film, 1934 to 1937*. New York: Harcourt Brace Jovanovich, 1985.
Koenig, Linda Lee. *The Vagabonds*. London: Farleigh Dickinson University Press, 1983.
Koppes, Clayton R., and Gregory D. Black. *Hollywood Goes to War*. New York: The Free Press, 1987.
Krasner, David. *A Beautiful Pageant*. New York: Palgrave, 2002.
La Farge, John Pen. *Turn Left at the Sleeping Dog*. Albuquerque: University of New Mexico Press, 2001.
Le Gallienne, Eva. *At 33*. New York: Longmans, Green and Company, 1935.
Levins, Hoag. "A Thoreau in Wood: The Making of Wharton Esherick." *Wharton Esherick*. http:/www.levins.com/esh5.html, 1–16. Accessed September 1, 2010.
Little Thunder, Julie. "Mixbloods and Bloodlust in *Cherokee Night*." *The Midwest Quarterly* 43, no. 4 (Summer 2002): 355–365.
Londre, Felicia. *The Enchanted Years of the Stage: Kansas City at the Crossroads of American Theatre, 1870–1930*. Columbia: University of Missouri Press, 2007.
Mackay, Constance D'Arcy. *The Little Theatres in the United States*. New York: Henry Holt, 1917.
Malone, Dumas, and Basil Rauch. *War and Troubled Peace: 1917–1939*. New York: Appleton-Century-Crofts, 1960.

McArthur, Benjamin. *Actors and American Culture, 1880–1920*. Philadelphia, PA: Temple University Press, 1984.
McElvaine, Robert S. *The Great Depression*. New York: Random House, 1993.
Miller, Henry. *Remember to Remember*. New York: New Directions, 1986.
Murdock, Henry T. "Behind the Hedgerow." *Theatre Arts* 36, no. 8 (1952): 41, 77.
Nearing, Scott. *The Making of a Radical*. New York: Harper Colophon Books, 1972.
O'Brien, Scott. *Ann Harding: Cinema's Gallant Lady*. Albany, GA: Bear Manor Media, 2010.
O'Neill, Eugene. *The Emperor Jones* in *Plays of Eugene O'Neill*. New York: Random House, 1954.
Pizer, Donald, ed. *Theodore Dreiser: A Selection of Uncollected Prose*. Detroit, MI: Wayne State University Press, 1977.
Poggi, Jack. *Theatre in America: The Impact of Economic Forces, 1870–1967*. Ithaca, NY: Cornell University Press, 1968.
"Racial Equality: Raising the Jim Crow Issue." *The Literary Digest*, September, 1935.
Rampersad, Arnold. *The Life of Langston Hughes, Vol. 1: 1902–1941*. New York: Oxford, 1986.
Reed, Penelope. "A History of the Training of Actors at the Hedgerow Theatre School under the Direction of Jasper Deeter and Rose Schulman." Master's Thesis, Marquette University, 1976.
Rideout, Walter. *Sherwood Anderson: A Writer in America, Volume 2*. Madison: University of Wisconsin Press, 2007.
Riggs, Lynn. *Big Lake*. New York: Samuel French, 1927.
———. *The Cherokee Night and Other Plays*. Norman: University of Oklahoma Press, 2003.
———. *A Lantern to See By*. New York: Samuel French, 1928.
———. *Roadside*. New York: Samuel French, 1930.
Rochberg, Gene. ed. *Drawings by Wharton Esherick*. New York: Van Nostrand Rheinhold Company, in association with the Wharton Esherick Museum, 1978.
Rotte, Joanna. "Jasper Deeter." *American National Biography Online* (February 2000). http://www.org/articles/18/18–01501/.html. Accessed October, 16, 2011.
Ryder, Andrew. *"To the Heart of It:* American Theatre from Hedgerow to the Oregon Coast." *Theatre Annual* 63 (2010): 27–44.
Saltmarsh, John A. *Scott Nearing: An Intellectual Biography*. Philadelphia, PA: Temple University Press, 1991.
Shandell, Jonathan. "The First *Emperor* of Pennsylvania: Wayland Rudd at Hedgerow Theater." Unpublished paper presented at the American Theatre in Higher Education Conference, Los Angeles, August 13, 2011.
———. "The Inheritors of *Inheritors*: How Susan Glaspell Inspired the Hedgerow Theater." *The Journal of American Drama and Theatre* 22, no. 3 (Fall 2010): 5–21.

Shaw, Bernard. *Too True to Be Good.* New York: Dodd, Mead and Company, 1934.
Sheaffer, Louis. *O'Neill: Son and Artist.* Boston, MA: Little, Brown and Company, 1973.
Smith, Wendy. *Real Life Drama.* New York: Grove Weidenfeld, 1990.
Sper, Felix. *From Native Roots: A Panorama of Our Regional Drama.* Caldwell, ID: Caxton Printers, 1948.
Stanlake, Christy. *Native American Drama: A Critical Perspective.* Cambridge: Cambridge University Press, 2009.
Stewart-Winter, Timothy. "Not a Soldier, Not a Slacker: Conscientious Objectors and Male Citizenship in the United States during the Second World War." *Gender and History* 19, no. 3 (November 2007): 519–542.
Swanberg, W. A. *Dreiser.* New York: Charles Scribner's Sons, 1965.
Tanner, Dolores. "The Hedgerow Theatre." Master's Thesis, University of Texas, 1957.
Taylor, Nick. *American Made.* New York: Bantam, 2008.
Thoreau, Henry David. *Walden or Life in the Woods.* New York: Dodd, Mead and Company, 1946.
Tucker, S. M. "Little Theatre: What Is It?" *Little Theatre Monthly* (February 1926): 180.
Van Gogh, Vincent. *The Complete Letters of Vincent Van Gogh*, Vol. Three. Boston, MA: Little, Brown and Company, 1958.
Weaver, Jace. *That the People Might Live.* New York: Oxford University Press, 1997.
Wentz, John C. "*An American Tragedy* as Epic Theatre: The Piscator Dramatization." *Modern Drama* (February 1962): 365–376.
———. "Anderson's *Winesburg* and the Hedgerow Theatre." *Modern Drama* (May 1960): 42–51.
———. *The Hedgerow Theatre: An Historical Study.* Doctoral Dissertation, University of Pennsylvania, PA, 1954.
White, Ray Lewis. ed. *Sherwood Anderson's Memoirs.* Chapel Hill: University of North Carolina Press, 1969.
Williams, Jay. *Stage Left.* New York: Scribner's, 1974.
Wilmeth, Don B., and Christopher Bigsby, eds. *Cambridge History of American Theatre, Vol II.* New York: Cambridge University Press, 1999.
Wilson, Garff B. *A History of American Acting.* Bloomington: Indiana University Press, 1966.
Witham, Barry. "Theatre, Environment and the Thirties." In *Readings in Performance and Ecology*, ed. Wendy Aarons and Theresa May, 13–22. New York: Palgrave Macmillan, 2012.
Yerkes, Andrew C. *"Twentieth Century Americanism."* New York: Routledge, 2005.
Ziegler, Joseph. *Regional Theatre: The Revolutionary Stage.* Minneapolis: University of Minnesota Press, 1973.

Index

Abraham Lincoln (Drinkwater), 9, 29
activism, 52, 69
Actors Studio, 106
African-American actors, 4, 27, 29–42, 63, 71, 76, 86, 122, 126, 156
Ah, Wilderness! (O'Neill), 48
American Federation of Labor (AFL), 37
American Laboratory Theatre, 77
American Negro Theatre, 42
American Tragedy, An (Dreiser-Piscator)
   controversy surrounding, 59–61
   Deeter and, 3, 50, 59, 65–72
   German performances of, 64–65
   Group Theatre and, 68–69, 106
   Hedgerow performances of, 3, 69–72, 127, 145–47, 152
   Hedgerow Story and, 116
   Nearing and, 69–72
   as propaganda, 61–62
   Shubert and, 67–68
   Speaker in, 65–67
   success of, 67
Anderson, Maxwell, 48
Anderson, Sherwood
   actors and, 104, 106
   Barton and, 159
   Both Your Houses, 48
   Deeter and, 3, 44, 46–57, 106
   Dreiser and, 50, 63, 72
   Naill and, 96
   Nearing and, 71
   Rideout on, 49
   Rose Valley and, 23
   theatre and, 11, 23
   Theatre Guild and, 47–48
   transitions, 49
   Van Gogh and, 52
   Winesburg, Ohio, 3, 43–57, 65, 84, 106, 145–46
Anna Lucasta, 42
Artef Theatre, 63
Arts and Crafts movement, 5–7, 9, 22, 110, 137
Ayers, Lew, 94
Ayers, William Smallwood, 94

Barber, X. Theodore, 162
Barsam, Richard, 168
Barton, Arthur, 47–48, 159
Bascom, Mansfield, 31, 160
Basehart, Richard, 10, 55, 160
Beach, Lewis, 15
Beaux Arts Theatre (Los Angeles), 63
Bellamy, Ralph, 81
Bentley, Eric, 120–27
Ben-Zvi, Linda, 155
Biberman, Herbert, 4
Big Lake (RIggs), 77, 79
Black, Cheryl, 156
Black Empire (Ames), 38
blackface, 22, 29
Blackhawk, 13, 16–17, 75, 84
Bledsoe, Jules, 32–33
bohemianism, 13, 25, 30, 44, 95
Both Your Houses (Anderson), 48

Boyle, Sheila Tully, 156
Brecht, Bertolt, 3, 73, 121–22, 123–25
Broad Street Theatre (Philadelphia), 32
Bromberg, Joe, 68
Bunin, Norman, 116–17
Bynner, Witter, 76–77

Camp Waldport, (OR), 98
Campbell, Louise, 65, 67
Can You Hear Their Voices? (Flanagan), 59, 61, 63, 65, 144
Candida, 3, 22, 87, 89–90, 136, 143–47, 149, 151–52
Capek, Karel, 21
Carnahan, Peter, 55, 74, 103, 109–10, 114, 139, 154, 155, 160, 171
Carnicke, Sharon, 166
Carnovsky, Morris, 4, 22, 68, 105–6
Case of Clyde Griffiths, 64, 68–69, 162
Caucasian Chalk Circle (Brecht), 3, 121, 124, 125, 127, 147
Chambers, Whittaker, 60
Chaudhuri, Una, 163
Chekhov, Anton, 4, 45, 47, 51, 101–2, 107–10
Cherokee Night, The, (Riggs), 73–86, 145, 147
Cherry Lane Theatre, 131
Cherry Orchard, The, (Chekhov), 148
Christopher, Michael, 137
Civic Theatre (New York), 30
civil rights, 11, 22, 31, 37–38, 69–72
Civil War, 82, 86
Civilian Conservation Corps (CCC), 98
Civilian Public Service (CPS), 95, 98
Clark, Ann, 66
Clark, Barrett, 79
Clark, Silas, 14
Clift, Montgomery, 106
Clurman, Harold, 68, 123–25
communism, 37, 44, 52, 60–61, 70–71, 118, 121, 168
Congress of Industrial Organizations (CIO), 37

Conroy, Frank, 14
contracts, 48, 55–57, 89, 160
Conway, Curt, 59
Cook, Jig, 15–16, 18, 21, 28, 83
Copeau, Jacques, 47, 159
Coxe, Maria, 112
Cullen, Countee, 4, 36, 38–39, 41, 158
cyclorama (cyc), 2, 8, 49, 84, 126, 141

Darby, Jaye, 164
Davis, Betty, 79
Davis, Owen, 21
De Grazia, Clyde, 64
Deeter, Jasper
  acting classes, 133–34, 137, 139
  American Tragedy and, 3, 50, 59, 65–72
  Beckwith and, 116
  Brewer and, 139
  Can You Hear Their Voices? and, 60–63, 65
  Cherokee Night and, 77–80, 83–86
  Cherry Lane and, 131–32
  death, 140
  Dreiser and, 67
  early acting career, 15–16
  Emperor Jones and, 16, 19, 21, 28
  Esherick and, 23–25, 31, 48
  festivals, 130–31, 149
  financial troubles, 129–34
  Gilpin and, 27–29
  Glaspell and, 22–23
  Great Depression and, 43–44
  Greenwich Village and, 13
  Guyer and, 45–47
  Hedgerow and, 2–11, 21, 25, 74, 129–40
  Hedgerow Corporation and, 135–36
  Hedgerow Story and, 116–27
  impressions of, 14–15, 25–26
  In Abraham's Bosom and, 32–34
  Inheritors and, 13, 16, 18–20
  leave of absence, 134–35

legacy, 141–42
love of theatre, 21–23
Machet and, 29–30
O'Neill and, 29
One Way to Heaven and, 38–41
politics and, 60–65
production methods, 74–76
race and, 30–36, 41–42
Rancour and, 80–81
Rich and, 28, 35, 41
Riggs and, 75–86
Roadside and, 81–82
Rose Valley and, 6–8
Schulman and, 1–2
Shaw and, 3, 87–100
Too True to Be Good and, 87–100
tours, 129–32
Uncle Vanya and, 101–14
Virginia Plan and, 53–55, 132
Winesburg, Ohio and, 44–57
Division of International Motion Pictures (IMP), 115–16, 117–18, 168
Doctor's Dilemma, The (Shaw), 87, 145–46
Domino Parlor, The, (Riggs), 80
Dreiser, Theodore, 3, 9, 11, 50, 63–67, 71–72, 106
Drinkwater, John, 29
DuBois, W.E.B., 38, 71

Ellis, Charles, 29
Emperor Jones, The (O'Neill), 16, 19, 21–22, 27–42, 116, 130–32, 136, 143–48, 151–52
Epic Theatre, 64
Erhard, Thomas, 81
Esherick, Letty, 7, 23–24, 52
Esherick, Ruth, 35, 70, 100, 117–18, 126, 140, 160
Esherick, Wharton, 7, 11, 23–24, 31, 48, 50–52, 65, 100, 110, 123, 125–26, 133, 137, 154, 160
Experimental Theatre, 19, 59

Fairhope (AL), 23, 31
Farley, Morgan, 64
Farmer, Virginia, 4, 69, 96, 105
Federal Theatre Project, 38, 59, 61, 63, 85–86, 161
Ferber, Edna, 15
Ficke, Arthur Davison, 163
Fitzgerald, Eleanor, 32
Flanagan, Hallie, 59–63, 65, 161
Follman, Ann, 57
Free Born (Nearing), 71

Gainor, J. Ellen, 155
Garland, Robert, 67
Garrick Theatre, 33
Ghosts (Ibsen), 98
Gilpin, Charles, 19–21, 27–30, 35, 37, 156
Gistirak, Joe, 98–99
Glaspell, Susan, 11, 13, 15–20, 22–24, 30, 41, 75, 83, 87, 94–95, 99, 127, 142
Goldschmidt, Lena, 64
Goodman, Edmund, 16
Goodman, Henry, 121–25
Gorelick, Mordecai, 14–15, 68
Gould, Laurence McKinley, 169
Great Depression, 1, 43–47, 60, 100
Green Grow the Lilacs, (Riggs), 75–76
Green, Paul, 4, 9, 32–34, 97
Greene, Stanley, 41
Greenwich Village, 13–15, 20, 30, 32
Greenwich Village Theatre, 14
Group Theatre, 4, 25, 64, 68–69, 96, 105–6
Guyer, John, 45–46, 53

Hagedorn, Hermann, 31
Hairy Ape, The (O'Neill), 19, 21, 144–45, 171
Haiti (DuBois), 38
Harding, Ann, 3, 10, 18–20, 22, 25, 32, 54, 88–89, 132, 155
Harlem Renaissance, 38

Harris, Jed, 159
Harris, Lester, 40
Harrisburg Community Theater, 21, 103
Hatch, James, 157
Haworth, Dorothy, 14
Hedgerow Corporation, 135–36
Hedgerow Story, The (film), 115–20
Hedgerow Theatre
   American Tragedy and, 59, 64–71
   authenticity and, 74–75, 81
   Broadway theatre and, 73–74
   Can You Hear Their Voices? and, 61–63
   Chekhov and, 101–6
   Cherokee Night and, 81, 83, 85–86
   closing of, 141–42
   community and, 23–26
   creation of, 13–14, 21–26, 69–70, 73
   Deeter and, 2–11, 21, 25, 73–74, 129–40
   Emperor Jones and, 29–42
   Esherick and, 23
   founding of, 1
   Harding and, 19
   Hollywood and, 115–27
   Inheritors and, 18
   money and, 129–40
   Philips and, 2
   racial equality and, 31–42, 71
   rehearsals, 110–12
   repertory 1923–1956, 143–48
   repertory calendars, 151–52
   Riggs and, 81–86
   Rose Valley and, 6–7
   Schulman and, 2, 111–12
   Shaw and, 8, 11, 45, 47, 51, 87–90, 120–22, 127
   Shaw Festival 1937, 149
   unique nature of, 3–6
   Virginia Plan and, 113–14
   Winesburg, Ohio and, 43–57
Herndon, Angelo, 34

Hershey, Lewis B., 96–97
Hill, Abram, 42
Hollywood, 3, 19, 32, 55, 79, 88, 115, 132
Holman, Libby, 48, 51
Holmes, Phillips, 64
Hoover, Herbert, 61
Hopkins, Harry, 63
Hopkins, Miriam, 64
House Committee on Un-American Activities (HUAC), 118
House of Connelly, The, (Green), 105
Huey, Richard, 34
Hughes, Kevin, 10, 140, 158
Hughes, Langston, 34, 37–38, 41, 157

Ibsen, Henrik, 4, 21, 25, 31, 98, 120, 122
Idiot's Delight (Sherwood), 92
IMP *see* Division of International Motion Pictures
In Abraham's Bosom, 32–33, 35–36, 144, 146
Inheritors, 3, 13–26, 30, 75, 83, 87, 92, 94–95, 97–99, 116–18, 129–30, 143–47, 151–52
integration, 30, 32, 36, 38, 40, 121, 156, 169

Jim Crow, 30, 94
John Ferguson, (Ervine), 15
Jones, Robert Edmond, 19
Joslyn, Allan, 22

Katz, Robert, 168
Kearney, Patrick, 64, 68
Keats, John, 38
Kinnard, Jack, 132
Kirkland, Alexander, 22
Kline, Herbert, 59, 69
Krasner, David, 156
Krigwa Players, 157

La Farge, John Pen, 163
Lafayette Theatre (Harlem), 28

Le Galliene, Eva, 4, 22, 25, 30, 43, 156
Leberman, Joseph, 98, 135
Light, James, 15–16, 19, 30, 38, 156
Lippa, Louis, 10, 101, 112, 136–37, 140, 166
Little Theatre (Philadelphia), 14
"little theatres," 4–5, 79
Little Thunder, Julie, 82
Lucky Sam McCarver (Howard), 144

Macgowan, Kenneth, 19, 32, 79
Machet, Sydney, 22, 29–30, 156
Man Who Died at 12 O'Clock, The (Green), 34–35, 144
Master Builder, The (Ibsen), 25
Mather, Eleanor Price, 24
McCarter Theater, 142
McCarthyism, 100, 118
McCarthy, Tom, 10
McClendon, Rose, 32, 34, 38–39, 158
McCranie, Abe, 32
McGuire, Dorothy, 160
Metcalf, Audrey, 54
Metcalf, David, 94, 101, 135
Method acting, 103, 106, 108–9
Miller, Arthur, 112
Miller, Henry, 15, 21
Mitchell, Abbie, 33
Mitchell, Loften, 42
Moscow Art Theatre, 77, 96
Murdock, Henry, 57, 91, 160
Mycka-Stettler, Joyce, 112

Naill, Mahlon, 94–96
Nathan, George Jean, 105
National Association for the Advancement of Colored People (NAACP), 32, 37
Nearing, Scott, 11, 69–72, 99, 133, 160
Negro Theatre Unit, 4
New Deal, 37
 see also Federal Theatre Project; Works Progress Administration

New Theatre, 15
Nofer, Ferd, 45, 48, 132, 159

O'Brien, Scott, 19, 165
O'Casey, Sean, 45, 96
O'Neill, Eugene, 4, 11, 16, 19, 27–30, 34, 41, 48, 122, 127, 129, 139, 155, 156, 171
Odets, Clifford, 68
Office of War Information (OWI), 115–16
Oklahoma, 76, 79
Oliver, Ruth, 66
One Way to Heaven (Cullen), 36–40, 146
Othello (Shakespeare), 34, 122, 144, 157
Owen, Chandler, 71

Paradise Lost (Odets), 68
People's Light and Theatre Company, 10, 139
Perex, Isaac Loeb, 61
Phillips, Miriam, 10, 24, 52, 99, 123, 167
Phoenix Theatre (New York), 35, 127
Piazza, Ben, 160
Piscator, Irwin, 3, 63–65, 67, 97, 106
placiality, 7
Playwright's Theatre (New York), 13
Polish Laboratory Theatre, 21
Pollock, Arthur, 132
Porgy, 34
Prager, June, 141
Price, David, 69
Price, The (Miller), 112
Price, William, 5–7, 21, 25
Princess Theatre, 155
Princess Turandot, 32
Producing Managers Association, 15
Provincetown Players, 4, 171

Ralphe, David, 10, 87, 102, 105, 137–40, 142
Randolph, A. Philip, 71

184   Index

Rauh, Ida, 76–77
Raynal, Paul, 92
Red Scare, 70
 see also McCarthyism
Reed, Penelope "Penny," 10, 103, 107, 109, 113, 142
Reiser, Catherine, 101
Reynolds, R.J., 48
Rich, Arthur, 28, 35, 40–41, 131, 157
Richmond Virginia Community Theatre, 42
Rideout, Walter, 49, 51
Rieser, Catherine, 45, 48
Riggs, Lynn, 3, 20, 47, 73–86
Roadside (Riggs), 20, 76, 81, 85, 144–46, 177
Robeson, Paul, 34, 38, 124, 156
Rockefeller Foundation, 41, 132
"rooted growth," 7–8, 35
Rose Valley Association, 5–6
Roseman, Ralph, 137
Rudd, Wayland, 34–35, 157
Ruskin, John, 5

Schulman, Rose, 1–2, 10, 102, 111–13, 117, 123, 127, 129, 132–33, 138–39, 141
Seagull, The (Chekhov), 101–2, 127, 145, 147–48, 152
segregation, 29, 31, 34, 36, 157
Sergel, Christopher, 160
Shakuntala, 14
Shandell, Jonathan, 22, 155, 157
Shanghai People's Theatre, 62
Shaw, George Bernard
 Androcles and the Lion, 22, 87, 136, 143–49
 Arms and the Man, 3, 87, 89, 92, 98, 114, 144–49
 Back to Methuselah, 95, 146
 Candida, 3, 22, 87, 89–90, 136, 143–47, 149, 151–52
 Deeter and, 3–4, 6, 8, 20, 29, 69, 87–100, 107, 142

Devil's Disciple, The, 89, 144–46, 149, 167
 festivals, 130–31, 135–36, 149
 Getting Married, 89, 146, 149
 Harding and, 88–89
 Heartbreak House, 3, 87, 90, 92, 100, 122, 144–49
 Hedgerow and, 8, 11, 45, 47, 51, 87–90, 120–22, 127
 Man and Superman, 3
 Misalliance, 8, 43, 87, 89, 143–45, 149
 repertory for *Shaw Festival*, 1937, 149
 Saint Joan, 90, 145–47
 Too True to Be Good, 3, 87–100, 135, 146, 148–49, 151–52
 You Never Can Tell, 89, 144–46, 149, 151–52
Sheils, Frank, 36
Sheppard, Harry, 66
Shubert Brothers, 4
Sidney, Sylvia, 64
Simi Valley Repertory Theatre, 139
Sinclair, Upton, 70–71
Smedley, Morgan, 97
Smithers (character), 16, 22, 27, 29–30, 131
Spring, The (Cook), 16, 83, 155
Stanislavski, Constantin, 103, 105–6, 108, 166
Stanlake, Christy, 82, 86, 163, 164
Stewart-Winter, Timothy, 94
Strasberg, Lee, 68, 103, 105
Strudwick, Sheppard, 48
Suitcase Theatre, 41
sustainability, 7–10, 23, 127

Tanner, Dolores, 10–11, 118–19, 138–39, 141
Taulane, Joe, 48, 66, 68
Theatre Guild, 4, 15, 48, 87
"Theatre in the Dirt," 140
Theatre Union, 67

Index 185

Theatrical Syndicate, 4–5, 15
Thoreau, Henry David, 18, 23–24, 63, 100, 142
Tinnin, Alvis, 121–25, 127, 169
Tomorrow's Yesterday (Kinnard), 132
Trial of Dr. Beck, The, (Allison), 38

Uncle Vanya (Chekhov), 101–27, 147–48, 152
Unknown Warrior (Raynal), 92, 145

Van Gogh, Vincent, 52, 160
Van Vechten, Carl, 30, 36, 41, 158
Virginia Plan, 53–55, 113, 132
von Sternberg, Joseph, 64

Wade, Jack, 49, 154, 159
Waiting for Lefty, (Odets), 62
Waldorf, Willeta, 132
Walnut, Charley, 138–39
Ward, Audrey, 101

Washington, Booker T., 71
Washington Square Players, 4, 15
Weaver, Jace, 82
Wentz, John, 49, 66, 68, 132, 134, 159, 161
When We Dead Awaken (Ibsen), 31
Whitmore, James, 160
Williams, Frances, 36
Wilson, Frank, 34
Winesburg, Ohio (Anderson), 3
Wonder Boy, 47, 159
Workers Theatre (China), 63
Works Progress Administration (WPA), 38, 63
World War I, 35, 47, 93
World War II, 81, 96, 106, 115, 122, 169
Wright, Frank Lloyd, 133
Wright, Richard, 10, 113

Yiddish Art Theatre, 111

GPSR Compliance

The European Union's (EU) General Product Safety Regulation (GPSR) is a set of rules that requires consumer products to be safe and our obligations to ensure this.

If you have any concerns about our products, you can contact us on

ProductSafety@springernature.com

In case Publisher is established outside the EU, the EU authorized representative is:

Springer Nature Customer Service Center GmbH
Europaplatz 3
69115 Heidelberg, Germany

www.ingramcontent.com/pod-product-compliance
Lightning Source LLC
LaVergne TN
LVHW051912060526
838200LV00004B/98